# Microsoft Application Virtualization Advanced Guide

Master Microsoft App-V by taking a deep dive into advanced topics and acquire all the necessary skills to optimize your application virtualization platform

**Augusto Alvarez**

BIRMINGHAM - MUMBAI

# Microsoft Application Virtualization Advanced Guide

First published: March 2012

Production Reference: 1190312

Published by Packt Publishing Ltd.
Livery Place
35 Livery Street
Birmingham B3 2PB, UK.

ISBN 978-1-84968-448-4

www.packtpub.com

Cover Image by Stanford Murray (stanmoore@live.com)

# Credits

**Author**
Augusto Alvarez

**Reviewers**
Nicke Källén

Kevin Kaminski

Aaron Parker

**Acquisition Editor**
Amey Kanse

**Lead Technical Editor**
Hyacintha D'souza

**Technical Editors**
Aaron Rosario

Priyanka Shah

Naheed Shaikh

**Copy Editors**
Brandt D'Mello

Leonard D'Silva

**Project Coordinator**
Kushal Bhardwaj

**Proofreader**
Joanna McMahon

**Indexers**
Hemangini Bari

Rekha Nair

**Graphics**
Manu Joseph

Valentina D'silva

**Production Coordinator**
Alwin Roy

**Cover Work**
Alwin Roy

# About the Author

**Augusto Alvarez** is a computer geek and a fan of the latest IT platform solutions. He has been working with Microsoft TechNet and Microsoft Academics since 2006, collaborating on different technological events.

He is currently working as a Sr. System Integration Consultant in Dell LATAM where he is in charge IT services delivery and quality assurance directly to the datacenter, deploying multi-vendor technologies and solutions within Microsoft, Citrix, VMWare and Open Source. These solutions deal with the major business processes used to manage the overall enterprise. The tasks involved in his work usually requires integrating hardware, processes, methodologies, software, and the customer.

He has vast experience not only in App-V, but also in several Microsoft technologies for Windows Server: deployment, Active Directory, Hyper-V, virtualization solutions, clustering, System Center suite, security implementations, and so on.

He has also written the first complete reference plus step-by-step book about App-V: *Getting Started with Microsoft Application Virtualization 4.6 (ISBN 13 : 978-1-84968-126-1)*.

You can find out more info about him in his blog: http://blog.augustoalvarez.com.ar/ or following him on Twitter: @augustoalvarez.

# About the Reviewers

**Nicke Källén** is an App-V MVP from Sweden. He posts as *Znack* on the TechNet forums, where he's consistently the most active responder on App-V topics. His focus has always been on end-user experience within migration projects for several enterprises and utilizing Microsoft Application Virtualization as a means to faster, more accurate delivery, with less interference for a more continuous experience.

With over thirteen years of systems management experience, **Kevin Kaminski** is no stranger to the challenges enterprises can experience when managing large deployments of Windows systems. As an independent consultant, Kevin uses the opportunity to visit many diverse environments and see the challenges they face first hand.

His contributions to the community can be seen on many sites, such as the Microsoft TechNet Forums, `Appdeploy.com`, `MyItForum.com`, `AppVirtGuru.com`, `BrianMadden.com`, and the Calgary Systems Management User Group (CSMUG.ca). He has also co-authored a course and book with fellow MVP Tim Mangan.

**Aaron Parker** is a Solutions Architect with sixteen years of experience in the IT industry. An App-V MVP, MCSE, and CCIA/CCEA, he spent the last 10 years working on server-based computing, desktop, and application deployment and virtualization. He currently resides in London, where he's involved in deployments for various clients including Fortune Global 500 companies. You can find Aaron contributing to `AppVirtGuru.com` and TechNet App-V forums, or blogging at `stealthpuppy.com`, although he just might be snowboarding instead. Follow Aaron on Twitter: `@stealthpuppy`.

# www.PacktPub.com

## Support files, eBooks, discount offers and more

You might want to visit www.PacktPub.com for support files and downloads related to your book.

Did you know that Packt offers eBook versions of every book published, with PDF and ePub files available? You can upgrade to the eBook version at www.PacktPub.com and as a print book customer, you are entitled to a discount on the eBook copy. Get in touch with us at service@packtpub.com for more details.

At www.PacktPub.com, you can also read a collection of free technical articles, sign up for a range of free newsletters and receive exclusive discounts and offers on Packt books and eBooks.

http://PacktLib.PacktPub.com

Do you need instant solutions to your IT questions? PacktLib is Packt's online digital book library. Here, you can access, read and search across Packt's entire library of books.

## Why Subscribe?

- Fully searchable across every book published by Packt
- Copy and paste, print and bookmark content
- On demand and accessible via web browser

## Free Access for Packt account holders

If you have an account with Packt at www.PacktPub.com, you can use this to access PacktLib today and view nine entirely free books. Simply use your login credentials for immediate access.

## Instant Updates on New Packt Books

Get notified! Find out when new books are published by following @PacktEnterprise on Twitter, or the *Packt Enterprise* Facebook page.

# Table of Contents

# Preface

Microsoft's Application Virtualization technology has been emerging as one of the main platforms in application virtualization. This is mainly because more and more organizations are thinking about application virtualization as a valid implementation and also because App-V probably represents the most attractive solution. App-V introduces a new and efficient way to improve operating systems and application life cycles in organizations. However, if we want to maximize our investment, we must learn that every scenario and application differs from another, as does complexity.

With the *Microsoft Application Virtualization Advanced Guide*, administrators will find detailed topics for understanding App-V components, architecture, and implementation models, as well as step-by-step guidance to master App-V processes. There is also guidance on integrating App-V with other robust platforms, such as VDI, SCCM 2012, and even virtualizing server applications.

The *Microsoft Application Virtualization Advanced Guide* will start by giving readers the means to discover unfamiliar topics in App-V, as well as understanding App-V's architecture. By doing so, it will provide the baseline needed before shifting to advanced topics in App-V, such as complex scenarios for sequencing and deploying applications.

This book details scripting within App-V as well as handling the platform using the command line; there is a complete review of troubleshooting installations, sequencing, and deploying applications.

Integration is another key component that we will cover by introducing App-V in VDI and SCCM 2012. Server applications are not forgotten with Server App-V. Using this book, the reader will have a detailed understanding, with step-by-step instructions on how to virtualize server applications.

# What this book covers

*Chapter 1, Taking a Deep Dive into App-V*: In this chapter, we will review App-V architecture and detailed components as well as some advanced options available in the App-V environment.

*Chapter 2, Sequencing in Complex Environments*: In this chapter, we will review detailed and advanced options available in the sequencing process, handling applications with unsupported configurations, and using package accelerators.

*Chapter 3, Deploying Applications in Complex Environments*: In this chapter, we will understand how to deploy applications in scenarios where it normally is not an easy process.

*Chapter 4, Handling Scripting and App-V Command Lines*: This chapter will be your guide to using scripting in OSD files as well as handling command lines available in App-V to automate all processes.

*Chapter 5, Troubleshooting App-V*: In this chapter, we will review all the scenarios to understand and solve problems within App-V installations and application sequencing, as well as deploying virtual packages.

*Chapter 6, Scaling Up App-V Implementations*: In this chapter, we will cover the scenarios for designing your environments on a large scale.

*Chapter 7, Integrating App-V with Virtual Desktop Infrastructure (VDI)*: In this chapter, we will learn about VDI environments and how to integrate them with App-V. We will also use the shared cache feature.

*Chapter 8, Integrating App-V with System Center Configuration Manager 2012*: In this chapter, we will cover the new System Center Configuration Manager platform and how to integrate it with App-V.

*Chapter 9, Integrating Server App-V with Private Clouds*: In this chapter, we will review, the new concept appearing as Server App-V, as a possibility to improve our private cloud environment.

*Appendix, Reviewing App-V Microsoft and Third-party Tools*: In this chapter, we will take a look at the tools available from Microsoft and third-party vendors to complement and improve App-V scenarios.

# What you need for this book

You will the following software for this book:

- Operating systems:
    ◦ Server: Windows Server 2003 R2 SP2 or superior
    ◦ Client: Windows XP SP3 or superior

- Software:
    ◦ Microsoft Application Virtualization 4.6 SP1
    ◦ SQL Server 2005 SP3 or superior

- Platform:
    ◦ Active Directory domain

Please note that as we will also be reviewing App-V integrations with other platforms (such as VDI and SCCM 2012), there are going to be some specific requirements for those scenarios. Each of those integrations will have their requirements outlined in the relevant chapters.

# Who this book is for

This book is for system administrators or consultants who want to master and dominate App-V and gain a deeper understanding of the technology in order to optimize App V implementations. Even though the book does not include basic steps, such as installing App-V components or sequencing simple applications, application virtualization beginners will receive a comprehensive look into App-V before jumping into the technical process of each chapter.

# Conventions

In this book, you will find a number of styles of text that distinguish between different kinds of information. Here are some examples of these styles, and an explanation of their meaning.

Code words in text are shown as follows: "The `content` folder is the location where this server requests for the packages."

A block of code is set as follows:

```
<DEPENDENCY>
  <SCRIPT TIMING="PRE" EVENT="LAUNCH" WAIT="TRUE" PROTECT="TRUE">
    <HREF>C:\Windows\System32\cmd.exe</HREF>
  </SCRIPT>
</DEPENDENCY>
```

Any command-line input or output is written as follows:

```
SFTMIME LOAD APP:application [/LOG log-pathname | /GUI]

SFTMIME UNLOAD APP:application [/LOG log-pathname | /CONSOLE | /GUI]
```

**New terms** and **important words** are shown in bold. Words that you see on the screen, in menus or dialog boxes for example, appear in the text like this: "we will receive a summary of all the notifications in the **Completion** section".

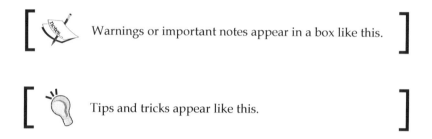

Warnings or important notes appear in a box like this.

Tips and tricks appear like this.

# Reader feedback

Feedback from our readers is always welcome. Let us know what you think about this book—what you liked or may have disliked. Reader feedback is important for us to develop titles that you really get the most out of.

To send us general feedback, simply send an e-mail to feedback@packtpub.com, and mention the book title via the subject of your message.

If there is a book that you need and would like to see us publish, please send us a note in the **SUGGEST A TITLE** form on www.packtpub.com or e-mail suggest@packtpub.com.

If there is a topic that you have expertise in and you are interested in either writing or contributing to a book, see our author guide on www.packtpub.com/authors.

# Customer support

Now that you are the proud owner of a Packt book, we have a number of things to help you to get the most from your purchase.

# Downloading the example code

You can download the example code files for all Packt books you have purchased from your account at `http://www.PacktPub.com`. If you purchased this book elsewhere, you can visit `http://www.PacktPub.com/support` and register to have the files e-mailed directly to you.

# Errata

Although we have taken every care to ensure the accuracy of our content, mistakes do happen. If you find a mistake in one of our books—maybe a mistake in the text or the code—we would be grateful if you would report this to us. By doing so, you can save other readers from frustration and help us improve subsequent versions of this book. If you find any errata, please report them by visiting `http://www.packtpub.com/support`, selecting your book, clicking on the **errata submission form** link, and entering the details of your errata. Once your errata are verified, your submission will be accepted and the errata will be uploaded on our website, or added to any list of existing errata, under the Errata section of that title. Any existing errata can be viewed by selecting your title from `http://www.packtpub.com/support`.

# Piracy

Piracy of copyright material on the Internet is an ongoing problem across all media. At Packt, we take the protection of our copyright and licenses very seriously. If you come across any illegal copies of our works, in any form, on the Internet, please provide us with the location address or website name immediately so that we can pursue a remedy.

Please contact us at `copyright@packtpub.com` with a link to the suspected pirated material.

We appreciate your help in protecting our authors, and our ability to bring you valuable content.

# Questions

You can contact us at `questions@packtpub.com` if you are having a problem with any aspect of the book, and we will do our best to address it.

# 1
# Taking a Deep Dive into App-V

Microsoft's Application Virtualization technology is emerging as one of the main platforms in application virtualization. This is mainly because more and more organizations are thinking about application virtualization as a valid implementation and also because App-V represents probably the most attractive solution.

With App-V 4.6 Service Pack 1 came an important variety of improvements, and most of them focused on the experience of sequencing. This made it possible for sequencer engineers and practitioners to quickly improve their techniques and share most of them with the community.

But, as you already know, App-V does not depend only on the sequencing process to work properly. There are several components in the App-V servers and App-V clients that are interacting. There are also several models available to implement and complement application virtualization in our company. Prior to starting implementation, we should be aware of and understand these components and possibilities in order to take full advantage of the complete platform.

The App-V server components and sequenced application files represent, probably, the pieces you already know about. The App-V client components are way larger than most App-V admins think they are, and if they know about their existence, they have probably not been fully used to optimize the platform.

A good example is using the App-V Client Management Console properties, from where we can configure the basic operations in the client and also several other important tasks, for example, configure the App-V client cache, add the SFT directories for cached content, configure permissions in the App-V Client Management Console for non-administrators, and so on.

The App-V deployment possibilities are also something you should already know about. But, there are some misleading concepts that we will review in this chapter about the use of each of these models.

Also, as an important section of this chapter, we will go through the detailed steps involved in the main processes in App-V, that is, publishing refresh and launch/load.

As a quick review, in this chapter, we are going to take a deep dive into the following topics:

- Latest improvements in App-V 4.6 SP1

- Server components in App-V and the files present in sequenced applications

- Take a detailed tour of the App-V client components:
    - Virtual environment
    - App-V Client Management Console
    - Global Data and User Data directories
    - App-V client cache
    - App-V client registry options

- Deployment methods available in App-V

- Understand the App-V client and publishing interaction: Publishing refresh and launch/load processes

# What's new in App-V 4.6 SP1?

The Microsoft Application Virtualization 4.6 build appeared a while back, introducing several enhancements with new features and possibilities to use virtual applications more efficiently. Some of the new features included were supporting 64-bit environments, including the "shared cache" feature for VDI environments, tight integration with Microsoft Office 2010, and so on.

This time, with the Service Pack 1 release, the improvements focused on the sequencer side, providing several new possibilities for the sequencer engineers to make their job easier and with several embedded best practices. Let's take a look at these improvements:

- **Package accelerators**: This major improvement simplifies the distribution of best practices and customizations used among applications in the sequencing process.

  A package accelerator, created by a sequencer engineer, contains all necessary files and customizations in a virtualized application. It makes it possible not only to share with the community, but also for a sequencer trainee to capture a complex application just by using this accelerator.

- **Best practices applied by default**: There are several common best practices that all of the experienced sequencer engineers know about. But, this time, the App-V Sequencer applies some of them by default, making it a lot easier to set our environment efficiently.

    - **Using the Q drive**: When we launch the App-V Sequencer installation, we have the option embedded into the wizard to select the *Q* drive as a default for the virtual drive. And, if we don't have any *Q* drive available, the installer creates this virtual drive automatically.

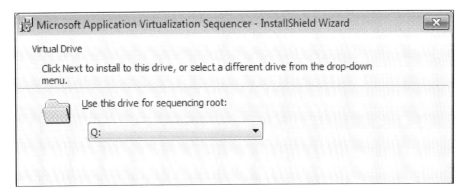

There is a known issue in App-V Client 4.6 SP1 RTM that causes the "symbolic link" *Q* drive to register DLLs improperly. This behavior can appear inconsistently in App-V clients.

It is recommended to use 4.6 SP1 Hotfix 4. More information is available at the following Microsoft KB: `http://support.microsoft.com/kb/2586968`.

° **Installing a dummy ODBC (Open Database Connectivity):** This is one of the common best practices we mostly didn't have deployed in several environments. The App-V Sequencer creates one as soon as the installation completes.

Remember that having an ODBC prior to sequencing an application can avoid creating several registry settings that would be captured by the sequencer in the current package (if this application tries to create an ODBC entry).

Also, if the default ODBC entries are not present, then the virtual application will only see the **Data Source Names (DSNs)** installed by the application; none of the local DSNs, due to registry overrides by the App-V client, can be seen.

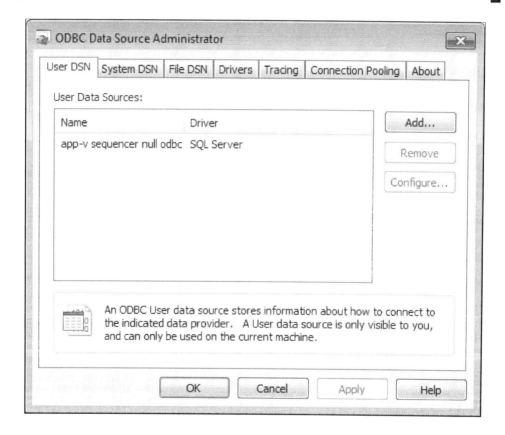

The App-V Sequencer does not create a dummy printer. This activity remains as a best practice to apply in your environment.

- ° **Verifications prior to sequencing an application**: Just before the App-V Sequencer wizard starts capturing a new application, it verifies that the OS image is clean and has no other capture launched before, no disruptive services are running in the background, or no other application is running.

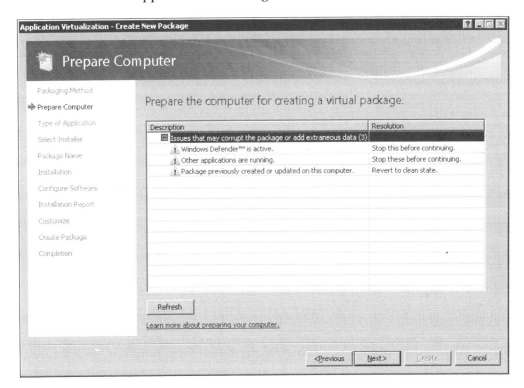

By double-clicking on each observation, we will also receive the recommendation to solve the warning.

- ° When we are capturing an application, we will also receive several guides during the stage to maintain common best practices, for example, the App-V Sequencer, by default, selects the installation path in the *Q* drive.

- **Several improvements in the App-V Sequencer GUI to improve sequencing workflow**: If you are just starting with App-V and trying to capture an application for the first time, the options available in this new App-V Sequencer will make the process much easier.

  As soon as we start the Sequencer wizard, we'll be given the option to choose the type of application we would like to sequence: **Standard**, **Add-on or plugin**, or **Middleware**. Depending on what we select, the capturing workflow will be modified.

  If we try to update/modify an existing captured application, then we will receive the options **Apply an update**, **edit a package**, or **add a new application**.

- **Quickly review important information regarding the sequencing process**: Starting with SP1, the Sequencer includes several important notifications when we are in the capturing process. For example, a driver that was not captured, or shell extensions not supported, and of course, the files excluded from the package.

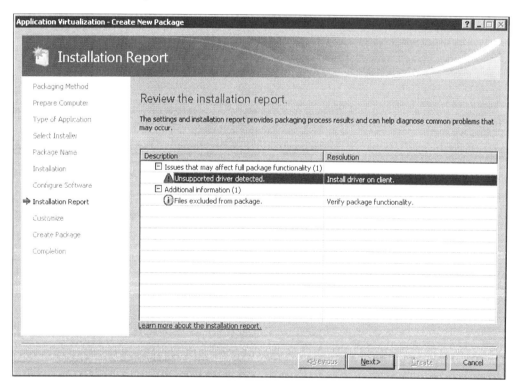

In this example, we receive the notification as soon as we complete the installation of the application, and we will receive a summary of all the notifications in the **Completion** section.

In this section, by double-clicking the information, we will get a detailed look for each message. With the **Unsupported driver detected** message, the App-V Sequencer will show us the driver and files detected that will not be included in the package.

 For more information on sequencing an application with drivers, review *Chapter 2, Sequencing in Complex Environments*.

- **Include "Templates" in the Sequencing process**: When we have some customized options that are commonly used for capturing applications (such as the server name in charge of deployment and the port used), we can apply them in a template and use it in all of our sequencing processes.

  The options we can use in templates to customize and maintain in our environment are:

    - **Parse Items**
    - **Exclusion Items**
    - **Package Deployment Settings**
    - **Advanced Monitoring Options**
    - **General Options**

- **Relax application isolation when we are virtualizing it**: This option appeared in earlier versions of App-V (by using the LOCAL_INTERACTION_ ALLOWED tag in the OSD files) but was required to be applied manually in all OSD files that we would want to use. Now, we can enable and disable it by using the App-V Sequencer options, which will apply to all packages. The default option is disabled, of course.

The option is called **Allow all named objects and COM objects to interact with the local system** and should only be applied when necessary, as the application will no longer work completely inside its "bubble" and will receive interaction from the OS components.

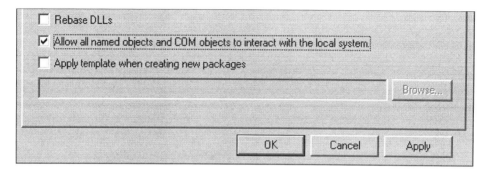

# App-V components and architecture

In this section, we are going to take a good look at the App-V components and architecture in order to understand how we can achieve a proper design, implementation, and maintenance of the infrastructure.

We are going to divide these concepts and components into those belonging to the server and those for the client machines. We will also review the sequenced application components, including all the files used in a virtual application.

# Understanding App-V server components

We are going to summarize all the server components including App-V, as well as some of the options available in the App-V Management Console that should be analyzed in order to get a correct implementation.

## App-V management server

The management server represents the service from which the App-V Full Infrastructure model controls application permissions, licenses, and policies as well as the statistics data.

The management server needs an SQL data store (multiple management servers can access the same data store), where it retrieves information such as application assignments and licenses, records, and permissions within the App-V management environment. The authorization phase, which we administer from the App-V management server, is integrated with Active Directory groups.

If we are including the streaming process with the App-V management server, the default ports used by this server are RTSP 554 and RTSPS 322. The `content` folder is the location where this server requests for the packages, but it does not necessarily have to be located in the management server.

Also, the management server gathers all the performance and metering information within the environment. This information is stored in the SQL data store, although it can be stored on a separate server.

 It is highly recommended that both of these servers, management and SQL, interact on the same network segment, because of the high amount of data that is transferred.

## App-V management system

The App-V management system is composed of the App-V Management Console and the App-V management service. This web service represents the communication channel between the MMC and the SQL data store, controlling any read/write requests to the database. It can be installed together with the management server or on a separate computer with IIS.

The MMC console can also be installed on a separate computer; the software requirements are MMC 3.0 with the .Net Framework 2.0 installed. Additionally, we need to configure a few settings in Active Directory. Take a look at the article *Running the App-V Management Console from a remote Computer* at `http://blog.appvtraining.com/Blog/tabid/87/EntryId/2/Running-the-App-V-Management-Console-from-a-remote-Computer.aspx`.

 We will also review the steps of "Trusted Delegation" in Active Directory and **Service Principal Names** (**SPN**) in *Chapter 6, Scaling Up App-V Implementations*.

Here's a quick overview of the interaction of the App-V management server components:

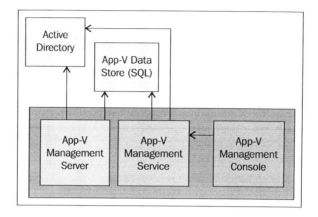

# App-V Streaming Server

This server will serve the role of streaming applications to the clients who do not have an acceptable connection to the management server, such as a branch office. Streaming applications is the only functionality enabled for this server, and it is represented, in most cases, as an optional role to be installed.

 It is important to note that only using the RTSP/RTSPS protocols in the Streaming Server requires an App-V installation. Using HTTP or SMB streaming does not need any App-V role installation.

# App-V Management Server Console options

In this section, we are going to understand some options that could be useful when we are working with the App-V Management Server Console.

We will not cover the App-V management server operations and features, such as managing providers' policies, in this section. Those processes will be covered in other chapters of this book.

## The Reset Administrators option

The App-V Management Console includes an option embedded to reset administrators for the App-V database. This option "in theory" would bring the administration back in control of the platform and change the location of the database, if required.

But "in theory" is the right term used, because, in the actual process, the UI does not work. This is a known error in the App-V Management Console. Microsoft states that this error will be fixed in a later release of the App-V management server.

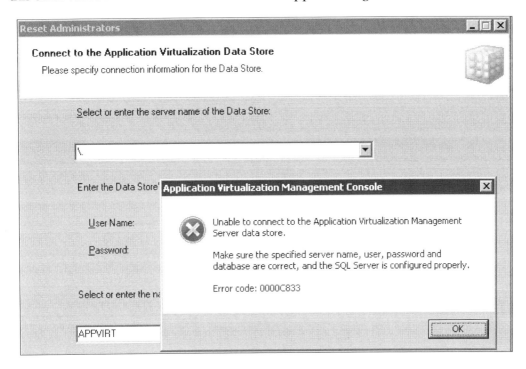

For more information on how to solve this situation, check *Chapter 5, Troubleshooting App-V*.

 Microsoft includes a process we can use to move the SQL database to another SQL server. Check the article *How to Migrate the App-V SQL Database to a Different SQL Server* at the following link: http://technet.microsoft.com/en-us/library/gg252515.aspx.

## Understanding memory and core processes utilization

There are some situations where we might experience performance issues in the App-V management server when we have a lot of clients connecting to this server to retrieve applications; one of the possible reasons could be related to the memory and core processes resources allocated in the Management Console.

In the App-V Management Console, when we access the **Server Groups | Properties** of the selected server, then in the **Advanced** pane, we can check some of the resource options available.

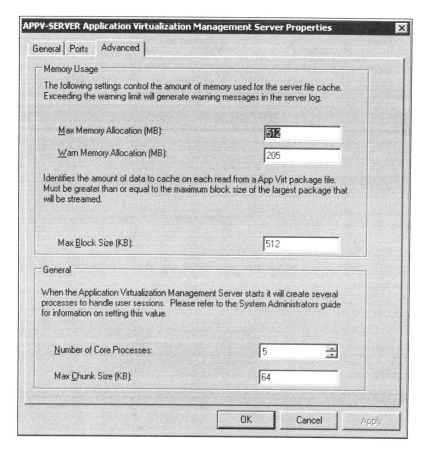

The **Max Memory Allocation (MB)** (defaults to **512**) represents the memory used by the App-V management server dispatcher core processes (shown as `sghwsvr. exe` in **Task Manager**). When we have several clients connected to the server and requesting applications constantly, we will see these processes repeated and consuming a lot of memory.

It is highly recommended to increase the **Max Memory Allocation (MB)** value when we have an App-V management server experiencing slow performance. For example, if we have an App-V management server with 8 GB of RAM, we should be considering using values such as 4096 to optimize the resources in the server.

Also, as a symptom, which could be related to the memory utilization, the App-V clients will show *timeouts* when they are trying to stream an application.

The **Number of Core Processes** represents the quantity of dispatchers (`sghwsvr.exe` processes) that will be used by the App-V management server to handle the clients' requests. **5** is the default value used.

If we have "crash dumps" (or also known as **BSOD, blue screen of death**), then it is recommended that we use it to reduce the value in **Number of Core Processes** to **1**. This will let us analyze only one core process in order to find the problem.

If we have a large App-V environment with several App-V management servers, we must configure these values, **Max Memory Allocation** and **Number of Core Processes**, consistently across all servers.

If we don't follow this consistency, some of the issues that might appear are periodic/intermittent loss of database connectivity, services failing to start, general performance issues, and so on. For more information, have a look at the article *Pre-creation of Server objects may yield certain sub-optimal values in the App-V SQL Database* at the Microsoft TechNet Blog: `http://blogs.technet.com/b/appv/archive/2010/05/10/pre-creation-of-server-objects-may-yield-certain-sub-optimal-values-in-the-app-v-sql-database.aspx`.

# Understanding sequenced application components

App-V applications do not act as normal applications and, of course, do not contain the normal files we can find in any given application. Once the App-V Sequencer captures the application, the following files are created:

- **SFT**: The SFT file is the container for the original files used by the application. In the capturing process, the App-V Sequencer packs these files in a form that can be streamed by the App-V server, without altering any configuration or source code. The SFT file is composed of two sections: the feature block 1 (FB1), which represents the applications most used features (or in this case, most used files), and the feature block 2 (FB2), which represents the rest of the application.

The behavior on the clients of these two blocks is as follows: the FB1 is streamed the first time the App-V client launches the application, and the FB2 is streamed by the client only on demand.

° **DSFT**: Also, there is a differential version for the SFT called the DSFT file. This file is the one that we create when we need an active upgrade of the published application. The DSFT contains the delta files between the original SFT. Using DSFT, we can reduce the bandwidth impact when we perform a significant change in an already-delivered application; the App-V server only streams the file that the client does not already have.

The DSFT feature appeared in App-V during the Release Candidate version of 4.5, which included an option in the UI of the App-V Sequencer to generate this type of file (**Generate Difference File**). Later, in the RTM version, this option in the UI was removed, but the option is still present, as seen when using an executable file included in the `Program Files` folder of the App-V Sequencer.

We can find the executable to generate DSFT at the following path: `%PROGRAMFILES%\ Microsoft Application Virtualization Sequencer\mkdiffpkg.exe`. For more information about using DSFT files, visit the article *How to Use the Differential SFT File* at Microsoft TechNet: `http://technet.microsoft.com/en-us/library/dd351395.aspx`.

- **OSD**: The OSD file (**Open Software Description**) represents the link for the SFT file, providing all the necessary information to the client for locating and launching the application.

  The OSD file translates to the App-V client the location of the SFT file for the application, the name and place of the executable file in the virtual environment, supported operating systems, and so on.

- **SPRJ**: The SPRJ is the XML-based project file. Once the application is sequenced, we can save the project for a future change in the application. It contains the list of files, registry keys, and directories that are being excluded by the sequencer, as well as the parse items.

- **Manifest file**: This XML file stores information for the sequenced application regarding the application shortcuts (**Desktop**, **Start Menu**, and **Quick Launch**) and the application file type associations.

  The manifest file is always saved in the sequencing process and uses the same name as the SFT and the SPRJ file, adding the `_manifest.xml` at the end of the filename.

  The use of this manifest file occurs on important phases in the App-V delivery deployment:

  - Loading and running a virtualized application using a script or command line with the `SFTMIME` command.
  - The MSI, which you can create to deploy applications to offline users, contains the manifest file.
  - The XML manifest is needed when you import App-V applications to System Center Configuration Manager 2007 R2.

- **ICO**: The icon file is created on the sequencing process and represents the file that App-V is using to deliver clients the proper shortcut for the App-V package as well as the file type associations. The ICO file always uses the same file from the original application.

- **MSI**: The MSI file is optional in most cases. The main role of this file is for offline users, in those scenarios where we need them to provide a file from which we deliver the application without the intervention of a streaming server.

  MSI files contain a copy of the manifest, OSD, and ICO file.

 It is important to note that the SFT file is not included in the MSI (due to restrictions in the MSI file format), and we are no longer able to quickly edit the OSD file to make a change in the virtual application. Therefore, we will need to re-sequence it.

# Understanding App-V client components

Now that we've arrived at the App-V client, in this section, we will understand which of the components are interacting on the client side.

The App-V client is actually a simple component in the platform, basically working as a **filter driver**, redirecting and comprehending requests from the virtual environment to the operating system. The App-V client contains several options and components interacting to execute the processes efficiently:

- **Virtual environment**: Called "SystemGuard" in App-V, this environment summarizes all the components virtualized that are redirected by the App-V client.
- **App-V Management Console**: Within this console, we can configure several options and behaviors in the App-V client.
- **Global Date and User Data directory**: These two directories are vital in App-V; common and user-specific data is kept in these locations.
- **App-V registry keys**: The client machine operates with several parameters that can be easily modified in the registry. Some of these parameters can be modified using Group.
- **App-V client cache**: Client cache is another key component in App-V; applications, icons, and OSD files will be stored here for re-utilization.

# Understanding the virtual environment

An important remark regarding virtualized application architecture is that it provides App-V clients with several virtual environments, which isolates the applications and generates all the necessary virtual components for a proper functionality. As we've seen earlier, this is the main difference between normal applications and virtualized applications.

These virtual settings created are packaged in one environment called SystemGuard, where we can find:

- **Virtual drive** or **virtual filesystem**: It is where the applications are stored, namely, the $Q$ drive. The virtual filesystem redirects the filesystem requests from the application, for example, where the application would normally be installed to the $C$ drive.
- **Virtual registry**: It is used for handling registry keys and requests for the application.
- **Virtual COM**: It is used for managing and redirecting COM objects to avoid conflicts with the already-existing operating system components.

- **Virtual services**: Embedded services in the application are captured in the sequencing process and maintained in the SystemGuard environment.
- **Virtual process environment**: It is where the path environment values are located.
- **Virtual fonts**: Each font created/added in the sequencing process exists only in this environment where the application can use it.
- **Virtual INI**: Here, each application has private settings within virtual copies of standard Windows .INI files.

# App-V Client Management Console

The App-V Client Management Console is rarely used by a normal user, but it could be quite helpful if we want to locally manage some of the options regarding the App-V client.

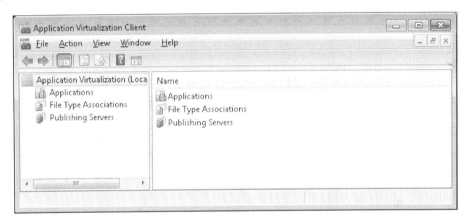

Following are the normal user tasks that can be executed in the App-V Management Console:

- **Handling applications associated with the user**: The applications listed here are those available for the user from which we can:
  - Add/remove.
  - Load/unload: This option loads/unloads the application into the client's cache.
  - Locked/unlocked: This locks/unlocks the selected application in the client's cache. Once it's locked, we cannot remove the application.
  - Clear: This option clears (not deletes) the current user's settings and publishing configurations for an application. None of the PKG files are deleted.

○ Repair: This option removes the user's settings applied to that application. Getting more specific, repairing an application deletes the `usrvol_sftfs_v1.pkg` from the user profile.

 A detailed explanation of the PKG files is included in the following sections of this chapter.

- **File type associations**: We can also modify the file type associations generated by the applications loaded.
- **Publishing servers**: Here, we have the chance to modify properties for the existing publishing servers available, as well as adding new ones.

The App-V Client Management Console can be accessed in the following `Program Files` path (64-bit environment): `C:\Program Files (x86)\Microsoft Application Virtualization Client\SftCMC.msc`.

So far, so good; handling these options did not present us with any advanced task in the client machines. But, the Management Console includes, in the **Properties** section, some important parameters we should consider. This is discussed in the next section.

 The App-V Client Management Console does not support remote management; we can access only the local computer when we are using it. This supportability changed in App-V 4.5 due to several security issues in this option.

As we have reviewed the App-V management server components, now let's take a look at the App-V client components' interaction. Within these components, we can find several services working together to make the virtual environment functional:

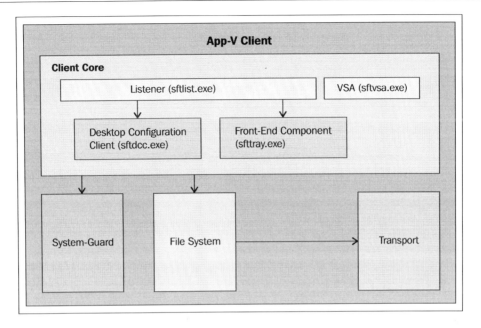

Here are the services and components included:

- Sftlist.exe: Represents the App-V client service
- Sftdcc.exe: In charge of publication refreshes
- Sfttray.exe: Handles the notification pop-ups placed in the system tray
- Sftvsa.exe: In charge of handling the virtual services included by the virtual applications
- **System-Guard**: The isolated environment for the virtual application
- **Transport**: Communicating channel to stream down the application into the client

# Reviewing Management Console properties

When we select **Application Virtualization (Local)** | **Properties**, we receive several new options available for the App-V client.

Let's take a look at some of the most important ones:

- **General** tab:
    - ○ Configure the **Logging** level in the App-V client, for both type of logs the `sftlog` and the **System Log** in the **Event Viewer**. More information about logging and errors are seen in *Chapter 5, Troubleshooting App-V*.
    - ○ Select the path for the **Global Data Directory**, which is the directory where common data for the computer will be kept. We are going to analyze this directory a little bit further in this chapter.
    - ○ Select the path for the **User Data Directory**, the location to keep the user-specific data for the virtual applications. We are going to analyze this directory a little bit further later in this chapter.

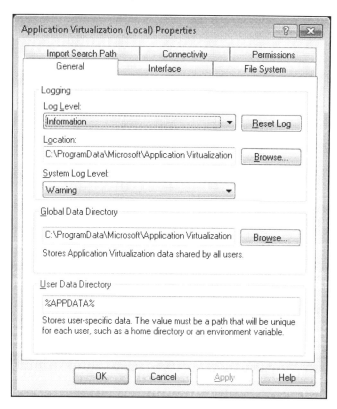

- **Interface** tab:
  - ° Configure the visibility that the user will have when the App-V applications are running.
  - ° Configure the time that the common App-V client pop-up messages appear.

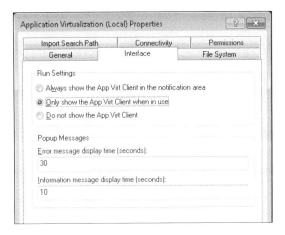

- **File System** tab:
  - ° In this tab, we can configure the **Client Cache**, using the same options we used when we installed the App-V client (and also when we added the current reserved cache size to avoid any misconfiguration).
  - ° Also, we can switch the drive letter assigned to the virtual drive. This option must not be changed if we already have our applications sequenced in the *Q* drive.

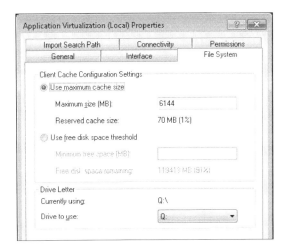

If we change the value of the maximum cache size to a lower one than the client already has, this will not change the actual size of the cache.

We will review the procedure necessary for resetting the App-V client cache size in the following sections of this chapter.

- **Permissions** tab:
    - ○ This is an interesting set of options we can use for our power users in the organization. We can define the tasks that can be performed in the App-V Management Console to normal users such as **Add applications** or **Publish shortcuts**.
    - ○ The complete set of these options is available to administrators, no matter the tasks we configure here.

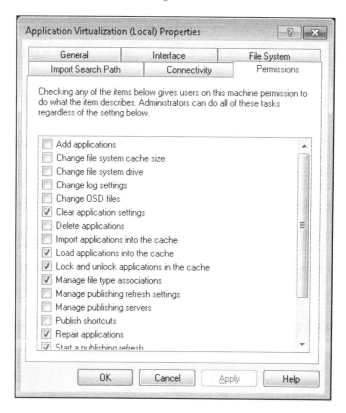

- **Connectivity** tab:
  - ○ In this tab, we can configure whether we want users to be able to execute applications when they can't establish the connection to the App-V Management or Streaming Server and just run it in the cache.
  - ○ We can also configure the time from which we will let the clients be able to use the "disconnected" option.

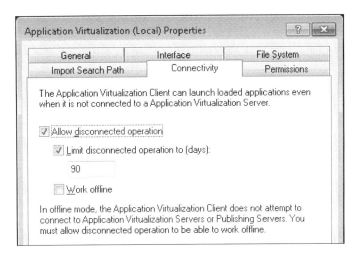

- **Import Search Path** tab:
  - ○ This tab represents a great alternative in App-V scalability; we can add directories that will let the App-V client scan for applications' SFT files that can be cached. The paths included here will be added into the cache beside the files the client receives from the App-V management server or the **Application Source Root** configuration.
  - ○ When we are using the Full Infrastructure model, it is not enough to make an application available in the client, as the authorization phase still occurs.

- When we are using the standalone model, caching SFT files in any directory added here won't require authorization.

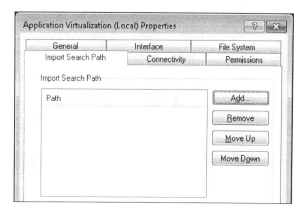

# Understanding Global Data and User Data directory

As we've reviewed earlier, the App-V client components are not only represented by the applications it receives from the server, this component includes several other elements used to handle App-V operations efficiently. With this are included the Global Data directory and User Data directory.

## Global Data directory

The Global Data directory is the container where the common computer data is stored and is available for all users in this operating system. The default location is `C:\ProgramData\Microsoft\Application Virtualization Client\`.

The default folders available in this directory are the `SoftGrid Client` and `Temp` folders, along with the `sftlog.txt` log file.

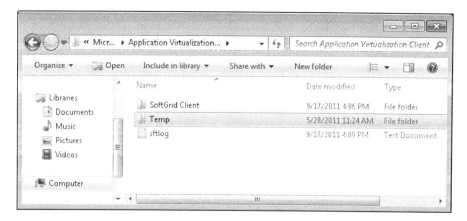

The `SoftGrid Client` folder is where all the necessary files are stored; here's a quick look at them:

- `Sftfs.eld` and `Sftfs.eld.old`: This is a log file used internally in the App-V cache; it is usually used by Microsoft Technical Support to detect possible errors.

- `Sftfs.fsd`: This is the App-V client SFT cache. It is a single file used by the App-V client to store all applications used in the computer.

- `Sftfs.fsG`: It is also a file related to the App-V client cache, but its use is undocumented at the moment.

- `shortcut_ex.dat`: This file is present in both directories, that is, the Global Data and User Data directories. It contains the list of application shortcuts present. This list is updated for every publishing refresh.

   The file in the Global Data directory is updated when adding a package using `SFTMIME ADD PACKAGE` with the `/Global` switch or adding an MSI-based package.

- `AppFS Storage` folder: Within this folder is kept information and personalization made in applications which are not user specific. Not all applications require storing particular computer information.

   The application-specific data in PKG files will be analyzed later in this chapter.

- `Icon Cache` folder: Stores the icons used in the machine when a package/application is added. This directory is populated in the publishing refresh workflow.

   There is also an `Icon Cache` folder created in the User Data directory for the same purpose.

- OSD Cache folder: As for the Icon Cache, this is the place where the OSD files of the applications involved and received from a server are stored.

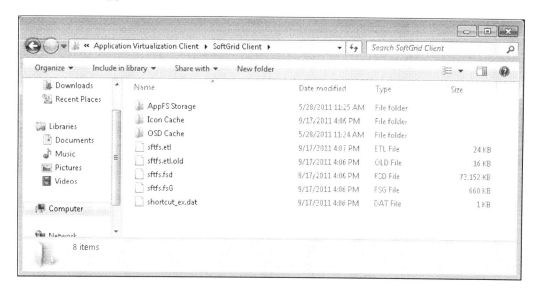

 If the computer had an earlier version of App-V, we could also see a Resource Cache folder, which is not necessary in this App-V client version.

## User Data directory

The User Data directory is the place where the applications store the user profiles associated with each application. Any particular configuration made by a user in an application is kept here.

The default location of the User Data directory is using the system variable %APPDATA%\SoftGrid Client, translated to C:\Users\username\AppData\ Roaming\SoftGrid Client.

| Name | Date modified | Type | Size |
|---|---|---|---|
| CHROME-D2D00519-1ACB-4F31 | 17/09/2011 10:05 ... | File folder | |
| FIREFOX6-C06AF524-837-44AC | 17/09/2011 10:17 ... | File folder | |
| FOXIT-1AFB4BEF-85FE-44BC | 16/09/2011 03:07 ... | File folder | |
| Icon Cache | 17/09/2011 05:51 ... | File folder | |
| IMGBURN-E9EB1D73-E8FF-4745 | 16/09/2011 12:09 ... | File folder | |
| KLITE-FD3E380A-7217-4072 | 16/09/2011 06:05 ... | File folder | |
| SKYPE-5C5ECF82-874A-49C2 | 16/09/2011 12:28 ... | File folder | |
| TWIHRL-4A08DB4B-DDB8-4481 | 17/09/2011 10:35 ... | File folder | |
| WINAMP-584F59A8-946F-4F1F | 16/09/2011 12:40 ... | File folder | |
| shortcut_ex.dat | 17/09/2011 05:51 ... | DAT File | 1 KB |
| userinfo.dat | 17/09/2011 05:03 ... | DAT File | 1 KB |

The folder also includes, as mentioned before, the **Icon Cache** folder for storing particular user published icons and the **shortcut_ex.dat** with the list of these icons.

The **userinfo.dat** file is used for storing each user identity.

## Using PKG files

We've discussed, in the last two sections, the common data appearing in virtual applications and stored in PKG files. App-V separates these files into two separate directories, Global Data and User Data, representing each change made in the operating system and in the user profile environment of the application.

How does App-V know where to store these changes? In the sequencing phase, each file captured includes a parameter regarding whether it is **User Data** or **Application Data**. So any change made to any of these files is stored as PKG in Global Data or User Data directories.

We can review this parameter in the App-V Sequencer using the **Files** tab:

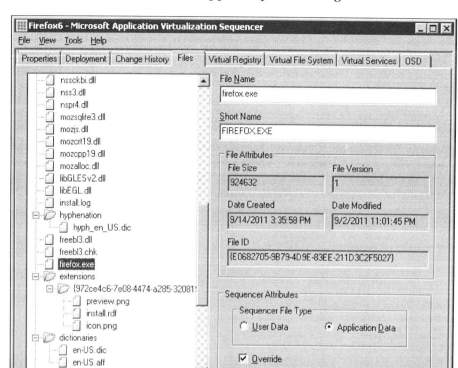

App-V already has an algorithm to decide whether the file belongs to **Application Data** or **User Data** and rarely will we need to change this value while editing a virtual application.

The PKG files created by each application are unique and can be differentiated in these directories, as it is using the package name plus the GUID associated with that package. Using a previous example, the Firefox directory is named **FIREFOX6-C06AF524-837-44AC**.

Within each package directory, we will also find several files, including two separate PKG files associated with User Data and Global Data. These files are present in the User Data and Global Data directories, respectively.

Here's an example of the Global Data directory of the Mozilla Firefox 6 package:

| | | | |
|---|---|---|---|
| GlblVol_sftfs_v1_S-1-5-18.pkg | 16/09/2011 12:06 ... | PKG File | 660 KB |
| GlblVol_sftfs_v1_S-1-5-18.tmp | 16/09/2011 12:06 ... | TMP File | 660 KB |
| GlblVol_sftfs_v1_S-1-5-20.pkg | 18/09/2011 10:26 ... | PKG File | 668 KB |
| GlblVol_sftfs_v1_S-1-5-20.tmp | 18/09/2011 10:26 ... | TMP File | 668 KB |
| GlblVol_sftfs_v1_S-1-5-21-334137358-1325371469-1414914945-1000.pkg | 18/09/2011 10:26 ... | PKG File | 672 KB |
| GlblVol_sftfs_v1_S-1-5-21-334137358-1325371469-1414914945-1000.tmp | 18/09/2011 10:26 ... | TMP File | 672 KB |
| UsrVol_sftfs_v1.pkg | 18/09/2011 10:26 ... | PKG File | 68 KB |
| UsrVol_sftfs_v1.tmp | 18/09/2011 10:26 ... | TMP File | 68 KB |

To understand a little bit more about these `GlbVol` and `UsrVol` files, here's an explanation:

- `UsrVol_sftfs_v1.pkg` contains new or modified user-specific data from a system process that is not associated with a specific user context but is associated with a specific package.

- `GlblVol_sftfs_v1_<SID>.pkg` contains application-specific files that are modified by any user process in the virtual environment. The SID of the user is appended to the volume name to uniquely identify it.

- `GlblVol_sftfs_v1_S-1-5-20.pkg` contains any application-specific data that is modified by a system process. The well-known SID for a system is appended to the volume. User modifications go instead to the application data isolation volume. The global package volume also contains the virtual environment configuration for system processes.

- `GlblVol_sftfs_v1_S-1-5-18.pkg` is only created when the package includes processes running in a different context besides the virtual, for example, a Windows service.

Regarding the User Data directory, we can find only one file:

- `Usrvol_sftfs_v1.pkg` contains user-specific files that are modified or new files that are created by any user process in the virtual environment. This volume also contains the virtual environment configuration, as modified by the user.

These files interact in several different ways during the normal processes of virtual applications such as the initial launch, shutdown, upgrade, and so on.

Microsoft developed a complete document where we can evaluate this behavior closely and understand how these files are used during each task.

The following is an example, taken from Microsoft documentation, of processes such as initial launch, shutdown, and subsequent launch:

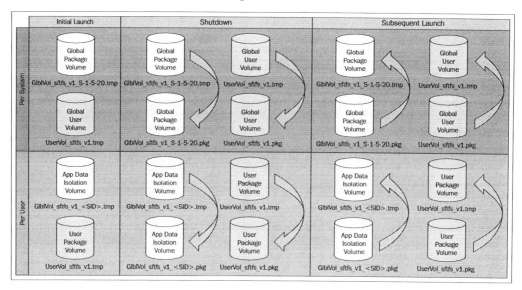

The process runs as follows:

1. When a user launches the virtual application, the TMP files are created in the Global Data directory to store any changes that occur while the application is launched, like we saw in the Firefox 6 package container.

2. When initiating a shutdown, the TMP files are merged with their respective locations, global and/or user, as PKG files. These files are stored for subsequent launches to preserve any changes that were made when the application was launched.

3. On subsequent launches, the PKG files are copied to TMP files for changes that are made while the application is launched.

We can find more information in the Microsoft document, *App-V Application Publishing and Client Interaction*, at: `http://download.microsoft.com/download/f/7/8/f784a197-73be-48ff-83da-4102c05a6d44/APP-V/AppPubandClientInteraction.docx`.

# Understanding the App-V client cache

As we've already seen, the App-V client cache performs a critical role in all App-V implementations. One of the main reasons is that most of the virtual application's usage occurs using the App-V client cache.

The client cache file, named as `sftfs.fsd`, contains the SFT files included in all the packages used by the App-V client.

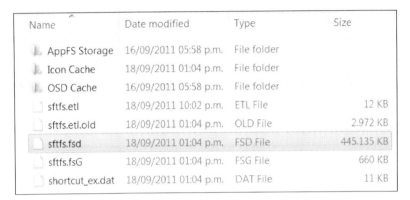

To summarize some of the characteristics regarding the App-V client cache:

- By default the App-V client cache is stored at `C:\ProgramData\Microsoft\ Application Virtualization Client\SoftGrid Client`.

- 1 TB is the maximum size permitted (it is 6 GB configured by default when we install the App-V client).

- Fixed size and minimum free disk space are the two limitations we can use in the App-V client cache.

In the App-V client cache, the following components are included: all the files and folders information, Feature Block 1 (FB1) of applications launched (complete packages are also stored when we configure auto load triggers), and virtual registry of the applications.

- When the App-V client cache is full and new applications need to be added, the oldest and unused files are removed from the cache in order to maintain the latest applications.

    ○ Applications "locked" into the cache are not considered for deletion.

    ○ When an application deleted from the App-V client cache is launched, the streaming process starts again.

- Sharing the App-V client cache among several clients is possible. It is only supported in VDI scenarios plus Full Infrastructure and RDS hosts. This "shared cache" feature is used as a read-only file.

 For more information about this, take a look at *Chapter 7, Integrating App-V with Virtual Desktop Infrastructure (VDI)*.

- Modifying the size of the cache is possible using the App-V Client Management Consoles **Properties | File System** tab.
- If we want to reduce the size of the client cache using the App-V Client Management Console and the current size exceeds our new value, then this will not reduce the size of the file. To do so, we must edit a registry.

## Reducing the size of the App-V client cache

As we discussed in the App-V Client Management Console, we can modify the size of the client cache, but the limitation is presented when we want to reduce the size of the cache and the current size of the file surpasses the value.

To accomplish this, the following procedure can be executed:

1. In the App-V client, access `regedit`.
2. In `HKEY_LOCAL_MACHINE\SOFTWARE\[Wow6432\]Microsoft\SoftGrid\4.5\Client\AppFS`, modify the "**State**" registry key to **0**.

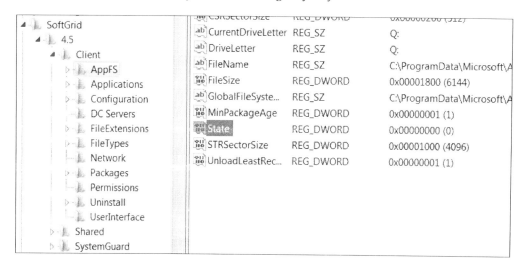

3. Reboot the operating system.

When the machine is rebooted, the FSD file is deleted and a new one is created. There's no need to change the registry value, as this is reconfigured by the App-V client.

# Registry keys available in the App-V client

The App-V client cache includes a complete set of registry settings we can modify manually, and several of them using Group Policy with the App-V ADM template. The registries can be found at the following path: HKEY_LOCAL_MACHINE\SOFTWARE\ [Wow6432Node\]Microsoft\SoftGrid\4.5\Client.

Microsoft already provides a complete review of each of the registry keys available; we can find *App-V Client Registry Values* at the link http://technet.microsoft. com/en-us/library/dd464849.aspx.

We are going to take a quick look at each of the sections included in the App-V client cache registries to understand the options available to configure:

- **Configuration** registry: This section is probably the most used, manually or using Group Policy, as it represents the behavior of the App-V client regarding the virtual environment parameters. Some of the important options we can find here are:
    - **ApplicationSourceRoot**: This is the option that overrides the location of the SFT files received by the applications in the OSD files.
    - The normal use of this value appears in, for example, branch offices. The clients here receive the application information from a management server in HQ, but by using registry or Group Policy, the location of the SFT file is overridden to use a local Streaming Server instead of accessing HQ resources.
    - **OSDSourceRoot** and **IconSourceRoot**: Also, we can change the default location from where these OSD files are retrieved.
    - **AllowIndependentFileStreaming** and **RequireAuthorizationIfCached**: These options are used when we need to configure the standalone model manually. For more information about the standalone model, review *Chapter 3, Deploying Applications in Complex Environments*.

This is an example of the **Configuration** setting with some default values:

| | Name | Type | Data |
|---|---|---|---|
| Shared Tools Location | (Default) | REG_SZ | (value not set) |
| SideShow | AllowIndependentFileStreaming | REG_DWORD | 0x00000000 (0) |
| Silverlight | ApplicationSourceRoot | REG_SZ | |
| SoftGrid | AutoLoadTarget | REG_DWORD | 0x00000000 (0) |
| 4.5 | AutoLoadTriggers | REG_DWORD | 0x00000005 (5) |
| Client | CoreInternalTimeout | REG_DWORD | 0x0000003c (60) |
| AppFS | CoreLongTimeout | REG_DWORD | 0x0000012c (300) |
| Applications | CoreMediumTimeout | REG_DWORD | 0x00000078 (120) |
| Configuration | CoreShortTimeout | REG_DWORD | 0x0000005a (90) |
| IncompatiblePro | GlobalDataDirectory | REG_SZ | C:\ProgramData\Microsoft\Application Virtualization Client\ |
| DC Servers | IconSourceRoot | REG_SZ | |
| FileExtensions | InstallPath | REG_SZ | C:\Program Files (x86)\Microsoft Application Virtualization Client |
| FileTypes | LaunchRecordMask | REG_DWORD | 0x00000000 (0) |
| Network | LogFileName | REG_SZ | C:\ProgramData\Microsoft\Application Virtualization Client\sftlog.txt |
| Packages | LogMaxSize | REG_DWORD | 0x00000100 (256) |
| Permissions | LogMinSeverity | REG_DWORD | 0x00000004 (4) |
| Uninstall | LogRolloverCount | REG_DWORD | 0x00000004 (4) |
| UserInterface | MaxHangedThreads | REG_DWORD | 0x00000014 (20) |
| Shared | OSDSourceRoot | REG_SZ | |
| SystemGuard | PreviousGlobalDataDirectory | REG_SZ | C:\ProgramData\Microsoft\Application Virtualization Client\ |
| Software | ProductCode | REG_SZ | {342C9BB8-65A0-46DE-AB7A-8031E151AF69} |
| Speech | ProductName | REG_SZ | Microsoft Application Virtualization Desktop Client |
| SQMClient | RequireAuthorizationIfCached | REG_DWORD | 0x00000000 (0) |
| Sync Framework | SystemEventLogLevel | REG_DWORD | 0x00000003 (3) |
| SystemCertificates | UserDataDirectory | REG_SZ | %APPDATA% |
| TableTextService | Version | REG_SZ | 4.6.1.20870 |
| TabletTip | | | |
| Tcpip | | | |
| Terminal Server Client | | | |
| TermServLicensing | | | |

- **Network** registry: Used to configure some of the network parameters in the App-V client.
    - **AllowDisconnectedOperation**: Also another option used for the standalone mode
    - Several network timeout values to configure

- **AppFS** registry: Controls the use of the drive, filesystem directories, and files used by the App-V client.
    - **State**: Changing it to 0 resets the App-V client cache when rebooted
    - **FileSize**: Maximum value for the App-V client cache
    - **FileName**: Filename used for the App-V client cache

- **Permissions** registry: The values here are the same ones used in the App-V Client Management Console available in **Properties | Permissions** (reviewed earlier in this chapter).

There are also other sets of registry settings available when some of the non-default configurations are present in the App-V client such as **CustomSettings** or **Reporting**. For more information on them, please visit the link http://technet.microsoft.com/en-us/library/dd464849.aspx.

# App-V deployment possibilities

Microsoft Application Virtualization offers administrators and decision makers tons of possibilities to implement it when we have already decided that virtualizing applications is our approach.

App-V implementation models consider pretty much all the scenarios in small, mid, and large-size organizations, making it possible to offer all users App-V applications. Scenarios such as branch offices with slow bandwidth, offline and/or roaming users, or when we already have other platforms to provide applications (such as SCCM, Citrix XenApp, or Remote Desktop Services) are also included as valid deployment models.

The deployment model used basically depends on the current infrastructure in place, understanding the requirement, and of course analyzing the cost-benefit equation. The deployment possibilities in App-V are as follows:

- Full Infrastructure model
- **Electronic software distribution (ESD)** model
- Standalone model

We are going to take a quick look at each deployment method available, but we are assuming that the basic concepts about App-V implementation are clear for the reader.

More information can be found in Microsoft's document *App-V 4.6 Infrastructure Planning and Design Guide* at http://go.microsoft.com/fwlink/?LinkId=160978.

In my previous book, *Getting Started with Microsoft Application Virtualization 4.6*, we've also covered App-V deployment models, replacing the Electronic Software Distribution to be reviewed in this book by the "Streaming Model".

There are several names that App-V experts use to list the deployment models, and practically these different approaches are the same, except that some of the information is reorganized.

For example, there are some articles, including Microsoft's, that include SCCM as a standalone deployment model. Others articles refers, that SCCM represents by itself a different deployment method; or even there are some approaches that refer to the ESD model as every implementation model which do not include an App-V management server.

In this book, we will consider the standalone model as the deployment model where the only requirement is the App-V client and the virtual application MSI, and the ESD as the deployment model using Streaming Servers (such as HTTP/S, File Server, SCCM, and any other third-party platform).

# Understanding the Full Infrastructure model

The full model contains the full set of components in App-V: management server (App-V SQL database included), Sequencer, Streaming Server, and App-V client.

In Full Infrastructure, clients interact with the App-V infrastructure by using the "publishing refresh" process, which is highly integrated with Active Directory. Here, users have access to their applications on logging in.

Other important features that you can benefit from by using this model are:

- **Reporting**: Detailed periodic reporting of the App-V package usage will provide us with significant information on improving our virtualized applications platform.

- **Central management for file type associations and shortcuts:** Using the App-V Management Console, we can control the behavior of these components in clients, which is crucial for the applications, deployment and maintenance. Other deployment methods require modifying OSD files or even the whole sequencing process in order to manage FTAs and shortcuts.

- **Central licenses management**: By using named licenses for each App-V package, you can guarantee that only users who have the appropriate license can run the application. And, if we are using concurrent licenses for the same application, the App-V licenses management will only let the application run the number of times permitted.

There are some known issues regarding the enforcement of licenses in App-V. Several customers complained that the behavior is not consistent.

The problem usually appears in scenarios where we have disconnected users, from which the system cannot verify whether the applications are running.

The App-V Full Infrastructure model is the most suitable when we are looking for a large, scalable, and dynamic platform in virtual applications within our organization.

In the following figure, we can see all of the App-V components interacting in the Full Infrastructure model:

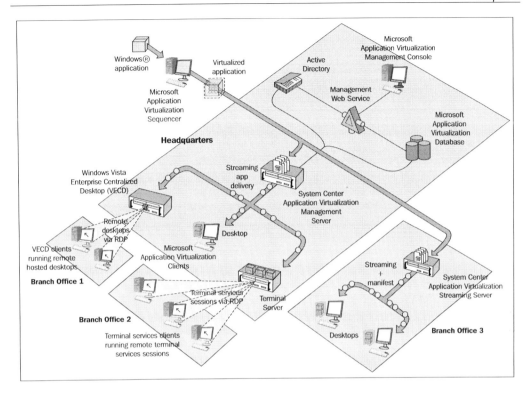

# Understanding the ESD model

The Electronic Software Distribution deployment model is focused on platforms that do not want/require management servers. The components present here are the Streaming Server, the sequencer to package applications, and the App-V client.

SCCM is the platform commonly used with ESD deployment methods. System Center Configuration Manager is highly integrated with App-V, providing a simple way to re-use an existing platform to deploy our virtual applications, optimizing our costs.

SCCM architecture is designed for large and scalable environments since it is not only in charge of deploying applications. Configuration Manager possibilities refer to all the life cycle in desktops, starting in the operating system deployment (OSD feature in SCCM), patch and application management, as well as hardware and software inventory, and so on.

This streaming process is not attached to SCCM. Other similar possibilities are also available:

- App-V Streaming Server: Using the RTSP/S native protocol to distribute applications
- HTTP/S Streaming Server: Configuring a web server such as IIS
- File Server

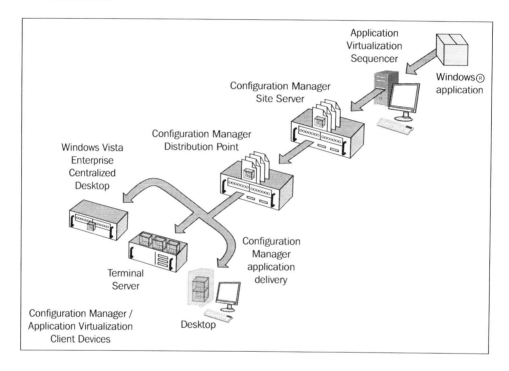

Third-party tools support publishing App-V applications such as XenApp. This Citrix platform publishes virtualized applications created by their own technology as well as Microsoft's App-V.

The key concept here is "publishing". This is not the same as deploying or streaming. Publishing represents the process of notifying clients about resources available (in this case, applications), but the delivery, deployment, or streaming process is still performed by this third-party tool or any other method supported by the vendor.

For more information about this interaction, take a look at the following links:

*How to publish an App-V-enabled application in Citrix XenApp*: http://support.microsoft.com/kb/931576

*Publishing App-V Sequences in XenApp*: http://support.citrix.com/proddocs/topic/xenapp6-w2k8-admin/ps-pub-app-v.html

# Comparing streaming methods

Streaming is the process of the App-V client obtaining the sequenced application package, starting with FB1 (feature block 1) and the rest; FB2 (feature block 2) is acquired on demand.

In the streaming possibilities, we already know about App-V. Here's a little summary on each of them that includes the pros and cons:

| Server | Protocol | Advantages | Disadvantages |
|---|---|---|---|
| File server | SMB | Simple, low-cost solution to configure an existing file server with the \CONTENT share<br><br>Supports enhanced security using IPSec<br><br>Familiar protocol | No active upgrade |
| IIS server | HTTP/HTTPS | Supports enhanced security using HTTPS protocol<br><br>Only using one port in the firewall<br><br>Familiar protocol | No active upgrade |
| App-V Streaming Server or management Server | RTSP/RTSPS | Active upgrade supported<br><br>Supports enhanced security using RTSPS protocol<br><br>If we are using RTSPS, only one port in the firewall is used | Server administration requirement. Can handle fewer simultaneous cached launches than file or IIS servers |

# Understanding the Standalone model

This is the minimalist mode of App-V with no infrastructure required, but App-V Sequencer, to generate the applications the first time and the App-V Desktop Client.

Sequencing the application adds all the necessary files into one package and generates an MSI file that you can use to deploy manually (distributing with a CD/DVD or USB drive), scripting and Group Policy (having GPO involved to distribute it will require, of course, Active Directory), or using the System Center Configuration Manager (SCCM).

This model is in use when you have several offline users. It also has several uses when the cost of distributing to branch offices with a small bandwidth is too high.

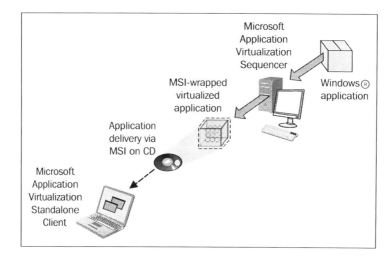

# Understanding the App-V client and publishing interaction

Having a deep understanding about the client-server communication is vital for every administrator.

The publishing interaction among clients and servers occurs in the Full Infrastructure model (even though we can configure the IIS server with a publishing configuration; for more information, take a look into *Chapter 3, Deploying Applications in Complex Environments*), where the database stores the list of the applications available and generates an XML file that is delivered to the App-V client and then the applications are streamed down.

In this section, we are going to take a good look at each step involved in the client and server processes regarding publication and refresh, and when an application is launched.

# Understanding the publishing refresh process

The publishing refresh process occurs, by default, when the user logs in or when the refresh is manually triggered using the App-V client or SFTMIME.

This process contains several steps to validate the applications available for each user. Let's take a look at this as soon as the publishing refresh is launched:

1. The client computer sends the user's Kerberos ticket, which contains all the **Security Identifiers (SIDs)** for the groups that this user belongs to, to the management server for authentication.

2. After a successful authentication, the client computer establishes a connection to the Management Server. The App-V client supports connections between the client and the server to commence using RTSP/RTSPS or a web-based provisioning service.

3. Next, the client will send a request for publishing information to the Management Server over RTSP or RTSPS, depending on the client configuration.

4. The Management Server will contact the data store and retrieve a list of the application records and build an XML file, named applist.xml, containing the applications that have been published for the requesting user.

    - Internally, the App-V management server works with an XML cache prior to sending a request to the database for the applications' information. Working with this XML cache is highly important for optimizing the workload in the App-V management server (consider the scenario with thousands of requests per hour; generating this XML every time could be very expensive).

    - If the XML cache is invalid (after a long period of time where the server did not receive any update) or if this is the first request, the process will continue normally.

5. The client computer will process the XML file from the Management Server that contains the location of the ICO and OSD files. These files will be copied to the client computer and populated into the OSD cache and icon cache directories.

6. The client computer creates the appropriate shortcuts and registers file type associations based on the publishing information from the server.

7. Finally, any offline reporting information will be sent to the management server to be placed in the data store for reporting.

# Understanding the application launch/load process

When a user double-clicks a published icon, the launch/load process occurs. This is a complementary workflow with the publishing refresh process.

Prior to the launch/load process, the publishing refresh process needs to be completed in order for the client to receive the icon in the desktop or the start menu.

We are going to examine the steps involved in this process, considering only the Full Infrastructure model where the client continues interacting with the App-V management server:

1. A user first double-clicks the application icon, or tries to open a file with an FTA associated to a virtual application.

2. The App-V client sends the initiating user's ticket to the management server for authorization to launch the application. The client will also send the GUID of the application to verify that the most current version of the package is delivered. Licensing will be checked if enforced by the assigned provider policy.

3. After successful authorization and licensing, the client will verify the cache space required for primary and secondary feature blocks of the package that is present.

   ° This applies when we are launching the application for the first time or any other situation when the streaming process needs to occur.

   ° If the application is already hosted in the App-V client cache, the application can continue the process within the client's cache.

 The phases of authorization, verifying a package's latest version, and the licensing enforcement still occur even when the application is completely loaded into the cache.

4. After ensuring that disk space is available, the client will stream the primary feature block of the package (SFT file) from a server with the appropriate package. App-V supports streaming package files from the following locations:

   ○ Using SFTMIME ADD or CONFIGURE PACKAGE with the /OVERRIDEURL switch allows an administrator to change the Streaming Server on an individual package.

   ○ This OVERRIDEURL is used in SCCM integration to let the client be able to interact directly with the SCCM client instead of a server pre-configured by the App-V client.

5. When the primary feature block is streamed to the App-V client, the application's virtual environment will be built and the client will attempt to launch the application.

6. The secondary feature block will be streamed to the App-V client when a user requests information from it on a block-by-block basis, called an **Out of Sequence Operation**, unless autoload settings are enabled.

## AutoLoad options

AutoLoad is a client runtime policy configuration parameter that enables the secondary feature block of a virtualized application to be streamed to the client automatically in the background.

We can modify this behavior by using the registry or Group Policy:

- Using registry, we can find the AutoLoad option in HKEY_LOCAL_MACHINE\ SOFTWARE\[\Wow6432Node\]Microsoft\SoftGrid\4.5\Configuration

- Using the App-V Group Policy ADM template inside **Microsoft Application Virtualization Client | Communication**, we can find two options to configure these parameters:

   ○ **Set Background Loading Triggers = AutoLoadTriggers**
   ○ **Specify What to Load in Background = AutoLoadTarget**

| Value | Default | Description |
|---|---|---|
| AutoLoadTriggers | 5 (OnLaunch and OnLogin) | This parameter will control the behavior when the FB2 will be streamed down by the client. |
| | | (0) Never: No bits are set (value is 0), no auto loading will be performed, as there are no triggers set. |
| | | (1) OnLaunch: Perform background loading when a user launches an application. |
| | | (2) OnRefresh: Perform background loading anytime a publishing refresh process occurs. |
| | | (4) OnLogin: Perform background loading for any application when a user logs in. |
| | | Default: 0x5 (OnLaunch \| OnLogin) |
| AutoLoadTarget | 1 (Previously Used) | This parameter indicates what will be autoloaded when any given AutoLoadTriggers occurs. Bit mask values: |
| | | (0) None: No autoloading, regardless of what triggers may be set. |
| | | (1) PreviouslyUsed (default): If any AutoLoad trigger is enabled and loads only the packages where at least one app in the package has been previously used by a user (pre-cached). This targets 'important' apps, meaning apps that have been used before are likely to be more important to a user than apps that have never been launched. |
| | | (2) All: If any AutoLoad trigger is enabled, all applications in the package (per package) or for all packages (set for the client) will be automatically loaded, regardless of whether they have ever been launched. |

These settings can also be configured during the App-V client installation using the `SFTMIME` command:

- Using the MSI installation file:
  - For setting `AutoLoadTriggers`, we can use the `AUTOLOADTRIGGERS=[0|1|2|4|5]` parameter. The numbers used are the same as we reviewed previously.
  - For setting `AutoLoadTarget`, we can use the following parameters: `AUTOLOADONLOGIN`, `AUTOLOADONLAUNCH`, and `AUTOLOADONREFRESH`.

 Using the `SFTMIME` command will be reviewed in *Chapter 4, Handling Scripting and App-V Command Lines.*

# Summary

In this chapter, we had the chance to take a complete tour of the App-V components and architecture. Learning about these concepts can introduce us to an optimized new implementation and healthy operations in App-V.

We've reviewed the App-V server components and the sequenced files present in each virtual package, and we also had a good look at the App-V client modules. This last topic is not usually used by most admins, ignoring the fact that some of the most important optimization parameters are included in the client.

We understood the Global and User Data directories present on each App-V client, and how the particular application's modifications are stored within these directories, including one of the key components in the App-V client cache.

We also took a quick tour of the deployment possibilities and differentiating them to understand which possibility (or possibilities) is best suited for our organization. In order to understand most of that, it is also important to understand the App-V client and publishing interaction processes.

We had a good glimpse at the App-V platform, and reviewed some key concepts that will probably clarify a lot of topics and highlight necessary information for a healthy App-V implementation and maintenance.

In the next chapter, we are going to keep up with some advanced topics; this time by using advanced sequencing techniques in App-V.

# 2
# Sequencing in Complex Environments

All of us working in the IT sector know that technology, platforms, infrastructure, and implementations do not always work as we would find in a step-by-step article. We know that every scenario that we could work in may require some tweaks to adjust our implementation.

App-V is one of the greatest examples of how a technology can adapt to almost any given scenario: integrating with other existing platforms, different implementation models, and the variety in the delivery methods.

If we are talking about the sequencing compatibility of applications, we are quite sure that almost any application is suitable for packaging, but sequencing complex applications could require several hours of analyzing, installing, packaging, and testing the virtual environment, to finally get it ready.

There are several parameters and options we can use in the sequencing process in order to complete an application virtualization, such as, editing the **Exclusion Items** used by default in the App-V Sequencer, handling drivers outside the virtual environment, working with the **LOCAL_INTERACTION_ALLOWED** policy for the application to interact with the operating system, and so on.

One important option about the complex applications scenario is the **package accelerators**, which is included in the App-V 4.6 SP1. With the package accelerators, we generate a new way of automating and simplifying the sequencing phase of an application. Once a complex application is captured, we can generate the necessary environment and guidelines within this package accelerator and share it with the community.

In this chapter, you will learn about:

- An overview of complex sequencing: applications not supported and sequencing best practices

- Complex scenarios in the sequencing phases: reviewing which applications could require more tuning than others

- Handling the virtual environment: the override and merge options, and local interaction policy

- Understanding and using **Dynamic Suite Composition (DSC)**

- Upgrading and editing an existing package with the new features of App-V 4.6 SP1

- Reviewing package accelerators

# Overview of complex sequencing

Most likely, almost all of the existing applications in your current operating system support virtualization, but as we said, not all of them will have the same, straightforward process to get it working properly.

It is important to note that:

- **Every application needs a deep understanding before capturing it**: Understand the application's usage, dependent components, requirements, and interaction with the operating system. If we don't have these things cleared up, the sequencing process will not be an easy ride.

- **App-V was not designed to solve incompatibility issues**: Even though virtualizing an application in Windows XP can actually allow it to run in Windows 7, the focus of this technology is not to solve incompatibility among operating systems. We have some great examples of resolving problems like this using App-V, but it's not 100 percent guaranteed.

- **Do not confuse "complex/advanced sequencing" with sequencing unsupported applications**: There are some applications that are not supported for sequencing; even though by editing and adding some tweaks you could probably get them working, it will surely not be a more stable scenario. In this chapter, we will take a look at some of these tweaks that we can accomplish, for example, in the "applications with drivers" scenarios.

# Applications not supported for sequencing

Here's a quick list of the applications not supported for sequencing that we should be aware of.

An interesting note about this list is that, as we are going to cover in this chapter, there are some workarounds we can apply in some applications which can be marked as "unsupported".

| Application type | Definition | Examples |
|---|---|---|
| Applications with drivers | Applications that install and rely on a system-level driver. As a workaround for this scenario, the driver portion of this application can be installed locally on the client system, allowing the other components of the application to be virtualized. | OEM hardware utilities |
| Applications that integrate closely with the operating system | Some applications, such as the Windows Internet Explorer browser, are closely tied to the operating system. As such, these applications cannot be sequenced. | Windows Media Player  Internet Explorer |
| Applications with shell extensions | Microsoft Application Virtualization does not support shell extensions that contain a custom dynamic-link library (DLL). This would require providing Windows Explorer access to the virtual environment. Shell extensions are in-process Component Object Model (COM) objects that extend the abilities of the Windows operating system. | WinZip |
| COM+ applications | COM+ is dynamic; it happens at runtime and is not captured. COM and DCOM, by contrast, are recorded in component services and are static. | BizTalk |

| Application type | Definition | Examples |
| --- | --- | --- |
| Applications with background tasks | App-V supports the virtualization of services; however, they must be started from within the virtual environment. Some applications install a service in the background, which is not captured. | PCAnywhere<br><br>Firewall Client ISA/TMG Server |
| Applications that integrate with many other applications | Applications with complex or unknown integration with other applications or operating system components need to be fully evaluated to identify and define interaction requirements. | Live Meeting 2007<br><br>Microsoft Office Communicator 2007 |
| Applications with licensing enforcement tied to a computer | Applications where the license is tied to system hardware or to the system's MAC address. | Computer-aided design (CAD) software |
| Applications that result in a `.sft` file greater than 4 gigabytes (GB) | App-V does not support sequences larger than 4 GB. | Microsoft Flight Simulator X |
| 16-bit application in 64-bit client | This is actually a restriction in the operating system. None of the Windows 64-bit clients supports 16-bit applications. | Pegasus Mail 16-bits version |

> Microsoft Office Communicator 2007 is not supported in App-V, but its successor, Microsoft Lync 2010, is. For more information about supportability in Lync 2010 check the following links:
>
> Client virtualization support for the Lync 2010 client and the Lync 2010 Group Chat client: `http://support.microsoft.com/kb/2560826`
>
> Client Virtualization in Microsoft Lync 2010: `http://www.microsoft.com/download/en/details.aspx?id=21129`
>
> Regarding applications with shell extensions, Aaron Parker developed a great article about how to add this feature for App-V packages — Adding Shell Extensions to App-V Packages. Check `http://blog.stealthpuppy.com/virtualisation/adding-shell-extensions-to-app-v-packages/`.

# Sequencing best practices

A good place to start would be the *Best Practices for sequencing* official knowledge base article from Microsoft (`http://support.microsoft.com/kb/932137/en`).

We can also find *Microsoft Application Virtualization 4.6 SP1 Sequencing Guide* at the Microsoft Download Center (`http://www.microsoft.com/downloads/en/default.aspx`).

I would like to mention some of the lessons I've learned so far, from the scenarios and applications I came across, when I had to work in sequencing and delivering virtualized applications:

- **Understand application requirements and installation process before capturing**: We should never start sequencing an application we've never installed before; we must review the requirements of each application and verify whether it needs other components or applications to use it. This will help us decide whether we need to use Dynamic Suite Composition or just one bundle with several applications.

- **Understand application usage**: Do we run the necessary tests once the application is running, to verify whether the user can actually use it?

  One common error appearing in several App-V implementations (and I must say in several IT implementations) is that the deployment application tester does not complete the right "use cases" to verify the successful implementation of the application.

  Ask an expert user which are the common activities a person executes once the application is launched; and include those in the moment of capturing it.

- **Before you start sequencing, close other programs**: The App-V Sequencer can capture changes generated from another application that is running. Some of those that might be a good idea to disable are:

  - Antivirus software
  - Windows Update
  - Windows Defender
  - Windows Search
  - Disk defragmentation tools
  - Software agents, such as, SCCM client, Dropbox, iTunes, Winamp, and so on

- Even though running an antivirus software on the sequencer machine is not a good idea, ensure that the computer is not infected with any type of malware. To do that without installing any antivirus, you can use the *Microsoft Malicious Software Removal Tool* from this link: `http://www.microsoft.com/security/malwareremove/default.aspx`.

  This tool is represented only by an EXE file that is updated frequently by Microsoft and automatically scans your computer to detect any malware presence.

 In *Appendix*, we will review some tools and add-ons we can use to complement App-V, including a few that can allow us to browse inside an SFT file. This way we can check whether there's any malware present in an App-V package.

- Use Windows Virtual PC or any other virtualization platform for the App-V Sequencer machines, using a virtual machine snapshot. This will give us the chance to work with a clean operating system. Do not reuse the same sequencer image, where you install and remove applications. Use snapshots to revert the system to a "clean" state, so that each capture contains as much information about the application as possible.

  Do not take the snapshot as soon as you complete the App-V Sequencer installation. The problem begins once the App-V Sequencer installation is completed, the App-V Sequencer launches. This assigns a unique GUID for the App-V package to be created. If you revert to the snapshot every time you want to capture a new application the same GUID will apply to the App-V application.

 Virtual PC does not support 64-bit guest operating systems. VMware Workstation/Server, Hyper-V, and other platforms do support this architecture.

- **Use the same operating system in the sequencer and client machines**: Use the same baseline, updates, and existing applications. Microsoft does not officially support deploying applications in an operating system other than from where they were captured.

- If the client/sequencer operating system is Windows Vista or Windows 7, consistently maintain the **User Account Control (UAC)** option. If the client machines have this feature enabled, maintain the same option in the sequencer.

- Ideally, place the application folder in the root drive, to avoid any inconsistencies among clients, for example, `Q:\MyApp`.

- Execute the application as many times as is necessary, to ensure that all the initial configurations that most applications perform, such as license agreement and file type associations, are completed successfully.

  There are some applications that, as soon as they are launched, will start generating unnecessary information and could also attach some configuration, specific to the current user and/or computer. This kind of application should not be run during the sequencing process.

- In the **Launch Phase** of sequencing the application, the FB1 (primary feature block) is created; a best practice in this phase is launching the application and executing it's normal use. For example, if the sequenced application is Microsoft Word, open the application and type and misspell a word; this will use grammar correction features.

  Also, consider not launching the application in the example mentioned earlier.

- Ensure that none of the application components are installed with the **Install on First Use** MSI option. Select either **Run from My Computer** (install this component) or **Not Available** (do not install this component).

- Remove **Automatic Updates** from a sequenced application. This could lead to deployment inconsistencies.

- Verify that the directory `%TMP%` or `%TEMP%` has sufficient space to store temporary sequencing data.

- **Increase RAM when the capturing process seems slow**: Sequencing an application is an intensive, memory-consuming process. If experiencing a slow process, consider adding more memory to the sequencer.

- If the application installation freezes or throws up notifications about errors encountered while the capturing process is running, re-run the sequencing procedure, even if the application seems installed correctly.

- **Install a dummy printer in the sequencer before starting any application capture**: This is another example of a common best practice for special applications that could install some virtual printers in the client operating system.

  If we are using an application that includes a virtual printer in the installation process, and if this is the first printer in the operating system, there are going to be several registries and files created in the operating system; these will be included in the App-V package.

- **Set user expectations**: The use of virtualized applications could result in losing some capabilities, such as "right-click options", of the application. It is important for us to explain to the users the functionalities that the application will have and the ones that it won't.

- **Create an App-V package accelerator when you consider necessary**: Package accelerators are created to maintain captured configurations needed for particular applications; creating those will give you the chance to share with the community and help your peers and yourself, the next time you need to sequence that application.

- **Document the sequencing process**: Do not expect that you will always hold the responsibility for sequencing an application; a good explanation document will facilitate our work and our teammates. The documents created here could be a guide for a new sequence procedure when a new application version appears.

# Reviewing complex applications

Understanding applications is a key element prior to starting with the sequencing process. Gaining deep knowledge about it will give us the necessary tools for proper sequencing, especially when we are dealing with complex applications.

In my previous book, *Getting Started with Microsoft Application Virtualization*, we took a closer look at the step-by-step process for virtualizing a seriously complex application such as Microsoft Office 2010. Even though we are not going to review it again, we'll talk about the important topics we must understand to achieve a happy ending while virtualizing a complex application.

Another important thing to remember about the applications and their sequencing process is that we should always maintain this process with the recommended best practices; this way we'll avoid common errors and misconceptions regarding this stage.

# Applications that require complex sequencing

If you have a bit of experience in App-V and in the sequencing process, you probably know that almost any application is suited for virtualization; however, every application is unique in how it interacts with the operating system or other applications, and the requirements included.

Here's a list of application types that require a complex capturing process:

- **Applications with device drivers**: As mentioned earlier, drivers are not suited for sequencing, but there are methods we can use to deploy these drivers manually or by automation (OSD or any other scripting process), to make those applications work smoothly.

- **Applications with non-virtualized extensibility points**: Good examples of those are applications with shell extensions, such as **WinRAR**. Also, by adding some parameters and changes to the packaging process, we can make most of them work properly.

- **Applications that cannot be installed on** *Q* **drive**: App-V supports these installations, since the virtual environment redirects the paths to the right directory; but there are some tweaks that might be necessary.

- **Applications with dependencies outside the virtual environment**: Some applications can contain particular and custom configurations that require, for example, paths outside their virtual environment. Depending on the application, we can solve this in different ways, such as, editing the sequencer exclusions list; using *merge* or *override* options within the package directories to edit the virtual application environment.

- **Web applications**: Internet Explorer does not support sequencing, but some web applications, such as **Java Runtime Environment** or **Silverlight**, can be captured. In these cases, we must guarantee that App-V can execute an instance of Internet Explorer correctly, in order to use these web apps.

- **Applications not compatible with the operating system**: As we said, we should not focus on using our App-V implementation to solve an incompatibility issue. But, if we find ourselves facing a compatibility problem, an efficient approach could be to understand exactly what went wrong in the configuration for it to be incompatible.

  For those scenarios, **Microsoft Application Toolkit** and deploying a "mitigation", by script or manually, can be very useful.

# About the Microsoft Application Compatibility Toolkit

One interesting tool we can use to complement App-V implementation is the **Microsoft Application Compatibility Toolkit**. This tool generates a complete analysis about the application we choose and verifies whether it is compatible with the Windows Vista and Windows 7 operating systems.

Not only we can save a lot of time by letting the Microsoft Application Toolkit find the incompatibility issues within the application and the operating system, but we can also use it to generate **mitigations** to solve the incompatibilities.

These mitigations can also be used as shim files (.sdb) that contain the actions that can solve these incompatibilities. By importing this shim into the operating system, the virtual package can interact with the operating system because of this new mitigation implemented.

As the application compatibility shim engine is an operating system feature that changes API behavior, these .sdb files must be installed outside of the virtual environment. This means that you must install the application compatibility fix(es) before sequencing, and then sequence the application, as you normally would. When it is time to deploy the application, you must install the shim database via a pre-launch script in the OSD or as a dependent SCCM advertisement. The installation requires administrator rights and the command line will look much like this:

```
sdbinst.exe -u C:\ApplicationFix.sdb
```

This, again, is no "silver bullet" to the real problem of incompatible applications. Consider this as a workaround but it is not guaranteed that it will solve the problem.

You can download the **Microsoft Application Compatibility Toolkit** from the Microsoft Download Center website http://www.microsoft.com/download/en/details.aspx?id=7352.

In the same link, you'll also find the **Step-by-Step Guide** and **Deployment Guide**.

# Understanding sequencing phases

Before we start working with the complex sequencing process, let's take a look at the sequencing phases included in App-V, which will facilitate our job while capturing.

When we are sequencing an application, as soon as the installation monitoring ends, the application goes through the following three phases:

- **Parsing**: Here's where the application becomes "portable" by removing all explicit names related to the computer or user name and transforming those into environment variables. For example, `appv-sequencer` (computer name) is replaced by `%COMPUTERNAME`, or `C:\Users\augusto` transforms into `%USERPROFILE%`.

- **Excluding**: In the excluding phase, selected directories are removed from the captured data, such as, the IE cache directory or recycle bin. Those are excluded not only to avoid any unnecessary data included in the package, but also because some of the directories are related to computer-/user-specific data, which must be avoided.

- **Classifying**: Depending on the category type, the data is classified and saved on a different PKG file; this is an important matter since this category will decide whether these components are shared with other virtual applications (application data) or not (user data).

Here's a figure about the phases interacting in the sequencing process:

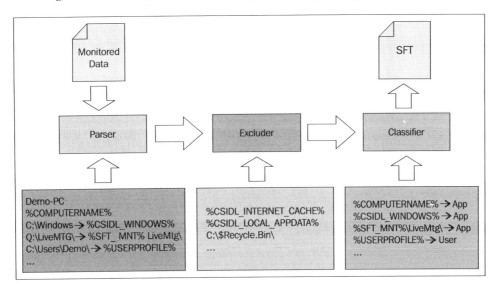

# Handling App-V Sequencer exclusions

As we've seen earlier, the App-V Sequencer needs to monitor specific data and directories to capture the application installation and, in this process, it also needs to exclude several directories to avoid unnecessary data as well as computer/user data.

The App-V Sequencer installation includes the default list for **Exclusion Items**, which it applies every time.

Microsoft's Network Monitor 3.4 is a good example of an application that requires editing of the App-V Sequencer **Exclusion Items**. Normally, this application is sequenced without any issue, but as soon as we start the virtualized package, we receive the error **Failed to load NPL script**.

In this example, the App-V Sequencer ignored a few files that are required for the application to function properly.

 We will review, in *Chapter 5, Troubleshooting App-V*, the normal process for finding these errors and the specific directory or files ignored by the App-V Sequencer, using Microsoft Sysinternal's **Process Monitor**.

To solve this issue with **Network Monitor**, we must follow the ensuing steps:

1. Open the App-V Sequencer with the machine in a clean state.

2. Select **Tools | Options | Exclusion Items**.

3. The missing files, in this case, are located in C:\Users\\*username*\AppData\ Local; in the list we can find them as **%CSIDL_LOCAL_APPDATA%**. Select and **Delete** this file.

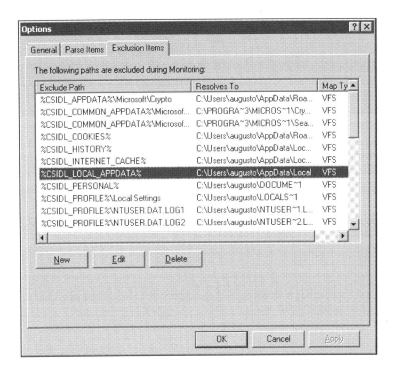

The change we just made will apply to the next package we capture; but, as soon as the virtual machine is reverted to a clean state, the configuration will be back to the default.

4. Sequence the application following best practices.

5. Deploy the application to clients and run it again.

**Q:** If I already have the application sequenced, do I need to re-sequence the package?

**A:** Yes. The change made only applies to new packages to be captured. We could also try to deploy the changes manually, but in most scenarios, this neither will be efficient nor recommended.

**Q:** Can I change the configuration of the exclusions so it overrides the default configuration?

**A:** Yes. The App-V Sequencer default configuration can be replaced by a new one; all we need to do is, when we've made the changes to the App-V Sequencer options, select **File** and then **Save as template**. The file will be saved as .sprt (Sequencer Template file).

Using this option, the following changes will be applied:

- Advanced Monitoring Options
- Package Deployment Settings
- General Options
- Parse items
- Exclusion items

# Using workarounds for applications with drivers

Network Monitor 3.4 is also a good example of an application that could be sequenced with a few tweaks, even if the software requires a driver to work properly.

Once we sequence the application and apply the workaround reviewed before editing the App-V Sequencer **Exclusion Items**, we will see our application running apparently normally; but, as soon as we try to capture it from the network, we will see the **None of the network adapters are bound to the netmon driver** message:

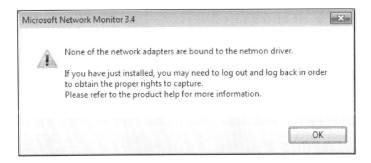

If we are working with an application and we don't know the exact driver that it is using, we can use Process Monitor again, to find the particular driver used. In this case, the network driver, used as a filter in communications, is named nm3.sys.

You can also easily find the latest driver installed by accessing C:\Windows\system32\drivers and looking for the latest files added.

In order to get this application working as virtual, we must do the following:

1. Sequence the application, as shown previously, using the App-V Sequencer exclusion.

2. When we sequence the application, the App-V Sequencer 4.6 SP1 detects an unsupported driver installed.

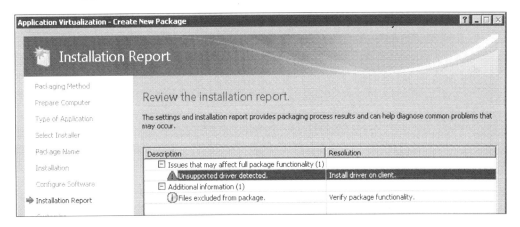

3. Deploy the applications to App-V clients.

4.  Install the Network Monitor driver manually or using a script.

    ○   If using a script, we must locate the `.inf` file to install it. The command line to execute, must be the following:

        ```
        Rundll32 syssetup,SetupInfObjectInstallAction DefaultInstall
        128 C:\pathToInf\netnm3.inf
        ```

5   After the driver is installed, we must bind it to the client's network card.

6.  Access **Network Control Panel** and double-click the network card.

7.  Select **Install | Service | Microsoft Network Monitor 3 Driver**:

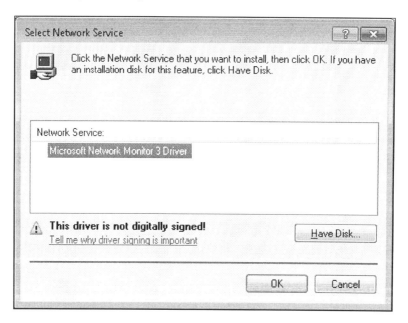

8.  Run the application and start a capture:

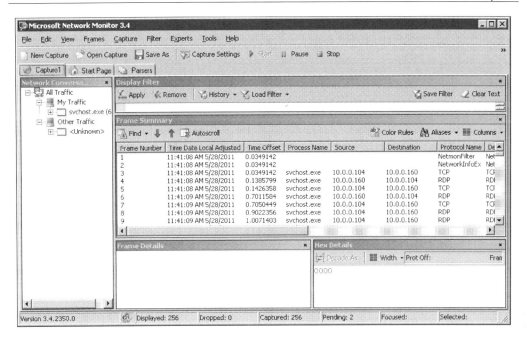

# Handling the virtual environment

Fortunately the flexibility that App-V provides lets us work and edit almost anything in the sequencing process, like we've seen by editing the parsed or excluded items, or by editing the virtual environment.

The virtual environment can be reviewed and edited using the SPRJ (Project File) of the application or as soon as we complete the sequencing wizard. The options we can edit in the virtual environment are as follows:

- **Files**: All the application files captured and included in the package.

- **Virtual registry**: The registry keys used by the application, which, again, are only going to be available for the application we are virtualizing.

- **Virtual file system**: A detailed view about the files stored in the $Q:\backslash$, including those which are redirected to the $C:\backslash$.

- **Virtual services**: Embedded services in the application that are captured in the sequencing process.

- **OSD**: This is a more practical view of the OSD file, which contains an XML-formed view. Using this tab, we can easily edit some important values about the application dependencies, behavior, and of course, embedded scripts.

# Using override/merge options

As we already know, virtual applications live in their "isolation bubble" but interact with other components (registry keys and files) within the operating system. Virtual applications are aware of these registry keys and files that are actually shared with other components in the operating system.

This *awareness* that we are talking about can basically be categorized into two modes:

- The virtual environment only sees what the application is using. This is called **Override Virtual View**.

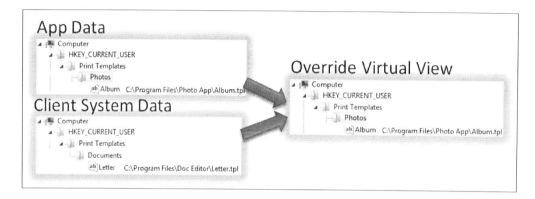

- The virtual environment shares this common space with the operating system by including those components, again, files or registry keys. This is called **Merged Virtual View**.

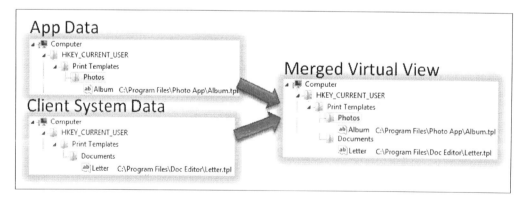

By default, App-V behavior (called *Opacity*) uses the following concept:

- If the file path/registry key existed already, then set to merge with local data
- If the file path/registry key did not exist, set to override (masking local data)

With those concepts cleared, we must know that there are some applications that, in this interaction, might need some changes to get things working properly.

While editing the virtual application, we can reference these options in both the virtual registry and virtual files.

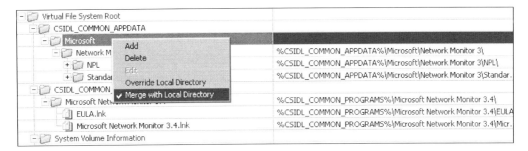

 An important note about overriding and merging options is that there are some applications, such as **Java Runtime Environment**, which could cause us some problems if there are previous versions of the runtime installed.

Without using the override options, the co-existence of registry keys in the *Virtual View* may result in some malfunctions when an application is using the incorrect version of, in this case, the Java Runtime Environment.

For those scenarios, we can also use interesting tweaks such as the following:

- Sequence the application normally.
- Look for the registry keys that could be causing the problem.

  This, again, can be done using Process Monitor, understanding whether the virtual application is querying for incorrect values.

- Use the virtual machine in a clean state again.
- Start sequencing the application and, in the monitoring phase, add and immediately remove the registry keys that you need the virtual application to ignore:

```
reg add HKLM\SOFTWARE\Companyname\registrypath1\setting1

reg delete HKLM\Software\Companyname\registrypath1\setting1 /va /f
```

  This execution will force the virtual environment to delete from its view the existence of these registry keys.

Using the /va parameter deletes any existing subkeys and their values; the /f option is used to execute the action without confirmation.

* Complete the sequencing process.

Another application that requires these types of changes in the virtual environment is Microsoft Office 2010, which we had the chance to review completely in my previous book *Getting Started with Microsoft Application Virtualization 4.6*.

# Understanding LOCAL_INTERACTION_ ALLOWED

Another option we can review in some scenarios is the ability to let the application interact with other applications or components of the operating system. This option is called **LOCAL_INTERACTION_ALLOWED**.

This feature always appears as disabled, by default, since the main purpose is to relax the isolation of the virtual application. There are some applications that could require specific features to communicate with other applications, for example, an application that requires Microsoft Outlook to send an e-mail.

This option should only be intended for use in particular scenarios and must not be enabled unless completely necessary.

To enable it in your virtual application, follow the ensuing steps:

1. Access the **OSD** tab from the virtual application package.
2. Expand **SOFTPKG | IMPLEMENTATION**.
3. Right-click on **VIRTUALENV**; select **Element | Add | POLICIES**.

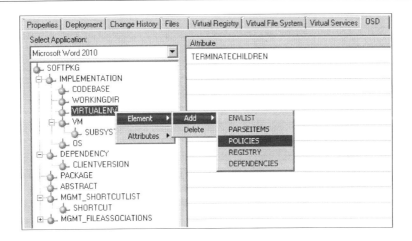

4. Right-click on **POLICIES**; select **Element | Add | LOCAL_ INTERACTION_ALLOWED**.

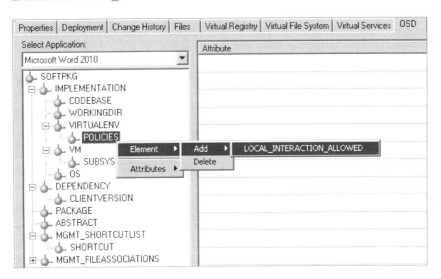

5.  Select **LOCAL_INTERACTION_ALLOWED** and, in the **Element Text** section, add the value **TRUE**.

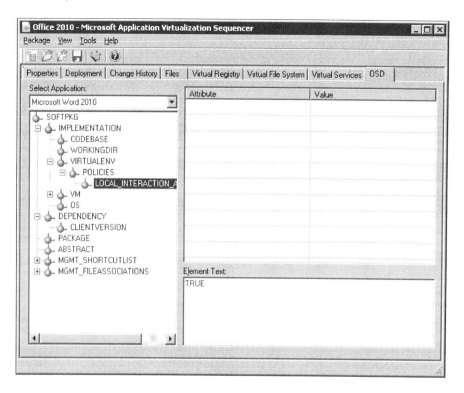

There's also the possibility of enabling this feature by default in every package we sequence. This can be done by accessing the App-V Sequencer options on the **General** tab.

The feature is named **Allow all named objects and COM objects to interact with the local system**.

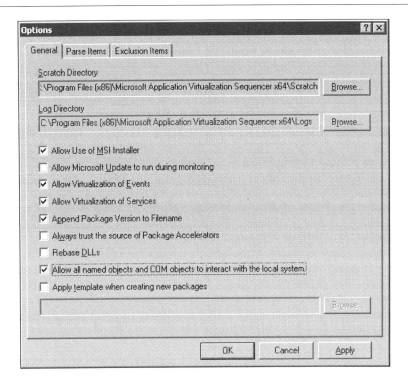

Enabling **LOCAL_INTERACTION_ALLOWED** does not permit the operating system to access the isolated environment; it only works one way.

If we enable this option, it works for the entire package. Meaning, if we have more than one application in the same sequencing process, the policy will be available for all those applications.

For more information about **LOCAL_INTERACTION_ALLOWED**, take a look at the article *A Look Under the Covers – The LOCAL_INTERACTION_ALLOWED Tag*, in the App-V TechNet Blog, here: http://blogs.technet.com/b/appv/archive/2007/09/20/ a-look-under-the-covers-the-local-interaction- allowed-tag.aspx.

There are several more options we can choose in order to customize our package, virtual environment, and application behavior, to fit our needs; important parts of this are the possibilities within the OSD scripting. That section will be covered later, in *Chapter 4, Handling Scripting and App-V Command Lines*. We will have the chance to include, for example, validation of a prerequisite in the operating system prior to the launch of the application, or starting a service outside the virtual environment that the virtual application may need.

# Using Dynamic Suite Composition

Dynamic Suite Composition represents the way in which administrators can define dependencies between App-V packages and guarantee final users transparent operability between applications.

In normal operating system use, we can find several applications that are dependent on other applications. The best example is probably that of web applications interacting (from a browser, of course) constantly with Java Runtime Environment, Silverlight, and other applications, such as PDF Reader. DSC is also very suitable in any plugin scenario for other large applications such as Microsoft Office.

Dynamic Suite Composition always identifies two type of applications:

- **Primary application**: This is the main application and is usually the full software product. It should be identified, as the application users execute primarily before needing a second application.

- **Secondary application**: This is usually a plugin/middleware attached to the primary application. It can be streamed in the normal way and does not need to be fully cached to run.

A primary application can have more than one secondary application, but only one level of dependency is supported. We cannot define a secondary package as dependent on another secondary package.

These application dependencies are customizable in the App-V configuration file of the virtual applications, the OSD, where we are going to use the <DEPENDENCIES> tag in the primary application, adding the identifiers of the secondary application. So, every time the main application needs this secondary application (such as a plugin), it can find the right path and execute it, without any additional user intervention.

In some environments, we find that secondary applications could be a "requirement" for normally using a primary application; with DSC, we can also use the variable MANDATORY=TRUE in the primary application OSD file. This value is added at the end of the secondary application reference.

# Sequencing applications in DSC

If we are using App-V Sequencer 4.6 SP1, we will notice that, as soon as we start the sequencing wizard, we are asked whether the application is: **Standard, Add-on or Plugin**, or **Middleware**. The last two options represent the scenarios when we usually apply DSC.

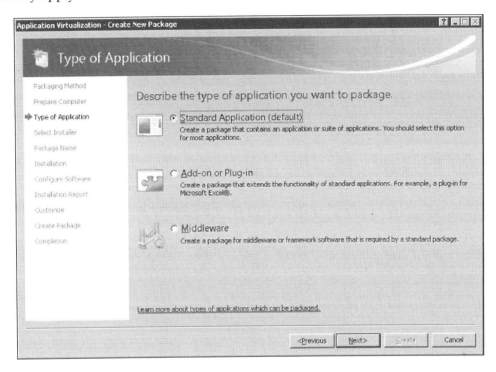

Basically, these options give us the easy path for proper sequencing in DSC. Depending on the type of secondary package, whether plugin or middleware, the process of installing the primary package will vary.

This is how to install a primary package for an **Add-on** or **Plugin**:

1. Sequence the primary app (for example, Microsoft Office).
2. Revert the virtual machine to a clean state.
3. Install a primary application without sequencing. Maintain the settings configured that you captured in the first step.
4. Sequence the secondary app (for example, the Microsoft Excel plugin).

5. Link any dependencies.

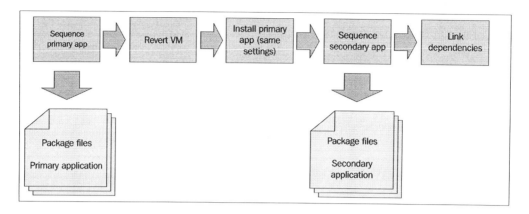

When we are using a **middleware** or a **framework** (such as .NET Framework 4.0) the sequencing workflow that we must follow is the following:

1. Install middleware or framework, without sequencing.
2. Sequence primary application.
3. Revert VM.
4. Sequence the secondary application (middleware or framework).
5. Link dependencies.

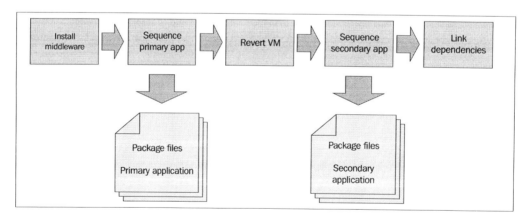

> Sequencing middleware and frameworks usually requires the use of the MANDATORY parameter in DSC.
>
> The App-V recipe for sequencing .Net Framework 4.0 can be found in the App-V Team Blog, `http://blogs.technet.com/b/appv/archive/2011/03/10/new-kb-guide-to-sequencing-net-4-0-with-app-v-4-6-sp1.aspx`.

# Using the Dynamic Suite Composition tool

This Microsoft tool provides a simple method for linking applications in the DSC process; we can straightforwardly accomplish the dependencies, without editing any OSD file.

The Dynamic Suite Composition tool does not need any installation; we just need to run the EXE file, and we'll be ready to start using DSC. You can download this EXE file from the Microsoft Download Center (`http://www.microsoft.com/downloads/en/default.aspx`).

Let's take a look at this simple process, using also the previous examples of Mozilla Firefox and Java Runtime Environment:

1.  Open the Dynamic Suite Composition tool and, in **Package Root(s)**, select the **content** folder in the App-V server.

    The applications existing in the folder will be loaded; they should be grayed out until we select a primary application.

2.  In **Primary Package**, select Mozilla Firefox.

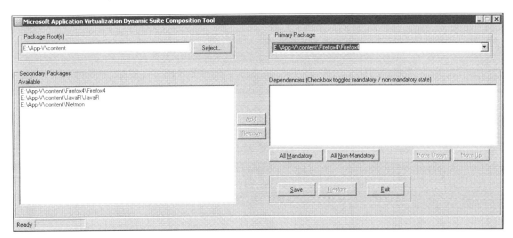

3. In **Secondary Package**, select **Java Runtime Environment** and click on **Add**.

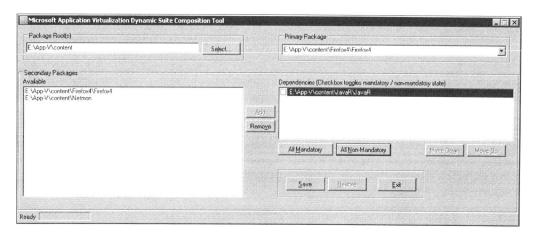

Java Runtime Environment is now added in the **Dependencies** area.

If we are using one primary package and several secondary packages, we just need to add them inside **Dependencies**.

4. Note that we can use the `Mandatory` variable, with just one click.

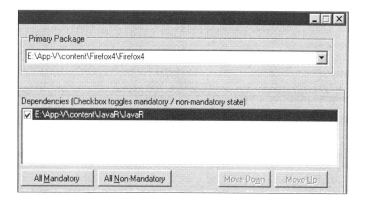

5. Click on **Save**; the change is ready to use in App-V clients.

If we check the Mozilla Firefox OSD file, we'll see that the following lines were added:

```
<DEPENDENCIES>
     <CODEBASE HREF="RTSP://appv-server:554/JavaR/JavaR.sft"
GUID="1CDCFD99-B83F-45D4-A13A-E85B2AE0B589" PARAMETERS=""
FILENAME="JavaR\bin\javaw.exe" SYSGUARDFILE="JavaR\osguard.cp"
SIZE="94749159" MANDATORY="TRUE" />
</DEPENDENCIES>
```

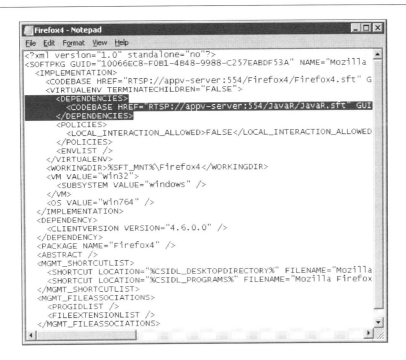

```
Firefox4 - Notepad
File  Edit  Format  View  Help
<?xml version="1.0" standalone="no"?>
<SOFTPKG GUID="10066EC8-F0B1-4B48-9988-C257EABDF53A" NAME="Mozilla
  <IMPLEMENTATION>
    <CODEBASE HREF="RTSP://appv-server:554/Firefox4/Firefox4.sft" G
    <VIRTUALENV TERMINATECHILDREN="FALSE">
      <DEPENDENCIES>
        <CODEBASE HREF="RTSP://appv-server:554/JavaR/JavaR.sft" GUI
      </DEPENDENCIES>
      <POLICIES>
        <LOCAL_INTERACTION_ALLOWED>FALSE</LOCAL_INTERACTION_ALLOWED
      </POLICIES>
      <ENVLIST />
    </VIRTUALENV>
    <WORKINGDIR>%SFT_MNT%\Firefox4</WORKINGDIR>
    <VM VALUE="win32">
      <SUBSYSTEM VALUE="windows" />
    </VM>
    <OS VALUE="win764" />
  </IMPLEMENTATION>
  <DEPENDENCY>
    <CLIENTVERSION VERSION="4.6.0.0" />
  </DEPENDENCY>
  <PACKAGE NAME="Firefox4" />
  <ABSTRACT />
  <MGMT_SHORTCUTLIST>
    <SHORTCUT LOCATION="%CSIDL_DESKTOPDIRECTORY%" FILENAME="Mozilla
    <SHORTCUT LOCATION="%CSIDL_PROGRAMS%" FILENAME="Mozilla Firefox
  </MGMT_SHORTCUTLIST>
  <MGMT_FILEASSOCIATIONS>
    <PROGIDLIST />
    <FILEEXTENSIONLIST />
  </MGMT_FILEASSOCIATIONS>
```

6.  Remember to refresh the server in App-V clients. With that, the applications are ready to work together.

We do not need to use the DSC tool to accomplish this configuration. This simple application just facilitates the manual work of setting the dependencies in the OSD file.

If we want to set DSC manually, we just need to access the primary application OSD, just above **/VIRUTALENV**, and add **DEPENDENCIES**, copying the **CODEBASE** line from the secondary application.

In my previous book, there was an entire chapter focused on Dynamic Suite Composition. This chapter is also available to download, for free; for more information check my related blog article at `http://blog.augustoalvarez.com.ar/2011/01/27/app-v-book-published-and-sample-chapter-available-for-download/`.

# Upgrading/editing an existing application

An important procedure we should always consider in our App-V deployment is that the application upgrade or modification in its life cycle.

There are different ways an application could need an upgrade or modification—a service pack or updated version, modification required within the options of the application, or adding a new feature/application to an existing package. For all of those options, the App-V Sequencer offers us a wizard.

The options available in the App-V Sequencer are:

- **Update application in an existing package**: This is the scenario for a new update, service pack, or for modifying a particular option within the application.
- **Edit the package**: This is the option we usually see, as soon as we are done with the capturing process. Here, we configure (or in this case, modify) the deployment settings, virtual environment (file system and registry), and so on.
- **Add new application**: This is the option for when we need to add a new application to an existing package.

Fortunately, the App-V Sequencer wizard simplifies every scenario, so that we will receive all the guidance we need. We are going to take a quick look at each of these options.

# Updating an application in an existing package

This option, as we said, applies when we need to update the application, but also applies for the scenario when we need to make specific changes in the options of an application; for example, removing the software option for "Auto Update".

We can probably review common virtual registry and file settings, just by using the **Edit the package** option; but, in some cases, editing the right components won't be a simple task.

To accomplish this, we will need the package files available for the App-V Sequencer. Here's a quick overview of the process:

1. Start the **Update application in an existing package** wizard.
2. Select the SPRJ file of the existing package.

   After the package is selected, the application is "re deployed" in the Q:\ drive, as we sequenced. This is necessary so that the proper files can updated.

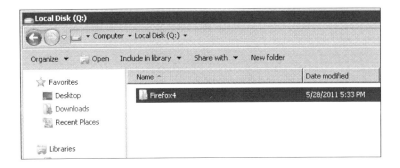

3. After this step, we can either select the update installation file or customize the installation.

> No matter what option we choose from here, the Sequencer starts preparing the machine to capture every change we make.

4. Run the update installation, or access the Q:\ drive where the application is located and execute the modification.

   In this case, I'm double-clicking the Firefox executable and modifying a few parameters in **Options** such as, **Override automatic cache management** to **1024**.

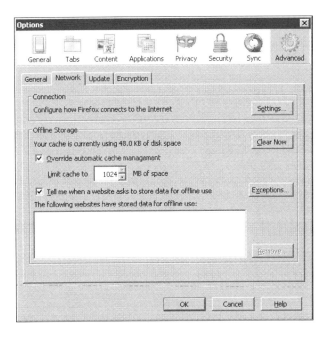

5. Select **I'm finished installing** and click on **Next**.

6. Complete the sequencing wizard.

We can see, in the sequencer options of the package, that the **Package Version** has changed, and so the **Change History** tab:

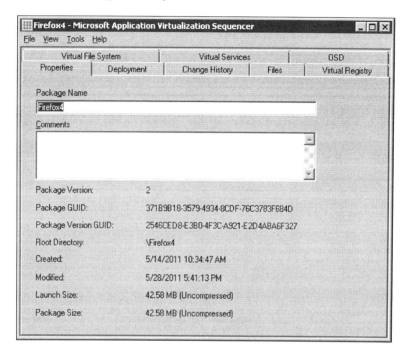

The filename of the SFT file has also changed; **_2** has been added (the number 2 is the package version).

 For SCCM/MSI deployment, it's recommended to append the version number to the filename of the .SFT file—especially SCCM—to avoid reusing an old SFT file.

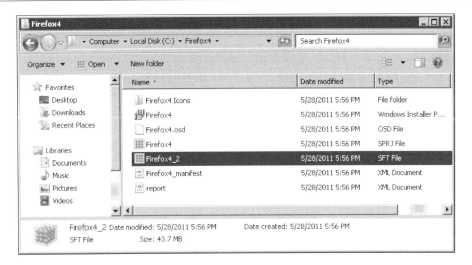

**Q**: Can I use this option to replace the entire application with a new version?

**A**: Yes. In some cases, the update could require replacing all the binaries from the application, for example, from Mozilla Firefox v3.x to v7; this is a supported scenario if the application supports the upgrade.

# Editing the package

This is the simpler option available, when we need to modify an existing package. Using this option, we get the chance to edit the same options used, when we are done with the capturing process:

- Package name and description.
- Deployment options: protocol, name of Streaming Server, operating systems, and MSI generation.
- Change history—revert to an older version of the package.
- Files—editing filenames and file category (user or application data).
- Virtual registry.
- Virtual file system.
- Virtual services.

- OSD—a nicer version of the OSD file. Remember that if we want to modify OSD options/parameters, we don't need to open the sequencer. Editing the OSD file directly also works.

  It is, however, recommended to edit the OSD with the App-V Sequencer UI. The changes we perform here will impact the Manifest and/or MSI.

# Adding a new application

This option is not that different from what we've seen in the first option, **Update application in existing package**; but, instead of monitoring when an update is running, we will configure a different application within the same package.

The procedure, using Mozilla Firefox and Java Runtime Environment, should be as follows:

1. Select the option **Add New Application**.

2. Select the existing package, in our case, **Mozilla Firefox**.

   This will also *redeploy* the application in the Q:\ drive.

3. Select the installer for the application we would like to add to this package.

4. The installer will start running, and since we are adding this application to an existing package that already had a monitoring folder in the Q:\ drive, we need to add this second application in the same folder, in this case, **Q:\ Firefox4**:

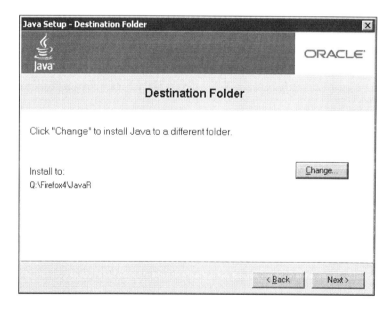

5. You should see that the package now contains all the applications within the same environment.

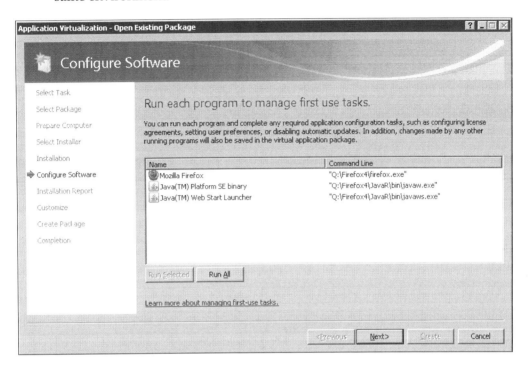

Remember that, at this stage, Feature Block 1 is created according to the actions we take when we launch the application; it is highly recommended that we configure this properly when we are handling a package with several applications, to avoid bandwidth impact.

6. Complete the sequencing wizard.

7. We will also notice that the package now has version 2, as does the name of the SFT file.

# Creating and handling package accelerators

One of the newest features in App-V 4.6 SP1 is the package accelerator, which appeared in order to help the App-V community share knowledge and common best practices for applications sequencing.

## What is a package accelerator?

Package accelerators represent a fast way to accomplish the sequencing of any given application by using the configuration files saved previously by a sequencer professional. These files can be used to rapidly create a new version of the sequenced application, saving a lot of time in the customization of this app.

Before package accelerators, sequencing a particular (most likely, complex) application and sharing that knowledge with the community implied that we write down that process in a detailed way, called an App-V recipe. These recipes are usually found in Microsoft TechNet and other App-V community forums.

A package accelerator is nothing more than a CAB file containing the following files:

- SPRJ
- OSD
- Manifest file for this particular application
- Modified information and files added in the sequencing process

## Creating a package accelerator

Creating a package accelerator does not require large additional steps, as compared to a normal sequencing process.

Basically, what we need to do is run the sequencing process normally, capturing data and customizing the package as we want, and then select the option **Create a Package Accelerator**.

There are two options for creating a package accelerator:

- **Using application installation media**: If we have the installation binaries, we can use them to generate the package once we already have the accelerator.

  This option is not suitable for all applications, since the App-V Sequencer tries to find the package files in the installation binaries; if the App-V Sequencer cannot find these files, we won't be able to create a package accelerator.

- **Using the installation folder**: Instead of using installation binaries, the App-V Sequencer can use the package with a locally installed version of the application to generate the package accelerator.

Both of these options still require the existence of the App-V package, in order to create the package accelerator.

Let's take a quick look at the process of customizing Mozilla Firefox:

1. Open the App-V Sequencer and select **Create Package** (default).
2. Select the installation as a **Standard application**.
3. Run the installation and capturing process normally.
4. Edit all changes necessary in the application, for example, I am not setting to search for software updates and am setting the home page as blank:

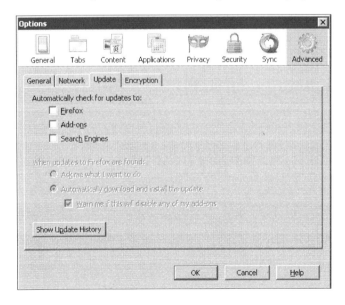

Also, I am including the **Windows Command Prompt** inside the package. This is a common best practice when we have complex applications that could require some troubleshooting inside the "bubble".

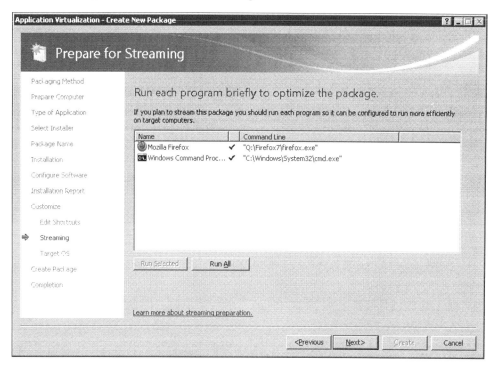

5.  In the Mozilla Firefox 7 scenario, once sequencing is complete, we need to delete two files included by default in the package—**VFS\CSIDL_ APPDATA\Mozilla\Firefox\profiles.ini** and **VFS\CSIDL_APPDATA\ Mozilla\Firefox\Crash Reports\InstallTime20110928134238**.

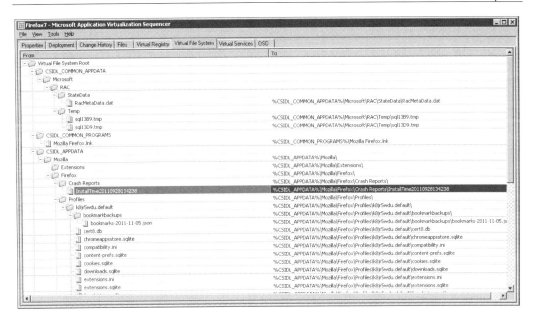

These two files are created during the installation and will differ, depending on the installation.

Since we will need to install the application again when we try to apply the package accelerator, these exact files won't be present; the creation will fail while looking for these two files.

6. Complete the sequencing process and save the package.

7. Revert the machine to a clean state, and run the App-V Sequencer with a fresh image.

8. In the App-V Sequencer window, select **Tools | Create a Package Accelerator**:

9. Browse for the SPRJ created earlier and click on **Next**.

10. In this step, we will be required to provide the installation file used by the application; select the folder where the application is located, or the folder where it was installed.

In my example, I've installed the Mozilla Firefox application, locally, in its default installation path (C:\Program Files\). If using the installer file for Firefox, the App-V Sequencer won't be able to find the necessary files to create the package accelerator.

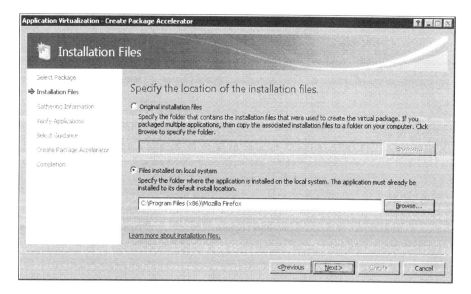

We can also copy the installation folder of the application from another computer.

11. Once we click **Next**, the process will start looking for necessary files in the package, in order to create the accelerator.

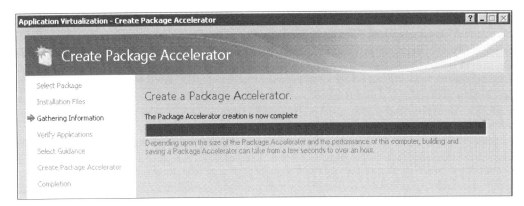

If, during this stage, we get the option to review missing files, we must carefully review whether the files presented here are actually necessary in the application; if not, we can remove them and continue with the process.

In the Mozilla Firefox scenario, if we choose to use the installation file for the application (the EXE file), App-V Sequencer will not be able to find most of the package files. If we remove them, the application will no longer work.

 The supported installation file types for creating package accelerators are MSI, CAB, ZIP, and the application files themselves.

Installation files with EXE or MSP extensions are not supported for the creation of package accelerators.

12. In the next window, we'll get a detailed look at the files that are going to be included in the package. We can also remove any of them:

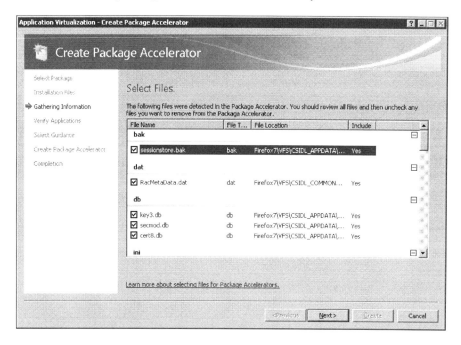

13. The **Verify Application** window simply verifies the App-V Sequencer with the applications detected:

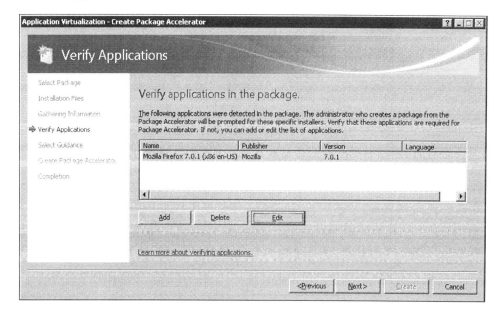

14. In the **Select Guidance** section, we will be required to provide a detailed guideline (`.rtf` file) for the administrators that will later be using this accelerator as a quick help guide.

15. Try to use this guideline to understand the pre requisites for the package, supported platforms included, details about the customizations made, disclaimers about the changes that will be necessary later, and so on.

    For example, a good document, that can help sequencer professionals later, should contain:

    ◦ A brief introduction of the package accelerator.

    ◦ A detailed version of the application to be sequenced.

    ◦ The platform used by the application and the App-V Sequencer and client.

    ◦ The operating system used for the sequencer and the client machine.

    ◦ A complete list of prerequisites to generate the package and the application itself. If there are any special parameters or configurations placed in the application or the sequencer, include it here. For example, a modified "exclusion items" list in the sequencer.

    ◦ Detailed steps for using this package accelerator.

    ◦ It would be nice to mention a way sequencer professionals can contact you to exchange feedback or queries.

16. The final step will let us save the accelerator as a CAB file.

The package accelerator is now created; since this `.CAB` file does not contain the SFT file, the size of this file should be considerably small.

When we are using package accelerators, as a recommended practice, test using the accelerator (in order to verify it), as soon as we are done with creation. If we excluded some necessary files in the creation of the accelerator, we should observe problems, as soon as we try to use it.

# Using a package accelerator

Using a package accelerator for a complex application represents a procedure far simpler than installing and capturing all over again; the SFT file will be generated automatically.

Using a package accelerator still requires installing the application; in this process, the SFT file will be created, following the parameters and configurations used in the package accelerator.

Please take note that there could be some configurations and parameters that could apply to specific information when the package was created, for example, server name or path. We can still edit those, as soon as we load the package accelerator.

Let's review the process for creating a package using an existing package accelerator:

1. Start the App-V Sequencer and select **Create a Package Using a Package Accelerator**.

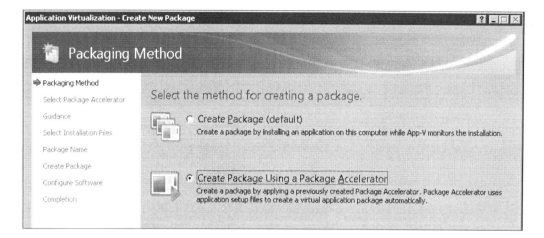

2. Select the CAB file created earlier.

3. Review the guidelines provided by the administrator who created the package.

4. In the next step, we will proceed to locally install the application and generate the files to be packaged in the SFT file.

   The application must be installed locally, using the default installation. In this step, the App-V Sequencer is not monitoring the installation process; it will only use the files created by the installation.

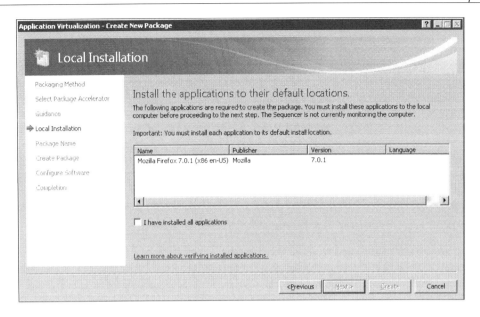

5. Complete the package name, description, and the path where it will be saved.

6. We are now ready to create the package. Select the path for the SPRJ file and also note the **Package Size** appearing in this window; it should match the size of the package we created earlier:

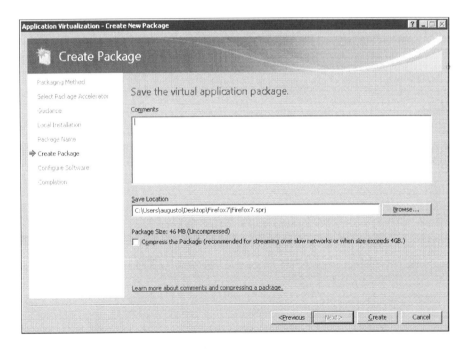

7.   Once the package is created, we can edit the final steps in this package creation process. In this example, I've selected **Configure Software**:

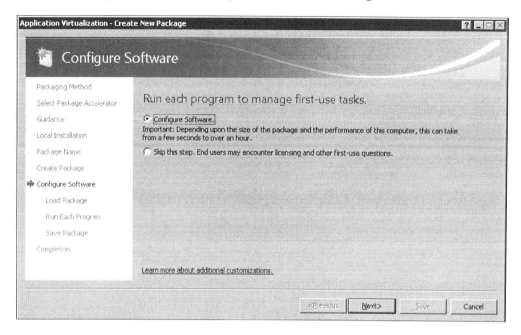

Using this option, the App-V Sequencer expands the application into the MNT install folder (directory in the Q:\); in this way, we can launch the application and perform any change we need to the package configuration.

8.   Configuring the application at this stage will also define the Feature Block 1 of this App-V package.

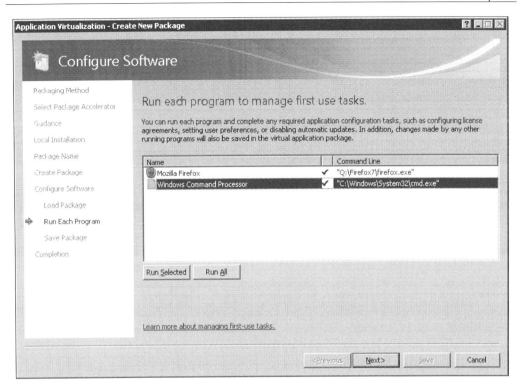

9. Click **Next** and save the package created.

# Reviewing package accelerators best practices

Package accelerators also include a set of best practices created by Microsoft in order to establish some guidelines to distribute them among the community.

Let's review them:

- Use a generic user account running in the App-V Sequencer when creating a package accelerator, for example, administrator. You should not use an account that is based on an existing username.

- Specify a general, non-identifying name for the computer running the sequencer.

- In the sequencer console of the App-V package, on the **Deployment** tab, use the default settings for the server URL configuration information (%**SFT_SOFTGRIDSERVER%**).

- If you do not want to share the list of applications that were installed on the computer running the sequencer when you created the package accelerator, you must delete the `appv_manifest.xml` file. This file is located in the package root directory of the virtual application package.

To retrieve some of the existing package accelerators developed by the community, review the TechNet Gallery available from Microsoft ("App-V" category) at `http://gallery.technet.microsoft.com/`.

# Summary

In this chapter, we had the chance to review important topics regarding complex sequencing and how to accomplish these in some scenarios where App-V is normally not supported.

There are some applications that require more tuning than others, including those that are not commonly supported in App-V, such as an application with drivers. A good example we reviewed here is Network Monitor; it requires editing the **Exclusion Items** of the App-V Sequencer, in order to include necessary files, and also requires the existence of a driver to function properly.

In complex sequencing, there are important concepts that we've had the chance to understand, in this chapter; for example, using the override/merge options and the ability to let the application interact with the operating system (using the LOCAL_INTERACTION_ALLOWED parameter).

We've also covered Dynamic Suite Composition, which lets us work with dependencies between different virtual applications. By handling the proper parameters in the OSD (the DSC tool from Microsoft helps us with this), two virtual applications can share a common space to improve user experience.

We've also reviewed the process of upgrading and editing an existing package, the difference between each scenario, and have looked at package accelerators—how to create and use them to facilitate jobs for all App-V administrators.

In the next chapter, we will also review scenarios where complexity is given by the virtual applications deployment, for example, including the possibility of using HTTP/S publication and streaming, handling standalone scenarios (with local and remote streaming), and some important topics about securing communications.

# 3
# Deploying Applications in Complex Environments

Complex scenarios can be defined by many things in the environment—adjusting communication ports for application delivery, handling particular applications, adapting company policies to the implementation, securing the environment, and so on. In this chapter, we'll be focusing on providing the necessary guidelines to adapt to each environment.

Other complexities we usually find are those related to the communication ports used by servers and clients, even when the environment requires no server interaction. App-V provides the necessary variety for us to adopt and handle these complications in a simple manner, using HTTP/S or SMB streaming, or even in the standalone scenarios.

Understanding and executing complex techniques to capture applications represents only half of the entire process of getting an application streamed down by clients; the publication and streaming process can get a little bit tricky.

Depending on the environment in which we are working, we can find several scenarios where it won't be possible to use the native **Real Time Streaming Protocol (RTSP)** to deliver applications remotely. Using HTTP/S, SMB, or standalone scenarios for App-V is possible, as we all know, but requires a few changes in the environment.

In this chapter, we will learn:

- Configuring HTTP streaming
- Configuring standalone mode for local and SMB streaming
- Configuring SSL communications in both clients and servers, using:
    ◦ RTSPS
    ◦ HTTPS

# Configuring and using HTTP publishing and streaming

Using HTTP protocol represents one of the best-suited scenarios for communication between App-V client and servers. HTTP protocol is a preferred method for communication between client and servers, because it is commonly used among networks and services.

As we saw in *Chapter 1, Taking a Deep Dive into App-V*, HTTP streaming offers the ability to use a single port for communication. RTSP protocol needs port 554 and one higher port (which is randomly used) open.

> This is why, when we are setting our Management and/or Streaming Server using the RTSP native protocol, we need to use "program exceptions", in Windows Firewall, instead of "port exceptions".
>
> The only possible way to use one port in Real Time Streaming is by using secure communications, RTSPS protocol; to be discussed later in this chapter.

Not only can we use these ports for streaming, but, with a few more steps in the configuration process, we can also publish applications and thus avoid using MSI files to distribute shortcuts and file associations.

The publication is achieved using an ASPX file, `publications.aspx`, which is used to list the applications contained in the `content` folder of the web server.

These are the steps we are going to follow:

1. Adding the Web Server role.
2. Configuring IIS options.
3. Adding MIME types.
4. Creating publication files.
5. Configuring App-V client.

# Adding the Web Server role

In this scenario, we are going to use Windows Server 2008 R2, with **Internet Information Services (IIS)**, to publish and deliver applications to users.

The following are the features we must add to the Web Server role:

- **Common HTTP Features**: All except **HTTP Redirection**
- **Application Development**: All features
- **Health and Diagnostics**: **HTTP Logging** and **Request Monitor**

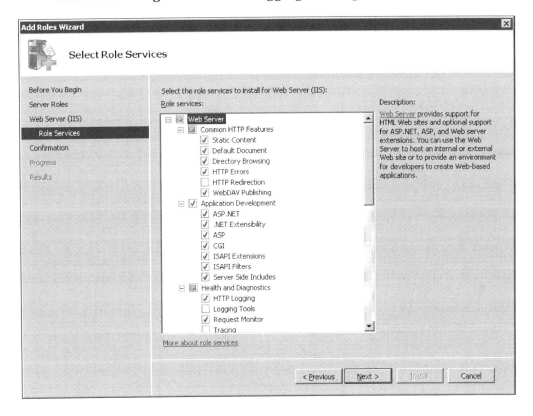

- **Security**: All except **IP Domains and Restrictions**

- **Performance**: All

- **Management Tools**: All, including **IIS 6 Management Compatibility** and sub-features

- **FTP Server** and **IIS Hostable Web Core** can be ignored

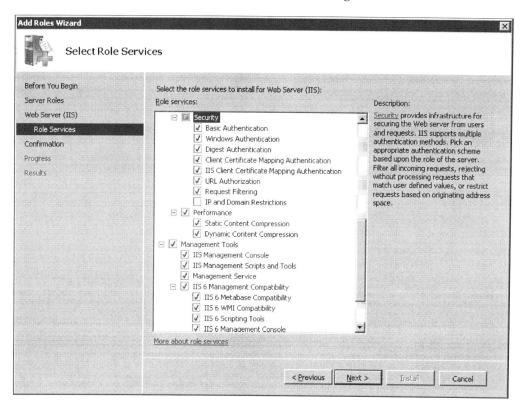

With those features, complete the **Web Server** role installation wizard.

# Configuring IIS options

Configuring IIS options basically requires adding the `content` folder as a virtual directory and making this directory suitable for placing the App-V applications.

1. Access the IIS console and in **Default Web Site**, select **Add Virtual Directory...**.

2. Specify an **Alias** and the path to the folder in the web server. In this case, I'm using **E:\content**.

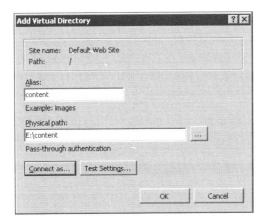

3. Now that the virtual directory is added, in the `content` folder of IIS options, select **Directory Browsing**.

4. In the right pane, click **Enable**.

Directory browsing is a necessary feature for the App-V clients to retrieve applications within this directory.

5. Again, in the `content` folder, select **Authentication**. Enable **Anonymous Authentication** and **Windows Authentication**.

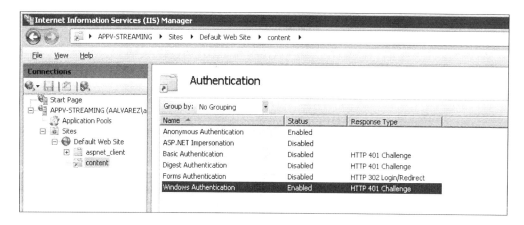

6.  Inside **Request Filtering**, remove the **.cs** file extension.

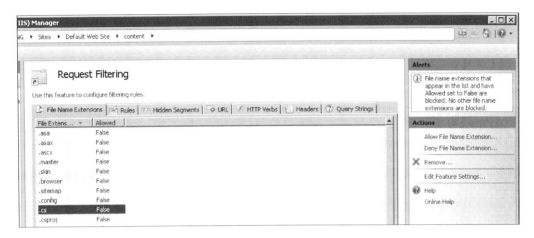

7.  Click on **Allow File Name Extension...** and insert **.cs** again.

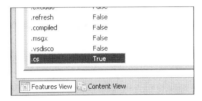

This **.cs** file extension will be used to configure HTTP publishing. If we are only seeking HTTP streaming, this last step is optional.

# Adding MIME types

**Multipurpose Internet Mail Extensions (MIME)** specify particular contents to be used in web servers, such as, e-mail content or web videos. In this case, we are adding these extensions to provide IIS the options for delivering App-V files, such as, OSD, SFT, and SPRJ.

In the `content` folder, select **MIME Extensions**, and add the following exceptions:

| File Extension | MIME-Type |
| --- | --- |
| .osd | application/softricity-osd |
| .sft | application/softricity-sft |
| .sprj | application/softricity-sprj |

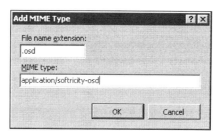

At this point, we can verify that the virtual directory we've just added is available, as well as listing the directory in the `content` folder. In a browser, access **http://**servername**/content**, and you should see something like this:

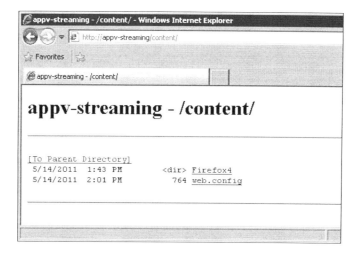

In this case, the **Firefox4** package is already included. The **web.config** file is created by default when we add the virtual directory.

# Creating publication files

For publication purposes, we are going to use a C# script that will generate the publications automatically, using the `publishing.aspx` file, which will receive information from the C# script, called `publishing.aspx.cs`. Here are the necessary steps:

1. Open a notepad file, copy the following and paste it into the file:

```
<%@ Page Language="C#" AutoEventWireup="true"
CodeFile="publishing.aspx.cs" Inherits="appv_publishing_service.
publishing" ContentType="text/xml" %>
<DESKTOPCONFIG>
<POLICY
MANAGEDDESKTOP="TRUE"
REPORTING="FALSE">
<REFRESH
ONLOGIN="TRUE"
PERIOD="60"/>
</POLICY>
<APPLIST>
<%this.generate_app_xml(); %>
</APPLIST>
</DESKTOPCONFIG>
```

2. Save the file as `publishing.aspx`, and place it in the root of the `content` folder.

3. Open a new notepad file, copy the following C# script and paste it into the file:

```
// This is publishing.aspx.cs file
using System;
using System.Xml;
using System.IO;
namespace appv_publishing_service
{
public
partial class
publishing : System.Web.UI.Page
{
protected void generate_app_xml()
{
```

```
string root_phys = MapPath(".");
string[] dirs = Directory.GetDirectories(root_phys);
foreach (string dir in dirs)
{
try
{
string[] manifests = Directory.GetFiles(Path.Combine(root_
phys,dir), @"*_manifest.xml", SearchOption.TopDirectoryOnly);
foreach (string filename in manifests)
{
FileStream file = File.OpenRead(filename);
XmlDocument doc = new
XmlDocument();
doc.Load(file);
XmlNode applist = doc.SelectSingleNode(@"/PACKAGE/APPLIST");
Response.Write(applist.InnerXml);
}
}
catch (Exception ex)
{
// Output
Response.AppendToLog(ex.Message);
}
}
}
}
}
```

4. Save the file as `publishing.aspx.cs`, and also place it in the root of the `content` folder.

5. To verify the scripts we've just added, we only need to browse for the `publishing.aspx` file in a browser.

   If we don't have any application added to the `content` folder, you will see this:

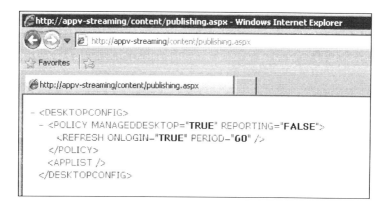

In this case, Firefox 4 has already been added and the publication file lists it as follows:

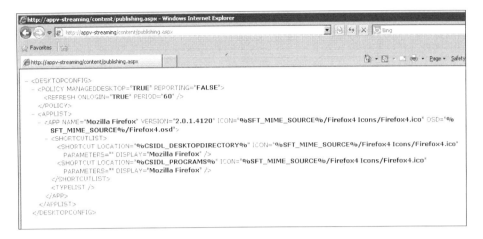

Now that we have the publications in place, we are going to make some changes to the manifest and OSD file in the application.

The file `publishing.aspx.cs` uses the manifest file from each package to complete the publication process.

Using the Firefox 4 manifest file, we can check the following information:

```
<APP NAME="Mozilla Firefox" VERSION="2.0.1.4120" ICON="%SFT_MIME_
SOURCE%/Firefox4 Icons/Firefox4.ico" OSD="%SFT_MIME_SOURCE%/
Firefox4.osd">
```

The variable `%SFT_MIME_SOURCE%` represents, in this case, the `content` folder used when I published this application on an App-V Management Server. Since I'm placing the `Firefox4` folder inside the `content` folder, we need to make some changes to the XML file.

6.  Edit the XML file (in my case, `Firefox4_manifest.xml`), replacing all instances of `%SFT_MIME_SOURCE%/` with `%SFT_MIME_SOURCE%/Firefox4` (this is the folder created that stores the App-V package).

If you already added the application to the `content` folder, editing the file could retrieve the error **The process cannot access the file because it is being used by another process**.

You need to stop the IIS service prior to making the change; once you save the file, you can start it again.

7.  Within the OSD file of the application, verify the `CODEBASE HREF` value. It should look like this:

    `<CODEBASE HREF="HTTP://servername/content/Firefox4/Firefox4.sft"`

Note that we are adding the **/content** section to be used with HTTP streaming.

8.  Within the OSD file, we can also find references to **%SFT_MIME_ SOURCE%**; replace it as we did before, using the name of the subfolder **%SFT_MIME_SOURCE%/Firefox4**.

```
VERRIDDEN="FALSE" DISPLAY="Mozilla Firefox" ICON="%SFT_MIME_SOURCE%/Firefox4/Firefox4_Icons/Firefox4.ico"/>
N="FALSE" DISPLAY="Mozilla Firefox" ICON="%SFT_MIME_SOURCE%/Firefox4/Firefox4 Icons/Firefox4.ico"/>
```

# Configuring the App-V client

Once the server and the application are ready, the only thing missing is configuring the App-V client to retrieve applications from the web server.

In this case, we are going to assume that the App-V Desktop Client is already installed.

1.  In the App-V client console, edit the **Publishing Server** properties to use the name of your web server and the HTTP protocol.

    Also, configure **Path:** with the value **/content/publishing.aspx**.

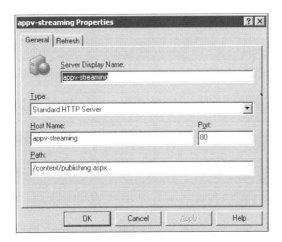

2.  We also need to change the default paths for the **Application Source Root**, **Icon Source Root**, and **OSD Source Root**. To do so, we can edit the registry settings of each client or using of course the App-V ADM Template (later in this chapter we will review how to use this ADM template).

    We need to change the paths, using the following values in the registry:

    ○   If the client is using a 64-bit operating system, locate the path
        `HKEY_LOCAL_MACHINE\SOFTWARE\Wow6432Node\Microsoft\SoftGrid\4.5\Client\Configuration\`.

     ◦   In case of a 32-bit operating system, use the path `HKEY_LOCAL_` `MACHINE\SOFTWARE\Microsoft\SoftGrid\4.5\Client\` `Configuration\.`

| | |
|---|---|
| **Application Source Root** | `HTTP://servername` |
| **Icon Source Root** | `HTTP://servername/content` |
| **OSD Source Root** | `HTTP://servername/content` |

3.   In the **Services** console, restart the **Application Virtualization Service Agent**.

4.   Access the App-V Management Console, and refresh the connection with the server. We should receive the application normally.

5.   Run the application.

# Configuring and using the standalone mode

As we know, another great option, when we can't (or just won't) use an App-V Management Server, is the standalone mode.

Working in standalone mode, we don't need anything more than the App-V Desktop Client to stream the applications from a local resource (such as a folder on the client's computer) or from a remote resource (such as a file server available on the network).

Since there's no server in charge of the publication process, in standalone mode, App-V clients cannot be aware that there are new applications available. This gives us three possibilities for importing applications:

1. **Standalone without streaming**: Here, we deploy the MSI file manually or using Group Policy. The MSI file contains the OSD and ICO files; in this scenario, the installer also uses the SFT file stored locally, on the client machine.

2. **Standalone with SMB streaming**: Here, we deploy MSI files using only the manifest file, and we can have the SFT placed on a file server for SMB streaming; using a particular parameter, the client can access the SFT file remotely.

3. **Standalone using SFTMIME**: This command line, included in the App-V client, handles virtual applications. SFTMIME supports having the package files remotely on a server. We'll learn more about this tool in *Chapter 4, Handling Scripting and App-V Command Lines*.

Using any of these mentioned scenarios basically requires two general steps: configuring the App-V Desktop Client and executing the MSI installer.

## Standalone without streaming

This scenario is preferred when we first start working with App-V, since it only requires the App-V Desktop Client and the packaged application that is placed locally. Using this scenario, we can guarantee that we won't have any complications in the communication process due to no client-server communication.

Configuring an App-V Desktop Client can be executed in the installation process of the client or by Group Policy (working with the App-V ADM).

# Manual configuration

To install the App-V Desktop Client to work directly as a standalone, run the installer with the following parameters:

```
setup.exe /s /v"/qb-! SWICACHESIZE=\"6144\" AUTOLOADTARGET=\"NONE\" RE
QUIREAUTHORIZATIONIFCACHED=\"FALSE\" SWIFSDRIVE=\"Q\"
```

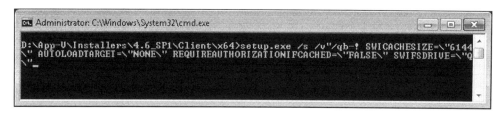

- **/s**: Used for silent installation
- **/v**: Used to interact with the MSI file of the App-V installation
- **SWICACHESIZE**: To set App-V Desktop Client cache size to 6 GB
- **AUTOLOADTARGET**: Not using the auto load target option
- **REQUIREAUTHORIZATIONIFCACHED**: If a connection to the server cannot be established, the client still allows the user to launch an application that has previously been loaded into cache. Setting this value to "FALSE", the authorization phase is skipped by the App-V Desktop Client
- **SWIFSDRIVE**: Selecting *Q* as the drive letter to be used for the App-V packages

# Group Policy configuration

We can access these Group Policy options by downloading the **Microsoft Application Virtualization Administrative Template (ADM Template)**, available at the Microsoft Download Center, here: `http://www.microsoft.com/downloads/en/default.aspx`.

> On how to import this ADM template, please review the Microsoft TechNet article, *Add or remove an Administrative Template* (`.adm` file), at `http://technet.microsoft.com/en-us/library/cc739134(WS.10).aspx`.

Once the Administrative Templates are imported, we can start working on the App-V group policies.

1. Create a Group Policy; link it in the organizational unit where standalone users will be working, and select **Edit**.

2. Expand **Computer Configuration | Policies | Administrative Templates | Classic Administrative Templates (ADM)**, and select either **Microsoft Application Virtualization Client** or **Microsoft Application Virtualization Client (64-bit)**.

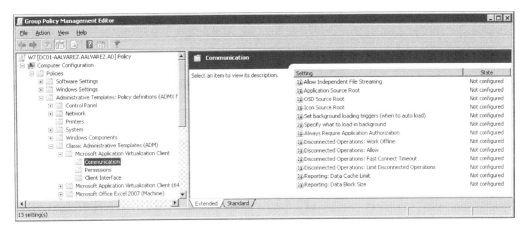

3. Select **Communication** and modify the following Policies values:

   ○ **Allow Independent File Streaming**: **Enabled**

   ○ **Always Require Application Authorization**: **Disabled**

   ○ **Disconnected Operations: Work Offline**: **Enabled**

   ○ **Disconnected Operations: Allow**: **Enabled**

   ○ **Disconnected Operations: Limit Disconnected Operations**: **Enabled**

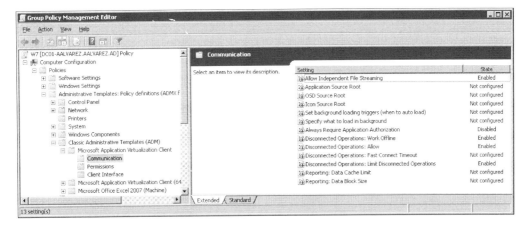

4. Under **Microsoft Application Virtualization Client**, select the folder **Permissions** and modify **Permissions to Toggle into Offline Mode**: **Disabled**.

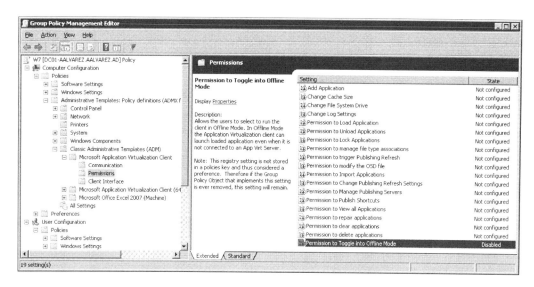

5. Once the values are set and the Group Policy linked, just use `gpupdate / force` on the client machines, to retrieve the latest configurations.

# Running the application in standalone mode without streaming

Once the App-V Desktop Client is installed and configured, we only need to place the MSI (which already contains the ICO, OSD, and manifest files) and SFT files locally.

Running the MSI file, as for any normal application, will provide the necessary shortcuts and file associations within the virtual package.

# Standalone with SMB streaming

As mentioned before, the standalone method can be used when we want to place the SFT file on a file server.

This is an important matter, since there are tons of applications, such as Microsoft Office, that can use SFT files up to 2 GB or larger; we can also consider a far more common example such as Adobe Reader, with nearly 300MB; these are examples that could result in huge costs to deploy, in scenarios with several large numbers of clients.

The configuration actually requires the same installation and settings for the App-V Desktop Client that we used for the standalone with no streaming; the actual difference appears when running the application MSI.

A good practice (though not particularly necessary) for this scenario is to enable the parameter AUTOLOADONLAUNCH and remove the AUTOLOADTARGET option used previously.

## Manual configuration

To install the App-V Desktop Client to work directly in standalone mode, run the installer with the following parameters:

```
setup.exe /s /v"/qb-! SWICACHESIZE=\"6144\" AUTOLOADONLAUNCH=\"1\" REQ
UIREAUTHORIZATIONIFCACHED=\"FALSE\" SWIFSDRIVE=\"Q\"
```

Enabling **AUTOLOADONLAUNCH** will guarantee that the full SFT file (Feature Block 1 and Feature Block 2) will be delivered as soon as the application is launched.

The option AUTOLOADTARGET sets it off, like it was in the previous scenario, automatically ignores the load triggers; we've ignored this option for this installation.

## Group Policy configuration

Since we maintain the same configurations as the previous scenario, the options to modify should remain the same, except for AUTOLOADONLAUNCH.

1. Create a Group Policy, link it in the Organizational Unit where the standalone users will be working, and select **Edit**.

2. Expand **Computer Configuration | Policies | Administrative Templates | Classic Administrative Templates (ADM)**, and select **Microsoft Application Virtualization Client** or **Microsoft Application Virtualization Client (64-bit)**.

3.  Select **Communication** and modify the following Policies values:

    ◦  **Allow Independent File Streaming**: **Enabled**

    ◦  **Set background loading triggers (when to auto load)**: **Enabled –** Load on Launch

    ◦  **Always Require Application Authorization**: **Disabled**

    ◦  **Disconnected Operations: Work Offline**: **Enabled**

    ◦  **Disconnected Operations: Allow**: **Enabled**

    ◦  **Disconnected Operations: Limit Disconnected Operations**: **Enabled**

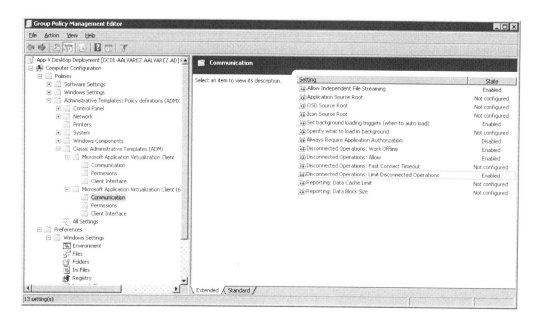

Note that we can find the AUTOLOADONLAUNCH option, using Group Policy, as **Set background loading triggers (when to auto load)**.

4.  Under **Microsoft Application Virtualization Client**, select the folder **Permissions** and modify the value **Permissions to Toggle into Offline Mode**: **Disabled**.

5.  Once the values are set, and the Group Policy is linked, just use the gpupdate /force, on the client machines, to retrieve the latest configurations.

# Running the application in standalone mode with SMB streaming

As we've seen, the App-V Desktop Client installation/configuration is quite similar in both scenarios, with just minor considerations to optimize file streaming. But, the real modification appears in running the application MSI.

Since we won't have the SFT file available locally, when installing the application using the MSI, we must use the `SFTPATH` parameter to set the path of the file:

```
~ Msiexec.exe /i \\virtualapp\packagename.msi SFTPATH=\\server\share\
package.sft /q
```

In this case, I'm using Mozilla Firefox 4 with the MSI placed locally in the App-V Desktop Client and the SFT placed in a network share.

# Configuring SSL communications

To accomplish a secured environment for App-V, there are several tasks we can execute. Of course, not all of them are mandatory and will depend mainly on two factors: the policies your organization already has and assuming or not the implementation's costs on security matters.

SSL communications are based in certificates, which are in charge of validating the integrity of the information sent and received by servers and clients. In most organizations, the distribution of those certificates is in charge of a server having the role **Certificate Authority (CA)**.

An alternative option, when we don't have a CA in place, is the use of self-signed certificates. This kind of certificate can be generated using the IIS Console. The procedure is covered in detail in my previous book *Getting Started with Microsoft Application Virtualization 4.6* and is not within the scope of this book.

# Certificate prerequisites

The certificate involved for communication must fulfil the common requirements for all environments we are attempting to use it in:

- The certificate must be valid
- The certificate must contain the correct **Enhanced Key Usage (EKU)** – Server Authentication (OID 1.3.6.1.5.5.7.3.1)
- The certificate FQDN must match the server on which it's installed
- Client and server must trust the root Certification Authority (CA)

But there's also an important and final requirement for using App-V with certificates:

- The certificate's private key has to have permissions changed, so as to allow the App-V Service account (by default, represented by NETWORK SERVICE) access to the certificate

For more information about the certification authority, there are several articles on the Microsoft TechNet website:

- *Building an Enterprise Root Certification Authority in Small and Medium Businesses* for Windows Server 2003: `http://technet.microsoft.com/en-us/library/cc875810.aspx`
- *Active Directory Certificate Services Step-by-Step Guide* for Windows Server 2008: `http://technet.microsoft.com/en-us/library/cc772393(WS.10).aspx`

# Setting RTSPS communications

Configuring a secure communication in RTSP can be done if we are using an App-V Management Server or an App-V Streaming Server, but the procedure will be different. This is because while the App-V Management Server configuration can be executed from the Management Console, the Streaming Server will require editing registry settings.

Let's take a look at both procedures:

## Configuring the App-V management server

Once the certificate is created and deployed on the server, the implementation process in the App-V Management Server is very simple and intuitive.

# Securing the App-V Management Server during installation

If we don't have the App-V Management Server installed already, we can secure the connections from scratch.

We can find this option in the installation process, in the **Connection Security Mode** step.

Just select the option **Use enhanced security**, and the drop-down will show you the certificate available. We will need to select, of course, the certificate with the FQDN of the server.

# Securing an installed App-V Management Server

Fortunately, the process of securing an already deployed platform does not provide complex steps or complicated changes in our environment.

1. Access the **Application Virtualization Management Console**. Expand **Server Groups | Default Server Group**, which is the default group created in the environment we are using.

2. Right-click the name of the server and select **Properties**.

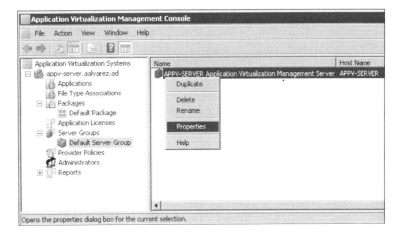

3.  In the new window, select the **Ports** tab. Remove the option for **RTSP port** connection and select **RTSPS port**. In this case, we are going to maintain the default port number for secure connections, **322**.

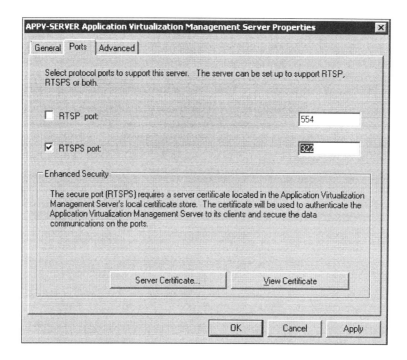

4.  Click on **Server Certificate...** and a new wizard will appear. Click on **Next**.

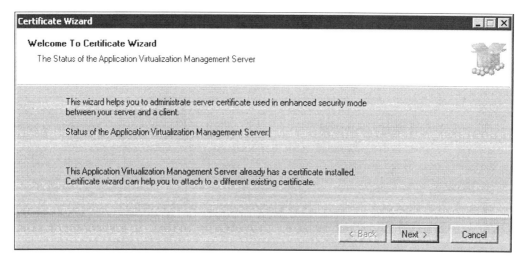

5. Select the certificate we've deployed earlier with the server FQDN. Click on **Next**.

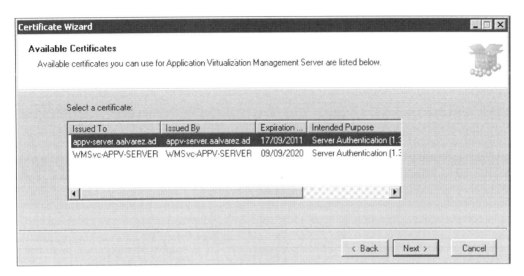

6. On the last window, click on **Finish**. We will receive a message saying we need to restart the **Application Virtualization Management Server service** to complete the changes made.

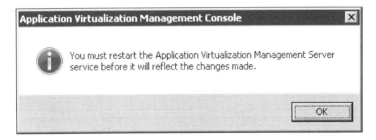

7.  We will only need to access the **Services** console; right-click the **Application Virtualization Management Server** service and click on **Restart**.

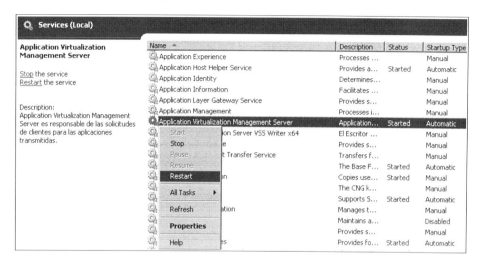

Once we finish these steps, the process for securing the connections used from the App-V Management Server is complete.

# Configuring the App-V Streaming Server

Configuring secure connections for streaming servers could be a little bit trickier, since we don't have an App-V console we can use to change the necessary configurations from there.

That's why we will need to change some registry values to accomplish this.

1.  Once the certificate is created and configured, select **Certificate | Properties | Details** and look for the **Thumbprint** value.

    Copy the value shown here:

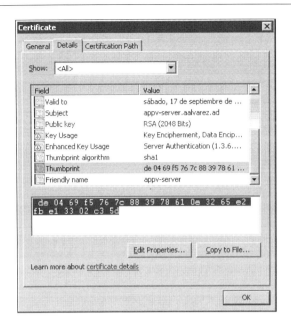

2.  Access **Run** and type `regedit`. Locate the path `HKLM\Software\Microsoft\`
    `SoftGrid\4.5\DistributionServer`.

    If this is a 64-bit operating system, the registry path should be: `HKLM\`
    `Software\Wow6432Node\Microsoft\SoftGrid\4.5\DistributionServer`.

3.  Double-click the key **X509CertHash** and paste the value from the
    **Thumbprint**, but remove all spaces.

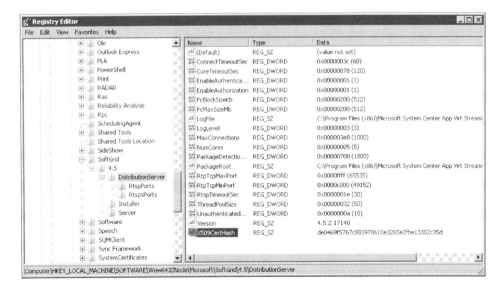

4. Now expand the registry folder **DistributionServer** and right-click **RtspsPorts**; select **New | DWORD (32-bit) Value**.

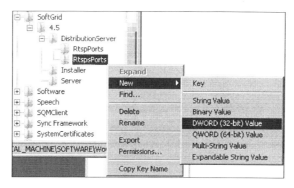

5. In the DWORD name, type **322**. Edit the value, selecting **Decimal**, and for **Value data** also, type **322**.

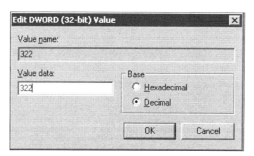

6. Restart the **Application Virtualization Streaming Server** service and the streaming server configuration is complete.

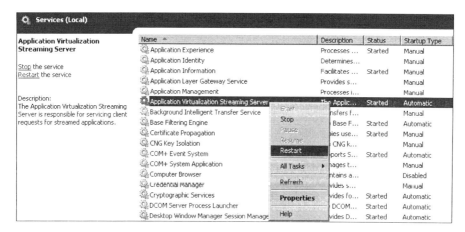

# Configuring the App-V Desktop Client

The procedure for securing the App-V Desktop Client is as simple as we've seen for the App-V Management Server. The possibilities are the same, configuring the client in the installation process or in a deployed client.

Again, if we are not using a Certificate Authority, we must import the certificate manually in the client OS, in order to make the App-V client trust in the App-V Server.

 Importing a certificate manually must be done by using the Computer Account, placing the certificate in the "Trusted Root Certification Authorities".

Let's take a quick look at the process:

1. Access the **Application Virtualization Client** console. Select **Publishing Servers** and right-click on the name of the App-V Server; select **Properties**.

2. In the **Type** drop-down, select the option **Enhanced Security Application Virtualization Server** and insert the host name for the server (in this example, **appv-server.aalvarez.ad**). Click **OK**.

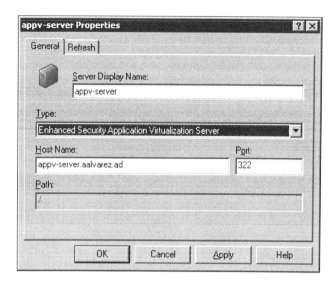

A very important thing to note is that you must use the FQDN of the App-V Server and not the NetBIOS name. This is because the certificate just imported is using the Fully-Qualified Domain Name to identify and trust in that server.

Remember that applying all these steps to the servers and clients will not automatically modify the virtual applications delivery options that are configured when the package is created. This parameter is set by either using the OSD file of each application or overriding that value using the registry keys.

Of course, the best approach to this is to use the App-V ADM Template to apply the necessary changes and distribute those among all App-V clients. We should try to avoid editing the OSD files of applications. It is a most uncomfortable solution and could lead to several problems if we do not edit the file correctly.

Using the ADM template, we must change the **Application Source Root** value to the server's secure URL, in my case, RTSPS://appv-server.aalvarez.ad:322. The **Application Source Root** value will override the URL placed in any application's OSD.

# Setting HTTPS communications

Configuring HTTPS can have two particular deployment benefits: securing the delivery of applications when we are using the HTTP protocol and securing the web service that we are using to connect with the App-V Management Console.

## Configuring the web service

We can also secure the communications between the Application Virtualization Management Console and the web service (in charge of managing the communication between the MMC and the SQL data store).

Since, in this example, we are using the Web Service, the MMC, and the SQL database in the same server, the procedure is really simple:

1. On the server, access the **Internet Information Services (IIS) Manager** console.

2. Expand the server name, and select **Sites | Default Web Site**.

3. In the **Actions** pane, select **Bindings**.

4. Click **Add**. In the type drop-down, select **https**, and in **SSL certificate**, select the certificate we'd created earlier. Click **OK**.

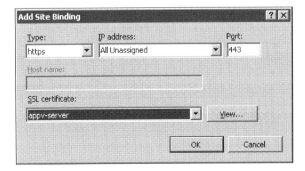

With that, we've configured our web service to accept HTTPS communications for the console.

5. We can test it by opening the **Application Virtualization Management Console** and selecting the **443** port.

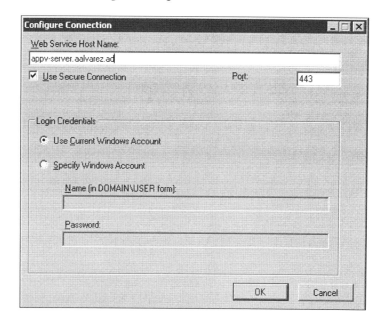

For more information about IIS and certificates, we can check the Microsoft TechNet article *Managing Microsoft Certificate Services and SSL*, at `http://technet.microsoft.com/en-us/library/bb727098.aspx`.

# Configuring HTTPS streaming

Configuring the website in charge of the secure delivery of the application is the same procedure as we have seen in securing the web service. We only need to import the certificate and configure the bindings in the website properties.

As an optional procedure for HTTP/S, streaming is the option to configure Kerberos authentication. Using this type of authentication, there is a mutual confirmation between client and server and it is highly recommended to use it.

For using Kerberos authentication between client and server, IIS must be configured to use **Service Principal Name (SPN)**, which is used by a client machine to uniquely identify an instance of a service.

To configure a SPN, we can use the command-line tool included in Windows Server 2008 R2, `setspn.exe`.

To configure it in your server, use the following example:

```
setspn.exe –A HTTP/appv-server.aalvarez.ad
```

For more information about the **setspn** tool, review the following links from Microsoft:

*Setspn Overview*: `http://technet.microsoft.com/en-us/library/cc773257(WS.10).aspx`

*Service Principal Name (SPN) checklist for Kerberos authentication with IIS 7.0/7.5*: `http://blogs.msdn.com/b/webtopics/archive/2009/01/19/service-principal-name-spn-checklist-for-kerberos-authentication-with-iis-7-0.aspx`.

# Using Providers Policies in App-V

One important aspect in the App-V deployment scenarios is based on how we can enforce security and legal compliance across our virtual applications. App-V includes the possibility of using Providers Policies and licenses in our environment.

In this section, we are going to take a good look at understanding this feature as well as configuring and applying Providers Policies in our environment, forcing licenses to achieve the mentioned compliances.

# Understanding Providers Policies and licenses

Providers Policies is a feature, included in the App-V Management Server, from which administrators can set rules for the users that connect to the environment for retrieving applications.

Using Providers Policies, we can basically set certain conditions to be fulfilled for the client connecting to the server, and if these conditions are not in place for a particular user, the application becomes unavailable. One important aspect of these conditions available is the applications licenses.

The following are the three types of licenses available in App-V:

- **Unlimited License**: This type of license offers the benefit of setting an expiration date for the applications included in this license. Being unlimited, there is no other restriction we can apply using this license.

- **Concurrent License**: The concurrent license allows setting a desired number of licenses to be used simultaneously for a certain application. Using this policy represents a common example we can use in organizations to maintain license compliance and protect us legally.

  An interesting tweak of this is that we can actually deploy the application to any desired number of clients, but the concurrency will focus in the "simultaneous" use of the application. This way, we can guarantee that all the applications are deployed on all the machines, but only the permitted users are accessing it.

- **Named License**: By using the named license, we can apply a particular license to a specific user; this way, we can permit a single user to run the application instead of configuring Active Directory Group access.

> Providers Policies and licenses can only be applied using an App-V Management Server. No other delivery method is supported for using these features.
>
> Licenses only apply per package; we cannot set different licenses for several applications included in the same package.

# Configuring and applying Providers Policies

Let's review the step-by-step process for creating and applying Providers Policies in App-V.

1. In the App-V Management Server Console, right-click on **Providers Policies** and select **New Provider Policy**.

2. Complete **Policy Name**, in this example **Devs** is used.

   ○ If the option **Manage client desktop using the Management Console** is selected, the settings defined at the App-V Management Console, for application shortcuts and file-type associations, will be applied to all clients that this policy applies to. If there are conflicting settings at the client, the server's settings will take precedence.

   ○ The option **Refresh desktop configuration when a user logs in** specifies that the client will look for updated information to the server whenever he logs in.

   ○ The option **Refresh configuration every** configures the client to refresh its configuration at a desired time interval.

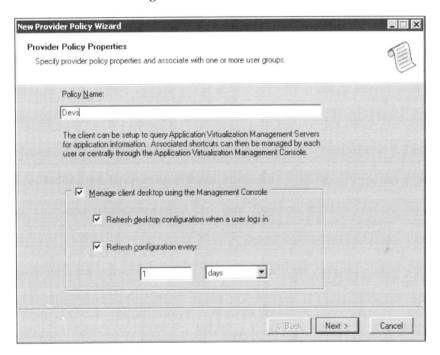

3. In the next window, select the groups where this policy will apply; **App-V Users,** in this case.

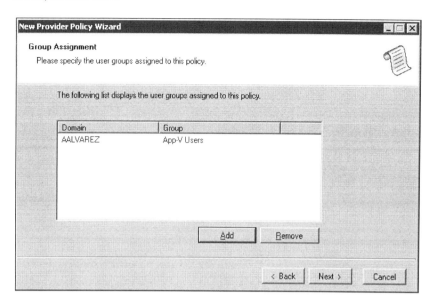

4. In the next window, we can configure the parameters for this policy:

   ° Enabling **Authentication** (the only suboption available is **Windows Authentication**) sets the normal behavior of the streaming process. The user is authenticated with credentials and domain. If we disable this option, it allows any user contacting the Management Server to launch the application.

   ° Also, by using **Enforce Access Permissions Settings** (enabled by default), access to all applications will be authorized against access permissions under the application parameters set in the App-V Management Server Console.

   ° By selecting **Log Usage Information**, every application running with this policy will start generating log information; this can later be retrieved by administrators to generate usage reports.

   ° **Licensing** has two options: **Audit License Usage only** does not prevent users from launching an application if licenses configurations do not match; on the contrary, using **Enforce License Policies** will require a valid license in order to allow the user to launch the application.

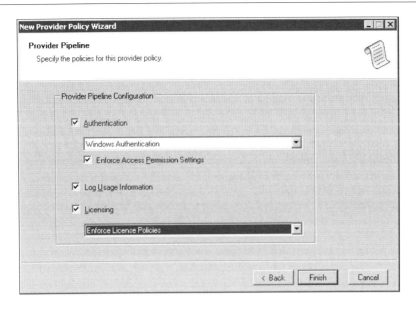

5. As soon as we click **Finish**, a message will pop up saying that the Application Virtualization Management Server services must be restarted. Execute this task in the **Services** console of the App-V Management Server OS.

6. There are two ways in which we can apply this newly generated policy to the applications/server:

   ○ By selecting **Properties** in the **Server Group** in the App-V Management Server Console: Enabling the policy, at this stage, will force all applications in this server group to use the same policy.

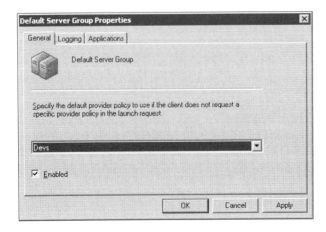

° Enabling the policy in OSD application files: Adding the Provider Policy parameter in the OSD file will apply the policy only to the selected application.

° The parameter we need to configure is in the CODEBASE section of the OSD file, adding `?Customer=ProviderPolicyName` at the end of the SFT reference.

° In this example, the CODEBASE line remains as follows:

```
<CODEBASE HREF="RTSP://appv-server:554/WinRAR/WinRAR.
sft?Customer=Devs"
```

So far, we've configured a Provider Policy, which will log application usage and enforce the use of an application license. In the next section, we are going to configure the licenses that can be attached in App-V packages.

# Configuring and applying App-V licenses

The Full Infrastructure model of App-V includes several features that can be used for App-V administrators and that are, in some cases, necessary in several organizations. One of them is App-V licenses.

Since virtual applications are abstracted from several operating system components and the normal process life-cycle of applications, it is virtually impossible to handle license enforcements in the same way that we did before.

Applying license policies in any App-V scenario can help us maintain legal compliance within our organization. These applications policies work together with Providers Policies; this last one is in charge of enforcing whether or not the existing license is applied to each application.

It is not possible to enforce licenses using the Default Provider Policy.

If we are using an App-V Management Server, but have configured the **Application Source Root** (**ASR**) setting (using registry settings or the App-V ADM template) in App-V clients, using a different Streaming Server (File Server, HTTP/S, or Streaming Server), enforcing licenses will not be possible.

Let's review the step-by-step process for creating, configuring, and applying App-V licenses. We are going to consider the three types of licenses in this process.

# Using an unlimited license

1. In the App-V Management Server Console, right-click on **Application Licenses** and select **New Unlimited License**.

2. Type an **Application License Group Name**. Licenses are stored in groups, so we can define several licenses for several applications with the same characteristics.

   In the **License Expiration Warning**, we can set the time the App-V application should wait for when it reaches the expiration.

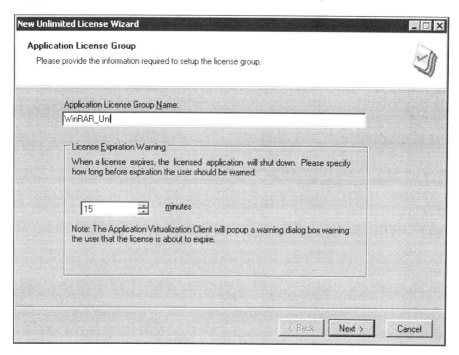

3. Insert a **License Description** (make sure **Enabled** is marked) and set the **License Key** and an **Expiration Date**, if it applies.

   Since this is an unlimited license, we do not define any restriction in the application concurrency.

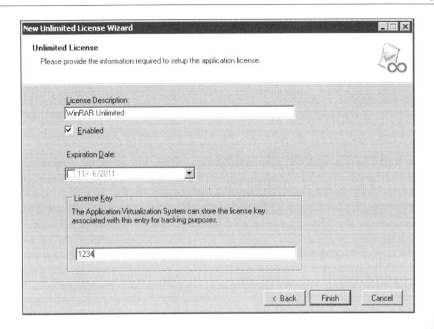

4. In the console, access the application properties, and in the **General** tab, we can select the existing applications licenses available.

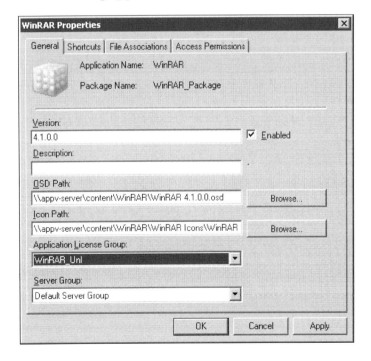

5.  As soon as we apply it, the license setting will start running. If users are running this application, the new license will apply as soon as they close the application and run it again (during the phase of **Checking for updates...**, new license properties are retrieved).

6.  If we disable this license, or if the expiration date arrives, users won't be able to run this application again and this message will appear in the App-V client: **You are not authorized to access this resource.**

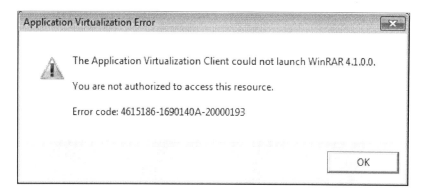

## Using concurrent licenses

The steps in all license types are the same; they just vary according to the options included:

1.  In the Management Server Console, right-click on **Application Licenses** and select **New Concurrent License**.

2.  Type the name for the license group and select the expiration time warning.

3.  In the next window, we can configure the number of concurrent licenses permitted for the application. We can also set an expiration date.

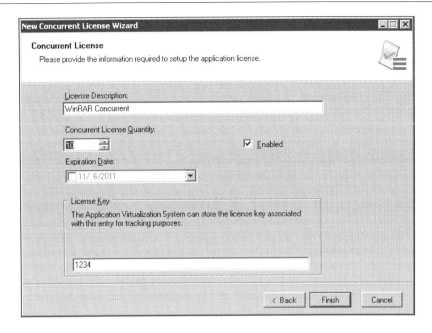

4.  Apply the license to the application's properties.

5.  The next time a user launches the application, the concurrency will start running and, in this example, a maximum number of **10** users will be allowed.

# Using named licenses

As we explained earlier, named licenses refer to attaching any license to a specific user; if we already configured user-access in our App-V implementation, setting this option could be unnecessary.

Let's review the steps for creating and associating a named license:

1.  In the Management Server Console, right-click **Application Licenses** and select **New Named License**.

2.  Type the name for the license group and select the expiration time warning.

3. Add a user in the Active Directory domain and attach, to this user, the specific license that applies.

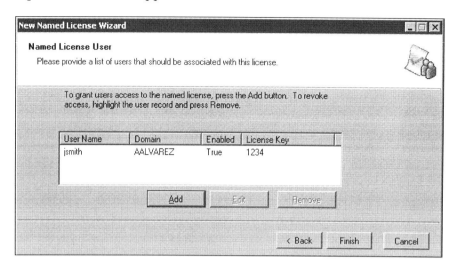

4. Apply the license to the application's properties.

 Whenever a license policy (any one of those mentioned) is not in compliance, is not enabled, or has expired, the "not authorized" error message is displayed if a user tries to launch the application.

# Summary

In this chapter, we covered the particular scenarios in which we need to customize our deployment methods without using the native Full Infrastructure model.

We've covered how to configure a streaming server using the HTTP protocol, which is highly necessary in several implementations, mainly because using a common protocol, such as port 80, facilitates communication between networks. We also had the chance to review an important matter, how to configure HTTP publishing in addition to streaming.

Standalone scenarios are also very common in App-V, which can be configured to stream applications located locally on each computer or to stream them from a file server. The main benefit of any of these two is that the implementation cost is really low since it does not require any server.

Securing communications is also covered in this chapter. We also covered configuring RTSPS and HTTPS communications, not only for a Management Server but also for streaming servers (Web or native App-V).

We've also reviewed the Providers Policies and license enforcements that we can provide if we are using the Full Infrastructure model or at least one App-V Management Server. Using these two options combined, we can guarantee that security and legal compliance are met, in our organization, using App-V.

In the next chapter, we will take a closer look at how to expand complex sequencing with OSD scripting; we will also look at adding some other concepts to work with virtual applications, using command lines and automation procedures.

# 4
# Handling Scripting and App-V Command Lines

Every IT professional, at some stage in their career, will ask or be asked this question: *Is there any way we can automate that process?* If we've never worked with scripts, we probably won't have a proper answer.

Handling scripts and automation processes can sound like an impossible thing to do, for some IT professionals; but, the truth is that scripting or the command line does not offer us a complexity beyond the technology itself. The real complexity resides in understanding the environment and the components we are working on.

The App-V architecture forces every application to work inside a "bubble", where it interacts with the operating system, but the operating system cannot modify or edit this virtual environment; this is necessary for maintaining the idea of application virtualization.

The important thing to remember when we are dealing with App-V and looking for a way to scale up our implementation, is that if you can do it with normal applications then you probably will be able to do it with virtual applications, as well. And scripting capabilities can help us achieve that goal.

Using the OSD file we generate every time an application is captured, we can introduce several ways to interact with the virtual and non-virtual environment of the client. Running scripts prior to an application launch, or in any other stage, makes it possible to, say, check for a prerequisite in order to guarantee the stability of my virtual application.

A different aspect of App-V and its scripting possibilities is the options it uses within command lines. App-V includes a set of tools that can be used in command lines and scripts to automate our normal App-V processes.

In this chapter, we will cover the following points:

- Understanding what OSD scripting is: the main differences between `<HREF>` and `<SCRIPTBODY>` and understanding the different scripting stages

- Using OSD scripting to interact with and modify the virtual environment of the application

- Using OSD scripting to interact outside the virtual environment

- Understanding the command lines that are included in App-V

- Using `SFTMIME` to handle applications, packages, and other client options

- Using `SFTSequencer` to run the same processes as the GUI in the App-V Sequencer

# What we can do with App-V scripting

When we think about scripting within App-V, we will be thinking about OSD scripting. As we know, the OSD file represents, in a virtual application, all the information that is necessary to launch it—package identifier, server and port name used to stream the application, dependencies set in Dynamic Suite Composition (DSC), the shortcuts, and file associations that will be applied in clients.

The possibilities of what we can do in this scripting scenario are many. We can handle several aspects of the virtual environment, making it possible to edit some of its components without resequencing the application; or, we can interact outside the "bubble" by starting a service prior to launching an application.

# Introducing OSD scripting

In this chapter, we will take a closer look at a powerful method App-V provides administrators to customize and optimize their virtual environment, adding some interesting options, such as, checking for a prerequisite before launching an application, adding environment variables, and so on. All of that is done using OSD scripting.

The OSD file is an XML-formed file, and we can find the following sections from which we can review the information mentioned:

| OSD section | Description |
| --- | --- |
| `<SOFTPKG>` | Package identifiers (GUID, name, and version) |
| `<IMPLEMENTATION>` | Server and port used to stream the application and other parameters to be used, when the client runs the application |
| `<DEPENDENCY>` | Specify the client version necessary and the scripts to run, prior to launching the application |
| `<PACKAGE NAME>` | Package name |
| `<ABSTRACT>` | Includes the notes added in the sequencing process |
| `<MGMT_SHORTCUTLIST>` | The list and location (using the virtual environment redirection paths) of the shortcuts to be included |
| `<MGT_FILEASSOCIATIONS>` | The list of file type associations to be used in the client |

Do not confuse the DEPENDENCIES tag used within IMPLEMENTATION and the DEPENDECY tag used later.

The first one is used to specify the package associations used in Dynamic Suite Composition; the second one, DEPENDENCY, runs the prelaunch scripts and verifies the App-V client version.

**Recommendation:**

Before editing an OSD, always back up the file. Any mistype or configuration error translates into virtual application malfunction.

# Understanding OSD scripting stages

All of the OSD scripts we would like to add must be inserted inside the DEPENDENCY tag, but we must know also that there are different stages at which we can execute this script.

Inserting different scripts within the application, and deciding when or where this command will execute, gives us a very dynamic and scalable environment that we will find easy to handle.

**When** we can launch a script, is defined in these stages:

- **Pre-Stream**: Runs the script before the program starts streaming, for example, checking for a prerequisite
- **Post-Stream**: Runs the script after authorization and after the program starts streaming but before the virtual environment is set up
- **Pre-Launch**: Runs the script inside the virtual environment before the program runs
- **Post-Launch**: Runs the script after the program is started
- **Post-Shutdown**: Runs the script after the program is shut down. For example, use this attribute to clean up configuration settings or to delete configuration files.

 There's no support for a pre-shutdown event. This is mainly because we cannot determine the exact moment at which a user will perform a shutdown.

**Where** we can launch, is determined by whether we want to run the script only in the virtual environment or outside the virtual environment; this is configured by the PROTECT attribute:

- PROTECT = TRUE: Runs only in the virtual environment, for example, for troubleshooting the virtual application
- PROTECT = FALSE: Runs outside the virtual environment, for example, starting a service in the client's operating system

Another behavior we can edit is "how much time" the script will run for. This configuration is set by using two values: TIMEOUT and WAIT:

- TIMEOUT = X: The client will wait X number of seconds for a response from the running script
- TIMEOUT = 0: There is no timeout; the client will wait indefinitely for the script to run and return a response
- WAIT = TRUE: The client will wait for the script to return with a response
- WAIT = FALSE: The client can continue executing the next step without expecting a response from the script

This is the workflow where we can identify the different instances of running scripts within the OSD file:

1. User clicks on the program shortcut for a virtual application.
2. **Pre-Stream script runs** (outside virtual environment).
3. Page streams FB1.
4. **Post-Stream script runs** (outside virtual environment).
5. Virtual environment is loaded.
6. **Pre-Launch script runs** (inside or outside virtual environment).
7. The virtual application launches.
8. **Post-Launch script runs** (inside or outside virtual environment).
9. If background streaming is enabled for the application, FB2 will stream into the client cache in the background.
10. User exits the virtual application.
11. The virtual environment is unloaded.
12. **Post-shutdown script runs** (outside virtual environment).

Inside the OSD scripting, there are two types of scripts we can use, and we must set them by using the HREF and SCRIPTBODY tags.

# Understanding <HREF>

Using HREF usually indicates that we need to execute a single command, for example, calling CMD to review directories and files within the virtual environment.

HREF is the simplest way to introduce a command line into the App-V client, but we have to be very careful; we must understand that there are several command lines that are not suitable for this category, for example, DOS commands that are non-executable, such as the command for creating a directory (md).

HREF can be used, for example, for running a .bat file in a local or remote path, since it supports using a network drive or share.

An example of the HREF script is as follows:

```
<DEPENDENCY>
  <SCRIPT TIMING="PRE" EVENT="LAUNCH" WAIT="TRUE" PROTECT="TRUE">
    <HREF>C:\Windows\System32\cmd.exe</HREF>
  </SCRIPT>
</DEPENDENCY>
```

*Quick question*: Without peeking at what we've seen earlier, answer these queries:

- In what stage exactly is this script running?

- Does it run outside the virtual environment?

- Is there a timeout?

# Understanding <SCRIPTBODY>

When we need to have a more complex type of execution that requires validations or launching a file, we must use SCRIPTBODY.

Take into consideration that SCRIPTBODY uses the \ character as an escape option for the script, meaning that, if we want to use that character for another purpose (for example, to use a network share), we will need to add an extra \ inside the command line.

Another difference in the use of SCRIPTBODY instead of HREF is that the script we run is actually being temporarily stored in a .bat file.

An example of SCRIPTBODY being used to reassign network drives by deleting any existing first is as follows:

```
<DEPENDENCY>
  <SCRIPT TIMING="PRE" EVENT="LAUNCH" WAIT="TRUE" PROTECT="TRUE">
    <SCRIPTBODY> @echo on \n
    net use z: /delete /y \n
    net use z: \\\\servername\share1 \n
    net use y: /delete /y \n
    net use y: \\\\servername\share2 \n
    </SCRIPTBODY>
  </SCRIPT>
</DEPENDENCY>
```

```
Firefox4 - Notepad
File  Edit  Format  View  Help
<?xml version="1.0" standalone="no"?>
<SOFTPKG GUID="10066EC8-F0B1-4B48-9988-C257EABDF53A" NAME="Mozilla Firefox" VERSION="2.0.1.·
        <IMPLEMENTATION>
                <CODEBASE HREF="RTSP://appv-server:554/Firefox4/Firefox4_2.sft" GUID="371B9|
                <VIRTUALENV TERMINATECHILDREN="FALSE">
                        <POLICIES>
                                <LOCAL_INTERACTION_ALLOWED>FALSE</LOCAL_INTERACTION_ALLOWED:
                        </POLICIES>
                        <ENVLIST/>
                </VIRTUALENV>
                <WORKINGDIR>%SFT_MNT%\Firefox4</WORKINGDIR>
                <VM VALUE="win32">
                        <SUBSYSTEM VALUE="windows"/>
                </VM>
                <OS VALUE="win764"/>
        </IMPLEMENTATION>
        <DEPENDENCY>
                <CLIENTVERSION VERSION="4.6.0.0"/>
                <SCRIPT TIMING="PRE" EVENT="LAUNCH" WAIT="TRUE" PROTECT="TRUE">
                        <SCRIPTBODY> @echo on \n
                        net use z: /delete /y \n
                        net use z: \\\servername\share1 \n
                        net use y: /delete /y \n
                        net use y: \\\servername\share2 \n
                        </SCRIPTBODY>
                </SCRIPT>
        </DEPENDENCY>
        <PACKAGE NAME="Firefox4"/>
        <ABSTRACT/>
        <MGMT_SHORTCUTLIST>
                <SHORTCUT LOCATION="%CSIDL_DESKTOPDIRECTORY%" FILENAME="Mozilla Firefox.lnk"
                <SHORTCUT LOCATION="%CSIDL_PROGRAMS%" FILENAME="Mozilla Firefox.lnk" OVERRII ▾
```

# Comparing <HREF> and <SCRIPTBODY>

To summarize what we've seen so far, here's a quick comparison between <HREF> and <SCRIPTBODY>:

| <SCRIPTBODY> | <HREF> |
|---|---|
| Can be used to call an executable by searching for it in the client's Path statement. | Can be used to call an executable by searching for it in the client's Path statement. |
| Uses \ as an escape character and, as such, requires an extra \ to pass the actual character. | Does not use \ as an escape character. |
| Can be used to pass non-executable commands such as the DOS make directory (md). This is actually a part of the COMMAND.COM. | Cannot be used to pass non-executable commands such as the DOS make directory (md). |
| When used, the contents of the script are copied to a temporary .bat file on the client's drive. | Does not create a temporary .bat file; instead, executes the contents of the script directly on the client. |
| When used, a DOS window appears on the screen during the execution of the script's .bat file. | No DOS window appears on the screen unless the process being called is a console application. |

# Interacting within the virtual environment

So far, we had a review about the OSD files, their components, and how we can insert scripts using `<HREF>` and `<SCRIPTBODY>`. In this section, we'll take a closer look at some practical examples and review other options within each OSD.

There are several options we can use to modify our virtual environment or application, in order to suit any given scenario; for example, adding parameters to the application executable, adding environment variables, editing registry settings, configuring the ability to interact with operating system variables, and so on.

# Adding parameters to the virtual application

There are some cases where we might need to modify the execution of our virtual application, for example, by adding a small tweak, in order to run with a specific parameter.

For example, we want the file to open, as soon as the user double-clicks the shortcut. This can be done since we can find, in the OSD, the executable file of the application with the reference `FILENAME`; adding `PARAMETERS` in this section will modify the execution to use the values used.

Taking that example, here's an OSD example of a Mozilla Firefox virtual application wherein, every time the user launches it, the company's website URL (`CompanySite. url`) will be opened:

```
<IMPLEMENTATION>
<CODEBASE HREF="RTSP://appv-server:554/Firefox4/Firefox4.
sft" GUID="xxx" PARAMETERS="%SFT_MNT%\Firefox4\CompanySite.url"
FILENAME="Firefox4\firefox.exe" … />
```

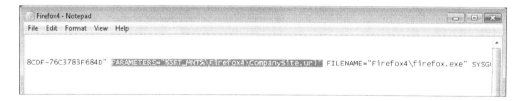

 Remember that `%SFT_MNT%` represents the `Q:\` drive used when we sequenced the application.

# Using WORKINGDIR

WORKINGDIR is commonly used with PARAMATERS since it references the directory where files will be looked, if no path is given.

Taking the previous example, if we already have the CompanySite.url file in a given directory, such as C:\Users, we can reconfigure our OSD, as follows:

```
<IMPLEMENTATION>
  <WORKINGDIR>C:\Users</WORKINGDIR>
  <CODEBASE HREF="RTSP://appv-server:554/Firefox4/Firefox4.sft"
GUID="xxx" PARAMETERS="CompanySite.url" FILENAME="Firefox4\firefox.
exe" ... />
```

# Adding environment variables

Another example of editing the virtual environment is the environment variables sometimes used by applications in the operating system to function properly.

We can add environment variables in two ways:

- Using a script in OSD that uses the SET command (or a .bat file called within a script in OSD)
- Using the ENVIRONMENT VARIABLE option inside the <VIRTUALENV> tag (located inside <IMPLEMENTATION>)

Working with ENVIRONMENT VARIABLE is quite simple, as well. Let's take a look at this example that is used when Visual Studio 2005 is sequenced changing the environment variable PATH to \vs2005\Microsoft\SDK\bin\ (vs2005 represents the folder name used when the application was sequenced):

```
<VIRTUALENV>
  <ENVLIST>
    <ENVIRONMENT VARIABLE="PATH">%PATH%;%SFT_MNT%\vs2005\Microsoft
SDK\bin\.;
    </ENVIRONMENT>
  </ENVLIST>
</VIRTUALENV>
```

Please remember that environment variables are captured in the sequencing process. So, if the application adds any variable, we should see it in our OSD file, inserted in the environment, as soon as the sequencing process completes.

Do not manually add any variable until you can complete a successful sequencing of the application.

When working inside the VIRTUALENV tag, or setting a script with the command SET, the environment variable will be added, but only in the virtual environment.

If we want to set those variables to be persistent in the operating system (outside the virtual environment), we will need to use the SETX command. For more information about SETX, check this Microsoft TechNet article: http://technet.microsoft.com/en-us/library/cc755104(WS.10).aspx.

Also note that any environment variable should appear in these registry paths: HKEY_CURRENT_USER\Environment and HKEY_LOCAL_MACHINE\SYSTEM\CurrentControlSet\Control\Session Manager\Environment.

# Editing the virtual registry

The App-V Sequencer has a very simple way for us to access and edit the virtual registry used by the application we sequenced; but, as a drawback of editing the registry of an existing package, when we save the changes, a new version of this package is created. That means that we must upgrade the application in our clients.

The OSD has the ability to edit the virtual registry without resequencing the application. For example, we can modify the application settings without either executing the application or re-deploying it.

The modifications within the OSD file must be executed also inside the VIRTUALENV tag. Let's take a look at an example:

```
<VIRTUALENV>
  <REGISTRY>
    <REGKEY HIVE="HKCU" KEY="Software\MyApp">
    <REGVALUE REGTYPE="REG_DWORD" NAME="EnableFileTracing">1</
REGVALUE>
    <REGVALUE REGTYPE="REG_DWORD" NAME="EnableDebuggerTracing">1</
REGVALUE>
    <REGVALUE REGTYPE="REG BINARY"
    </REGKEY>
  </REGISTRY>
</VIRTUALENV>
```

```
<POLICIES>
        <LOCAL_INTERACTION_ALLOWED>FALSE</LOCAL_INTERACTION_ALLOWED>
</POLICIES>
<REGISTRY>
        <REGKEY HIVE="HKCU" KEY="Software\MyApp">
            <REGVALUE REGTYPE="REG_DWORD" NAME="EnableFileTracing">1</REGVALUE>
            <REGVALUE REGTYPE="REG_DWORD" NAME="EnableDebuggerTracing">1</REGVALUE>
            <REGVALUE REGTYPE="REG_BINARY"/>
        </REGKEY>
</REGISTRY>
<ENVLIST/>
```

Here's a detailed explanation of what we do here:

1. Using REGKEY HIVE first, locates the registry path where we need to edit/ modify the values.

2. Then, using REGVALUE REGTYPE, we set the type of registry we need to access (in this case REG_DWORD).

3. By selecting NAME (for this example, EnableFileTracing), we've selected the registry we need to edit.

4. Adding the value 1, we modify the registry using that value.

 Using OSD files, we cannot set REG_MULTI_SZ values in the scripting process.

# Editing LOCAL_INTERACTION_ALLOWED

As we've seen earlier, enabling LOCAL_INTERACTION_ALLOWED reconfigures the virtual environment, allowing the components in this environment to be available outside the isolation bubble.

We've also seen how we can enable it using the App-V Sequencer. But, again this requires a new version of the application to be created, if this is an existing package. Editing the OSD, we can easily modify this option; it is turned off by default.

The value can be found inside VIRTUALENV, as well. Here's a quick example:

```
<VIRTUALENV>
  <POLICIES>
    <LOCAL_INTERACTION_ALLOWED>TRUE</LOCAL_INTERACTION_ALLOWED>
  </POLICIES>
</VIRTUALENV>
```

As a reminder, keep in mind that this feature should only be enabled when it's absolutely necessary. If we have to enable it, test the application properly since there could be some conflicts.

Other policies we can use are: VIRTUAL_SERVICES_DISABLED, VIRTUAL_REGISTRY_DISABLED, and VIRTUAL_FILESYSTEM_DISABLED.

Using those should be avoided, unless they are necessary.

Usually, we can enable any of those mentioned when we need to troubleshoot a virtual application. For example, by disabling any services that the application is using, we can find out whether there's an incompatibility.

# Editing TERMINATECHILDREN

Even though this option sounds a bit rough with the terminology used, what it basically means is that we can terminate all processes or services that might keep running after the application has shut down.

This value is set to FALSE, by default; we can edit it by accessing VIRTUALENV, as well; here is an example with the option enabled:

```
Firefox4 - Notepad
File   Edit   Format   View   Help
<?xml version="1.0" standalone="no"?>
<SOFTPKG GUID="10066EC8-F0B1-4B48-9988-C257EABDF53A" NAME="Mozilla Firefox" VERSION="2.0.1.4120">
        <IMPLEMENTATION>
                <CODEBASE HREF="RTSP://appv-server:554/Firefox4/Firefox4_2.sft" GUID="371B9B18-3579-4934
                <VIRTUALENV TERMINATECHILDREN="TRUE">
                        <POLICIES>
                                <LOCAL_INTERACTION_ALLOWED>FALSE</LOCAL_INTERACTION_ALLOWED>
                        </POLICIES>
```

```
<VIRTUALENV TERMINATECHILDREN="TRUE">
  <POLICIES>
...
  </POLICIES>
  <ENVLIST/>
</VIRTUALENV>
```

# Editing the Provider Policy

As we've seen, Providers Policies are used to set rules about the users/machines connecting and consuming each application; these rules are necessary when we need to have a detailed report about application usage and correctly handling the licenses within our environment.

To use and configure Providers Policies, an App-V Management Server is necessary, but editing the policies that are applied to each application can also be achieved by editing the OSD file. Editing the HREF reference to the SFT file does this.

Here's an example of applying the Provider Policy Office to Microsoft Office Word:

```
<CODEBASE HREF="RTSP://appv-server:554/Office14/WinWord.
sft?Customer=Office"
```

```
<IMPLEMENTATION>
        <CODEBASE HREF="RTSP://appv-server:554/Office14/winWord.sft?Customer=Office"
        <VIRTUALENV TERMINATECHILDREN="FALSE">
```

When we use the Default Provider Policy (which cannot be used to enforce licensing), usually we won't see any reference in the OSD file; so, an application configured to use the Default Provider Policy should look like this:

```
<CODEBASE HREF="RTSP://appv-server:554/Office14/WinWord.sft"
```

 For more information about Providers Policies and enforcing licenses in App-V, refer to *Chapter 3, Deploying Applications in Complex Environments*.

# Interacting outside the virtual environment

So far, we've seen some practical examples of editing the virtual environment used by applications, without the need for resequencing it, just by editing the OSD file. But, there are some cases where we are going to need to interact outside the virtual environment, in those situations we also can use the OSD file to accomplish this.

Every application has a unique way of working and interacting with other components, and this integration could sometimes require some tweaking in the virtual application life cycle. Using some scripts, we can get a chance to handle the "outside" environment.

# Launching local applications

There are some cases in which we might need to use external applications to accomplish a task with our virtual application; we can use the OSD file to execute this.

A quick example of this is when we want to deliver a web application—we need to execute a web browser prior to opening this virtual application. Here's how it should look in the OSD file:

```
<CODEBASE FILENAME="C:\Program Files\Internet Explorer\iexplore.exe"
HREF="RTSP://appv-server:554/webapp/webapp.sft"
GUID="xxx"/ … >
```

# Starting a service

There are some applications that need a particular service to be running in order to launch; if this service is not included in the sequencing process, we will have some problems.

Using SCRIPTBODY is the answer to getting this task done; the procedure is the same one that we would run in a command line. **QuickBooks** is one of the applications that require a service to be started prior to being launched. Here's an example:

```
<SCRIPT TIMING="PRE" EVENT="LAUNCH" PROTECT="TRUE" WAIT="TRUE">
  <HREF>cmd /c start /wait cmd /c net start QBCFMonitorService</HREF>
</SCRIPT>
```

# Checking for prerequisites before launching

Another excellent feature of OSD scripting is the ability to validate prerequisites prior to running the application.

We are going to take a look at an example of using .Net Framework 3.5 as a prerequisite. The idea is to return a value in case the Framework folder exists; if the path appears in the client, the application can be launched (SUCCESSFULRESULT = "1"), otherwise the process is aborted(ABORTRESULT = "0").

```
<DEPENDENCY>
  <SCRIPT TIMING="PRE" EVENT="LAUNCH" WAIT="TRUE" PROTECT="TRUE"
SUCCESSFULRESULT="1" ABORTRESULT="0">
    <SCRIPTBODY> @echo off  \n
    set net35loc=%windir%\\Microsoft.NET\\Framework\\v.3.5\n
    set file35=%net35loc%\\csc.exe\n
    if no exist &quot;%file35%&quot; (\n
      echo .Net Framework 3.5 must be installed to run this
application. \n
      pause\n
      exit 0 )\n
```

```
    exit 1
    </SCRIPTBODY>
  </SCRIPT>
</DEPENDENCY>
```

```
<CLIENTVERSION VERSION="4.6.0.0"/>
<SCRIPT TIMING="PRE" EVENT="LAUNCH" WAIT="TRUE" PROTECT="TRUE" SUCCESSFULRESULT="1" ABORTRESULT="0">
    <SCRIPTBODY> @echo off \n
    set net35loc=%windir%\\Microsoft.NET\\Framework\\v.3.5\n
    set file35=%net35loc%\\csc.exe\n
    if no exist &quot;%file35%&quot;  \n
        echo .Net Framework 3.5 must be installed to run this application. \n
        pause\n
        exit 0 \n
    exit 1
    </SCRIPTBODY>
</SCRIPT>
NDENCY>
```

App-V also includes a set of tools that lets us interact with the processes included in the platform and that we can also include in the automation process.

# Using App-V command lines

Besides working with OSD scripting to scale up our applications deployment, we can use several tools provided by App-V to automate normal processes.

The possibilities regarding the command lines available are pretty much the same as we could use in the App-V client and sequencer console.

In this section of the chapter, we will have a detailed review of what we can accomplish with tools, such as, SFTMIME, SFTSequencer, and SFTTRAY.

# Configuring client options with SFTMIME

Among all these tools provided by App-V, SFTMIME is the most powerful. By using this tool, we get the chance to execute all the normal processes of the App-V client that we usually would in the GUI—handle virtual applications, packages, publishing servers, and file type associations.

Since using SFTMIME provides a large set of possibilities; the verbs and parameters used will be plenty. What we need to remember is that the basic syntax of SFTMIME should be as follows:

`SFTMIME verb object [parameters]`

Additionally, we can use the following:

- /LOG log-path: Generates a log file for the action performed, placing the file in log_path.

  Starting with App-V 4.6, there's also the option to use the /LOGU variant, which is intended for use when we need the log output in Unicode format.

- /CONSOLE: This option is set by default and is used to display the output in the active window.

- /GUI: Any errors will appear in a pop-up window. This is important if we are expecting to run SFTMIME in a background script.

As with any command line tool, we can review the entire help section included by using SFTMIME /?" or SFTMIME /HELP.

> Some of the concepts we are going to encounter here about the command line options are detailed in *Chapter 1, Taking a Deep Dive into App-V.*

# Handling virtual applications with SFTMIME

Regarding applications, the actions we can execute are as follows:

- ADD APP
- CLEAR APP
- CONFIGURE APP
- DELETE APP
- LOAD/UNLOAD APP
- LOCK/UNLOCK APP
- REPAIR APP

Let's take a quick look at some examples of each.

## Using ADD APP

To add an application using SFTMIME, follow the ensuing syntax:

```
SFTMIME ADD APP:application /OSD osd-pathname [/ICON icon-pathname] [/LOG
log-pathname | /CONSOLE | /GUI]
```

 In my example, I'm using the /ICON parameter, but, as mentioned in the syntax description, this value is optional.

## Using CLEAR APP

The CLEAR APP option clears (not deletes) the current user's settings and publishing configurations for an application. None of the PKG files are deleted.

```
SFTMIME CLEAR APP:application [/LOG log-pathname | /CONSOLE | /GUI]
```

## Using CONFIGURE APP

CONFIGURE APP could appear to execute the more complex options of the application, but it basically lets the user change the icon file associated previously.

```
SFTMIME CONFIGURE APP:application /ICON icon-pathname [/LOG log-pathname
| /CONSOLE | /GUI]
```

## Using DELETE APP

DELETE APP removes the application from the App-V client.

```
SFTMIME DELETE APP:application [/LOG log-pathname | /CONSOLE | /GUI]
```

This command does not remove the user's settings configured in the application; shortcuts are also left in the Icon Cache, and file type associations are hidden but not deleted.

# Using LOAD/UNLOAD APP

This option loads/unloads the application into the client's cache.

```
SFTMIME LOAD APP:application [/LOG log-pathname | /GUI]

SFTMIME UNLOAD APP:application [/LOG log-pathname | /CONSOLE | /GUI]
```

When we execute the LOAD command, you will see the progress bar in the system tray; if we want to ignore this notification, we can use the LOAD PACKAGE feature.

# Using LOCK/UNLOCK APP

LOCK APP places and locks/unlocks the selected application in the client's cache.

```
SFTMIME LOCK APP:application [/LOG log-pathname | /CONSOLE | /GUI]

SFTMIME UNLOCK APP:application [/LOG log-pathname | /CONSOLE | /GUI]
```

# Using PUBLISH APP

When we use PUBLISH APP, we present the necessary shortcuts in order for the user to run the virtual application. Using the right parameters, we decide the places where we want to insert these shortcuts.

```
SFTMIME PUBLISH APP:application {/DESKTOP | /START | /TARGET target-path}
[/ICON icon-pathname] [/DISPLAY display-name] [/ARGS command-args...] [/
LOG log-pathname | /CONSOLE | /GUI]
```

Here's a detailed look at the parameters we haven't seen so far:

- /DESKTOP: The shortcuts are placed on the user's desktop
- /START: The shortcuts are placed in the user's **Start Menu** (Application Virtualization folder)
- /TARGET: The shortcuts will be placed in the desired absolute path given by target-path
- /DISPLAY: This option is used for the display name we would like to use in the shortcut, given by the display-name value
- /ARGS: Using this parameter, we can introduce the arguments we would like to use in the shortcut presented

# Using REPAIR APP

The REPAIR option basically removes the user's settings applied to that application. Getting more specific, repairing an application deletes usrvol_sftfs_v1.pkg from the user profile.

```
SFTMIME REPAIR APP:application [/LOG log-pathname | /CONSOLE | /GUI]
```

 Remember that repairing an application permanently deletes the user's settings applied to that package. So, if another application also exists in the same package, the user's applied settings will be lost as well.

# Differentiating between UNLOAD and DELETE

Both of these options, UNLOAD and DELETE, removes the UsrVol_sftfs_v1.pkg file, but the difference lies in that the UNLOAD option does not delete shortcuts and file type associations created by the application.

# Handling packages with SFTMIME

Handling packages is quite the same as handling applications; the only difference to understand is that "virtual applications" are not the same as "packages".

Handling virtual applications means handling what the OSD file is presenting to us for that single application; by using packages, we get the chance to handle all the applications included in the same package.

Packages depend on the manifest file, where we can edit the entire behavior of the applications presented in that package in terms of background loading, SFT location, which of the applications will use Auto Load, and so on.

Let's take a look at the options we can use with SFTMIME:

- ADD PACKAGE
- CONFIGURE PACKAGE
- DELETE PACKAGE
- PUBLISH/UNPUBLISH PACKAGE
- LOAD/UNLOAD PACKAGE

# Using ADD PACKAGE

This command adds a package; if the package already exists, this command will update the configuration of the existing package.

```
SFTMIME ADD PACKAGE:package-name /MANIFEST manifest-path [/OVERRIDEURL
url [/AUTOLOADONREFRESH] [/AUTOLOADONLOGIN] [/AUTOLOADONLAUNCH] [/
AUTOLOADTARGET {NONE|ALL|PREVUSED}] [/GLOBAL] [/LOG log-pathname | /
CONSOLE | /GUI]
```

Here's a detailed look at each of the parameters:

- /MANIFEST: Path of the manifest file (XML) where all the package information exists (list of applications and the publishing information)

- /OVERRIDEURL: If we want to override the location of the SFT, we can use this option

- /AUTOLOADONREFRESH: Background loading is performed after a publishing refresh

- /AUTOLOADONLOGIN: Background loading is performed when a user logs in

- /AUTOLOADONLAUNCH: Background loading is performed after a user starts an application from the package

- /AUTOLOADTARGET: We can select which application within this package we would like to autoload

- NONE: No auto loading will be performed, despite the presence of any / AUTOLOADONxxx flags

- ALL: If an auto load trigger is enabled, all applications in the package will be loaded into the cache, whether or not they have been previously started

- PREVUSED: If an auto-load trigger is enabled, the package will load — if any applications in this package have previously been started by a user

- /GLOBAL: Using this option, the package will be present for all users

# Using CONFIGURE PACKAGE

The CONFIGURE option lets us change any of the parameters we can use in an already-added package.

```
SFTMIME CONFIGURE PACKAGE:package-name [/MANIFEST manifest-path] [/
OVERRIDEURL url] [/AUTOLOADNEVER] [/AUTOLOADONREFRESH] [/AUTOLOADONLOGIN]
[/AUTOLOADONLAUNCH] [/AUTOLOADTARGET {NONE|ALL|PREVUSED}] [/LOG log-
pathname | /CONSOLE | /GUI]
```

The package-name variable also corresponds to the package GUID assigned at package creation, including the {} characters. We can find this variable in the App-V Client Management Console, accessing the added application properties:

We can also access the package name in the manifest file. In this case, the package name is presented as the package GUID, including the {} characters.

```
<?xml version="1.0" standalone="no" ?>
- <PACKAGE GUID="{9450B473-87D7-4BE0-8C4F-13B9F57E9357}" NAME="WinRAR"
  - <APPLIST>
    - <APP NAME="WinRAR" VERSION="4.1.0.0" ICON="%SFT_MIME_SOURCE%/WinR
      - <SHORTCUTLIST>
```

In the CONFIGURE PACKAGE example, using WinRAR, we have the following command line to change the Manifest file used:

```
Administrator: C:\Windows\System32\cmd.exe

C:\>SFTMIME CONFIGURE PACKAGE:{9450B473-87D7-4BE0-8C4F-13B9F57E9357} /MANIFEST C
:\apps\WinRAR_manifest.xml

C:\>_
```

If we reassign a new manifest file for a package, the package GUID included in this package must match the package GUID included in the new manifest file.

## Using DELETE PACKAGE

This option removes the selected package and all the applications within that package. Deleting a package always deletes it globally, meaning that no user in the machine will have access to it.

```
SFTMIME DELETE PACKAGE:package-name [/LOG log-pathname | /CONSOLE | /GUI]
```

## Using PUBLISH PACKAGE

As for the option used in APP, PUBLISH PACKAGE publishes the content of the entire package and all the included applications.

```
SFTMIME PUBLISH PACKAGE:package-name /MANIFEST manifest-path [/GLOBAL] [/
LOG log-pathname | /CONSOLE | /GUI]
```

The package must already have been added.

To use the GLOBAL parameter, the PUBLISH PACKAGE command must be run as the local administrator; otherwise, only ManageTypes and PublishShortcut permissions are needed.

Publishing without the GLOBAL parameter grants the user access to the applications in the package and publishes the file types and shortcuts that are listed in the manifest to the user's profile.

Publishing with the GLOBAL parameter adds the file types and shortcuts listed in the manifest to the **All Users** profile.

If the package is not global before the call, and the GLOBAL parameter is used, the package is made global and available to all users.

# Using UNPUBLISH PACKAGE

This option removes the shortcuts and file types associated with an existing package.

```
SFTMIME UNPUBLISH PACKAGE:package-name [/CLEAR] [/GLOBAL] [/LOG log-
pathname | /CONSOLE | /GUI]
```

The /CLEAR option is set to mark that the user settings will also be removed.

> To use GLOBAL, UNPUBLISH PACKAGE must be run as local administrator; otherwise, only ClearApp permission is needed.
>
> Using UNPUBLISH PACKAGE with the GLOBAL parameter removes any global file types and shortcuts for the package. CLEAR is not applicable for all users.
>
> Using UNPUBLISH PACKAGE without GLOBAL, removes the user shortcuts and file types for the package and, if CLEAR is set, also removes user settings and stops background loads, under the user's context.
>
> UNPUBLISH PACKAGE works on applications from the same package name or GUID that was used as the source ID for ADD, EDIT, and PUBLISH PACKAGE.
>
> UNPUBLISH PACKAGE always clears all the user settings, shortcuts, and file types, regardless of the use of the /CLEAR switch.

# Using LOAD/UNLOAD PACKAGE

These options load or unload the content of an entire package in the client's cache.

```
SFTMIME LOAD PACKAGE:package-name [/SFTPATH sft-pathname] [/LOG log-
pathname | /CONSOLE | /GUI]
```

```
SFTMIME UNLOAD PACKAGE:package-name [/LOG log-pathname | /CONSOLE | /GUI]
```

> Only the LOAD option can use a different SFT path.
>
> If no SFTPATH is specified, the client will load the package by using the path it has been configured to use, based on the OSD file, the ApplicationSourceRoot registry key value (configured also with the App-V ADM Template), or the OverrideURL setting.

# Configuring server options with SFTMIME

We can also configure the server properties in the App-V clients. The possibilities are as follows:

- ADD SERVER
- CONFIGURE SERVER
- REFRESH SERVER
- DELETE SERVER

## Using ADD SERVER

With ADD SERVER, we can add a publishing server to the App-V client.

```
SFTMIME ADD SERVER:server-name /HOST hostname /TYPE {HTTP|RTSP} /PATH
path [/PORT port] [/REFRESH {ON|OFF}] [/SECURE] [/LOG log-pathname | /
CONSOLE | /GUI]
```

Here's detailed information about each parameter:

- SERVER: Display name for the server we are adding
- /HOST: The host name or IP address for the publishing server
- /TYPE {HTTP|RTSP}: Indicates the streaming protocol we are going to use
- /PORT: Port to be used for streaming
- /PATH: The path portion of the URL used in a publishing request; if the TYPE parameter is set to RTSP, the path is optional and defaults to /
- /REFRESH {ON|OFF}: If set to ON, publishing information will be refreshed when the user logs in; default is ON
- /SECURE: If present, indicates that a connection with enhanced security should be established to the publishing server

Here's an example of adding the **appv-server**:

## Using CONFIGURE SERVER

Applying CONFIGURE, we can edit any of the information and configuration of an existing publishing server.

```
SFTMIME CONFIGURE SERVER:server-name [/NAME display-name] [/HOST
hostname] [/PORT port] [/PATH path] [/TYPE {HTTP|RTSP}] [/REFRESH
{ON|OFF}] [/SECURE] [/LOG log-pathname | /CONSOLE | /GUI]
```

## Using REFRESH SERVER

The REFRESH option updates publishing options from an existing server.

```
SFTMIME REFRESH SERVER:server-name [/LOG log-pathname | /CONSOLE | /GUI]
```

## Using DELETE SERVER

This option, of course, removes a publishing server from a client.

```
SFTMIME DELETE SERVER:server-name
```

# Handling file type associations

SFTMIME handles the file type associations as a separate object so we can add and edit in our environment. Using TYPE, we can do the following with SFTMIME:

- ADD TYPE
- CONFIGURE TYPE
- DELETE TYPE

# Using ADD TYPE

ADD TYPE adds a specific file type association and an optional icon file to the package.

```
SFTMIME ADD TYPE:file-extension /APP application [/ICON icon-pathname] [/
DESCRIPTION type-desc] [/CONTENT-TYPE content-type] [/GLOBAL] [/PERCEIVED-
TYPE perceived-type] [/PROGID progid] [/CONFIRMOPEN {YES|NO}] [/SHOWEXT
{YES|NO}] [/NEWMENU {YES|NO}] [/LOG log-pathname | /CONSOLE | /GUI]
```

Let's take a look at each of the parameters:

- TYPE: The file name extension that will be associated with the application specified

- /APP: Name of the application with the new association; optionally, we can add the version number of the application

- /ICON: Path of the icon file

- /DESCRIPTION: Just a user-friendly name for the new extension

- /CONTENT-TYPE: This is a MIME header used in App-V; Content-Type headers are used to specify the media type and subtype of data in the body of a message (such as, e-mailing or streaming) and to fully specify the native representation of such data; the default value is application/softricity-extension, and it is not recommended to change it

 For more information about MIME headers and content-type, please visit this Microsoft MSDN article: *MIME Headers* (http://msdn.microsoft.com/en-us/library/ms526943(v=exchg.10).aspx).

- /GLOBAL: If present, the file extension will be available for all users on this computer

- /PERCEIVED-TYPE: This is the perceived type of the file and defaults to nothing; it is used to identify the file type for Windows (and applications) as being an image, audio, document, or other type

- /PROGID: The programmatic identifier for the file type; this value is used to match file type association and defaults to App Virt.extension.File

- /CONFIRMOPEN {YES|NO}: Indicates whether users downloading a file of this type should be asked whether to open or save the file; defaults to YES

- /SHOWEXT {YES|NO}: Indicates whether the file's extension should always be shown, even if the user has requested that all extensions be hidden; defaults to NO

- `/NEWMENU {YES|NO}`: Indicates whether an entry should be added to the shell's "New menu"; defaults to `NO`.

## Using CONFIGURE TYPE

As for any of the objects we've seen so far, the `CONFIGURE` option is available to edit any of the existing information using the same parameters as `ADD`.

```
SFTMIME CONFIGURE TYPE:file-extension [/GLOBAL] [/APP application] [/ICON
icon-pathname] [/DESCRIPTION type-desc] [/CONTENT-TYPE content-type] [/
PERCEIVED-TYPE perceived-type] [/PROGID progid] [/CONFIRMOPEN {YES|NO}]
[/SHOWEXT {YES|NO}] [/NEWMENU {YES|NO}] [/LOG log-pathname | /CONSOLE | /
GUI]
```

## Using DELETE TYPE

We can use this option when we need to remove an existing file association.

```
SFTMIME DELETE TYPE:file-extension [/GLOBAL] [/LOG log-pathname | /
CONSOLE | /GUI]
```

# Handling queries and OBJ with SFTMIME

`SFTMIME` also includes the verb `QUERY` to be executed in order to retrieve information about the existing virtual environment in the client.

## Using QUERY OBJ

The `QUERY OBJ` parameter is probably one of the most powerful options to use with `SFTMIME`, or at least where we could start several other actions. `QUERY OBJ` returns a list of current packages, applications, file type associations, and publishing servers, available in the App-V client.

In `QUERY OBJ`, when we use it to retrieve current applications, the last column of the output tells us whether the application is currently published to the user (`PUBLISHED=1`). The publishing method of that application could be made by using a publishing server refresh, MSI installation, or any of the `SFTMIME` command lines.

Here's an example of running the query to retrieve current applications:

```
SFTMIME query obj:app
```

The result is tab-delimited and it might be a bit tough to read it when you have all that information. As a tweak, we can add the /short parameter to retrieve a simpler list of applications published.

```
SFTMIME query obj:app /short
```

The complete syntax is as follows:

```
SFTMIME QUERY OBJ:{APP|PACKAGE|TYPE|SERVER} [/SHORT] [/GLOBAL] [/LOG log-
pathname | /CONSOLE ]
```

To summarize, here are the parameters we can use:

- OBJ:{APP|PACKAGE|TYPE|SERVER}
- /SHORT
- /GLOBAL

## Using CLEAR and DELETE OBJ

When we use the CLEAR or DELETE options for OBJ, we can only apply it to applications and not packages, or any other object. These two options, CLEAR and DELETE, apply in the same way as reviewed before: CLEAR removes all the user settings and publishing information about each application, and DELETE removes all the application records.

```
SFTMIME DELETE OBJ:APP [/GLOBAL] [/LOG log-pathname | /CONSOLE | /GUI]

SFTMIME CLEAR OBJ:APP [/LOG log-pathname | /CONSOLE | /GUI]
```

# Using SFTSequencer

In the command lines provided by App-V, there are some commands also available, for those sequencing admins, who are seeking to automate processes regarding the capturing, update, and modification of an application. The SFTSequencer tool is provided when we install the App-V Sequencer.

This tool was included in earlier versions of App-V, but, with the new update of **Service Pack 1**, Microsoft updated SFTSequencer to support the latest improvements included in the Service Pack — defining and using package accelerators and the ability for the admin to set the **Feature Block 1 (FB1)** of the SFT.

The principal benefit of using the command line is its automation possibilities. There are some scenarios where we have a detailed and well-known installation procedure of an application; using this tool can help us speed up the process.

SFTSequencer applies in those particular scenarios, but it is not recommended to use this tool, if this is the first time you are sequencing an application. Even though we will have a SPRJ file as an output, which we can edit from the App-V Sequencer GUI, make sure you have a detailed understanding about the sequencing process first.

These are the actions we can execute using SFTSequencer:

- **Sequencing an application**: We will have all of the necessary parameters available to customize the capturing process, including the possibility of defining the FB1

- **Upgrading a package**: As for the wizard procedure, the command line works by generating a new sequencing process, starting with opening an existing package

- **Creating a package accelerator**: Here, we have two options — creating a package accelerator using an installation media and selecting a locally installed application

- **Creating a package from a package accelerator**: This option can be used also with the installer of the application or with a locally installed app

Note that, even though we get an SPRJ file as an output when we sequence an application, there are some possibilities, such as editing the **Virtual File System** or the **Virtual Registry**, that we won't be able to do unless we use the App-V Sequencer GUI.

# Sequencing an application using SFTSequencer

Using SFTSequencer with App-V 4.6 SP1, introduces a set of new options to use in the command line; the most important one is the ability to set the Feature Block 1 within this new package.

The following is the syntax we must use when we are using SFTSequencer to capture an application:

```
SFTSequencer /INSTALLPACKAGE:installpackage /INSTALLPATH:installpath /
OUTPUTFILE:outputfile [/FULLLOAD | /LAUNCHALL [/UPTIME:seconds] | /
LAUNCH:executable1.exe,... [/UPTIME:seconds] | /LAUNCHSCRIPT:scriptpath]
[/PACKAGENAME:packagename] [/BLOCKSIZE:4|16|32|64] [/COMPRESS] [/MSI] [/
DEFAULT:defaultproject]
```

 Remember that the parameters presented in [] are optional.

Here's a detailed look at the SFTSequencer parameters:

- /INSTALLPACKAGE: This is where we select the installation file for the new application
- /INSTALLPATH: The installation path where the application will be installed, for example, Q:\app
- /OUTPUTFILE: The path and name for the SPRJ file to be created
- /LAUNCHSCRIPT: Any scripts we would like to add in the installation process must be included here
- /PACKAGENAME: The package name we are creating
- /BLOCKSIZE: Here, we define the block size
- /COMPRESS: If present, the files will be compressed
- /MSI: If present, an MSI for the standalone installation will be created
- /DEFAULT:defaultproject: In this parameter, we can redefine the template we are using

The arguments /FULLLOAD, /LAUNCH, /LAUNCHALL, and /UPTIME, are the ones that can interact in the creation and definition of FB1.

## Defining FB1

Defining Feature Block 1 is possible with the new version of the SFTSequencer, and we can modify it by handling the proper arguments.

Let's take a look at each of these:

| Option | Argument | Description |
| --- | --- | --- |
| Do not put anything in FB1 | None | Default behavior if no FB1 arguments are passed. |
| Add entire package to FB1 | /FULLLOAD or /F | This can be used in several scenarios where we need to deliver the entire package to guarantee transparent usability. |
| Launch only these files for FB1 optimization. Files must be linked to shortcuts | /LAUNCH: executable1. exe [,filename2.xyz ...] | Each filename is separated by commas; command line arguments for each executable cannot be passed. |
| Launch all shortcuts for FB1 optimization | /LAUNCHALL | Equivalent to Launch All in GUI Sequencer: serially launches each application. |
| Run each application for exactly this amount of time | /UPTIME:seconds | Allows user to override default heuristics for how long an application will run before being shut down [min: 5; max: MAX_INT]. |

Here's an example of sequencing Mozilla Firefox 4, selecting the entire package as FB1, and saving the package in the C drive:

```
SFTSequencer /INSTALLPACKAGE:"C:\inst\Firefox Setup 4.0.1.exe" /
INSTALLPATH:"Q:\Firefox4" /OUTPUTFILE:"C:\Firefox.sprj" /FULLLOAD
```

When we press *Enter*, you will notice that the App-V Sequencer will start with the preparation process in the background:

Since I'm not selecting an unattended installation of Firefox (I would need to parameterize the installation), the installation wizard will appear, and we should manually complete the process.

Once we've completed the installation, the App-V Sequencer will understand that the installation has completed and will collect and save the environment automatically.

When that step is completed, we can check for the package files created in C:\.

# Opening a package for upgrade using SFTSequencer

Upgrading a package using SFTSequencer works in a similar way to sequencing the application, but the main difference lies in selecting an existing package prior to the capturing.

Here's the syntax — we have the parameter /UPGRADE to introduce the package we would like to modify:

```
SFTSequencer /UPGRADE:packagetoupgrade /INSTALLPACKAGE:installpackage /
OUTPUTFILE:outputfile [/DECODEPATH:path] [/FULLLOAD | /LAUNCHALL [/
UPTIME:seconds]| /LAUNCH:executable1.exe,... [/UPTIME:seconds] | /
LAUNCHSCRIPT:scriptpath] [/PACKAGENAME:packagename] [/COMPRESS] [/MSI]
```

# Handling package accelerators using SFTSequencer

Package accelerators are a new feature in App-V 4.6 SP1, and Microsoft introduced into the command line a quick way to handle these new objects.

For creating a package accelerator, we have two options: using a path for creating it through the installation media and by selecting a locally installed application.

Handling a package accelerator will require the following parameters:

- /INPUTFILE and /OUTPUTFILE: The SPRJ files to be introduced when we need to create a package accelerator or as an output file when we are creating a package from a package accelerator

- /INSTALLMEDIAPATH: The path of the installation media for the application

- /LOCALINSTALLPATH: The path for the locally installed application

- /PACKAGEACCELERATORFILE: The CAB file for the package accelerator

- /REMOVEMISSINGFILES: If present, the files that the application cannot find will be removed from the SFT; this, again, is a very delicate option—do not use unless you are absolutely certain

- /TRUSTPACKAGEACCELERATOR: Used when we are creating a package from a package accelerator; if present, the CAB file is accepted as trusted.

## Creating a package accelerator using installation media

The syntax of creating a package accelerator using installation media is as follows:

```
SFTSequencer /INPUTFILE:SprjFile /INSTALLMEDIAPATH:InstallMediaPath /PACK
AGEACCELERATORFILE:PackageAcceleratorCabFile [/REMOVEMISSINGFILES]
```

## Creating a package accelerator from a locally installed application

The syntax for creating a package accelerator using a locally installed application is as follows:

```
SFTSequencer /INPUTFILE:SprjFile /LOCALINSTALLPATH:LocalInstallPath /PACK
AGEACCELERATORFILE:PackageAcceleratorCabFile [/REMOVEMISSINGFILES]
```

## Creating a package from a package accelerator (installation media)

For creating a package from a package accelerator, using installation media, the syntax is as follows:

```
SFTSequencer /PACKAGEACCELERATORFILE:PackageAcceleratorCabFile /INSTALLME
DIAPATH:InstallMediaPath /OUTPUTFILE:SprjFile [/PACKAGENAME:Package Name]
[/COMPRESS] [/MSI] [/TRUSTPACKAGEACCELERATOR]
```

## Creating a package from a package accelerator (locally installed application)

For creating a package from a package accelerator, using a locally installed application, the syntax is as follows:

```
SFTSequencer /PACKAGEACCELERATORFILE:PackageAcceleratorCabFile /
LOCALINSTALL /OUTPUTFILE:SprjFile [/PACKAGENAME:Package Name] [/COMPRESS]
[/MSI] [/TRUSTPACKAGEACCELERATOR]
```

# Expand package to a local system

When we are working with Dynamic Suite Composition (DSC), in some cases, we need to work with an application that has been sequenced earlier, in order to capture the secondary file. For that, we use the EXPAND option to deploy the captured application in the Sequencer.

When we are working with App-V 4.6 SP1, this step is usually transparent for the user, since the App-V Sequencer wizard executes this step for us.

To expand an existing application, we can use the SPRJ or the SFT file; the syntax is as follows:

```
SFTSequencer /EXPAND:SprjOrSftFile
```

# What about SFTTRAY?

Besides using SFTMIME, App-V provides another tool from which we can run several actions in App-V clients. The variety of commands is not all that vast, compared to what we've seen in SFTMIME, but it could apply to some scenarios where we need a quick way to run particular actions, for example, launching an application.

```
SFTTRAY /hide /launch "Mozilla Firefox 2.0.1.4120"
```

SFTTRAY requires the full name used when the application was published by a server, whether MSI or SFTMIME; that's why the Mozilla Firefox includes the version number used when I imported the application in the App-V Management Server.

If you are having doubts about the application name, you can always check the properties from the shortcut.

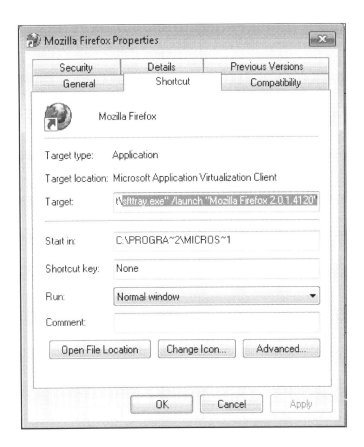

SFTTRAY represents the actual target application that is used by App-V application shortcuts when we are launching the application, that's why you will see it in the **System Tray** notification area or in the **Task Manager** of the client operating system.

Here are the parameters we can use:

| Parameter | Usage | Description |
|---|---|---|
| /launch | /launch "application name"<br><br>/launch "file_name. osd" | Specifies an application to be launched. You can specify the application by using a relative path, an absolute path, the path of a network share, or a URL. |
| /load | /load "application name"<br><br>/load "file_name. osd" | Specifies an application to be loaded in the cache. You can specify the application by using a relative path, an absolute path, a UNC path, or a URL. |
| /loadall | /loadall | Loads all applications completely in the cache. |
| /hide | /hide | Hides the App-V client in the notification area. Must be used together, with, and before, the /launch, /load, or /loadall options. |
| /sftfile | /sftfile "file:// path/file_name.sft" | Specifies a .sft file to import directly from the file. Must be used together with the /load option. |
| /exit | /exit | Exits all App-V -enabled applications and removes the icon from the notification area. |

# Reviewing possibilities using PowerShell

Unfortunately, to date, Microsoft has not provided much, officially, about **Cmdlets** using PowerShell to automate processes in App-V.

Recently, Microsoft published the *Microsoft App-V Server Snapln* on **CodePlex**, which includes almost any task we can execute in the App-V server GUI.

The cmdlets available are as follows:

- **System options:**
  - Get-AppVSystemOptions
  - Set-AppVSystemOptions

- **Packages:**
  - Get-AppVPackages
  - New-AppVPackage
  - Remove-AppVPackage

- **Application groups:**
    - Get-AppVApplicationGroup
    - New-AppVApplicationGroup
    - Remove-AppVApplicationGroup

- **Applications:**
    - Get-AppVApplications
    - New-AppVApplication
    - Remove-AppVApplication
    - Set-AppVApplicationPublishingSettings

- **Administrators:**
    - Get-AppVAdministrators
    - New-AppVAdministrator
    - Remove-AppVAdministrator

- **Server groups:**
    - Get-AppVServerGroup
    - New-AppVServerGroup
    - Remove-AppVServerGroup

- **Servers:**
    - Get-AppVServers
    - New-AppVServer
    - Remove-AppVServer

- **Providers:**
    - Get-AppVProviders
    - Remove-AppVProvider

For more information about *Microsoft App-V Server SnapIn*, take a look at http://posh4appv.codeplex.com/.

# Summary

In this chapter, we had the chance to take a good look at the possibilities around automation processes with the App-V command lines and how we can introduce several new options with OSD scripting.

OSD scripting provides high scalability in our deployment scenarios, making it possible to interact and modify several components in our virtual environment, without the requirement of resequencing our applications. It also gives us the alternatives, to be aware of components outside the virtual environment, to facilitate user experience.

Even though handling an OSD could be very familiar for most IT professionals, since it is XML based, we have to be very careful with the options we are using; any change not properly introduced will most certainly cause application malfunctions or unavailability.

As automation processes, App-V gives us several command line tools that we can insert in batch scripts. The stronger of all of those is SFTMIME, which delivers the same functionalities as the App-V client console (handling virtual applications, packages, publishing servers, and file-type associations), but from a command line.

SFTSequencer is improved, as well, including the App-V 4.6 SP1 features (handling package accelerators and the possibility to customize the Feature Block 1 (FB1) of our package) within the command line.

In the next chapter, we will take a closer look at most of the troubleshooting scenarios in App-V, such as, understanding and solving common errors in installation and configuration of the platform, application sequencing problems and how to mitigate them, and deployment errors and misconfigurations.

# Troubleshooting App-V

**5**

The larger the complexity of our environment, the larger the varieties of problems that can be found in our implementation.

Troubleshooting tasks are not always straightforward activities; we have to understand that a simple error message in a pop-up window cannot be the final analysis we need to solve it. We need to understand the problem from several points of view: reviewing the errors, checking the event viewer, platform logs, or even changing the logging mode included by default.

As for any of the Microsoft platforms, App-V contains several log files—server, sequencer, and client logs—that we can use to get a deeper understanding about the exact problem we are having. These log files can be used in addition to obtaining statistical analysis of the App-V applications.

Regarding the sequencing phase, we can retrieve from log files some of the common errors that may appear in the capturing process. But, what is to be done when the sequencing process is completed successfully but the application fails to work? Or even worse, the application works but exhibits erratic behavior? Process Monitor is the tool we can use to closely observe an application and modify our sequencing technique to fit it into App-V.

In this chapter, we will take a look at the following topics:

- Troubleshooting App-V implementations: reviewing server and common client problems, and how to solve them
- How to troubleshoot virtual application publications and delivery
- How to troubleshoot App-V application usage when the virtual version of the application is not working as expected
- Troubleshooting application sequencing: using not only log files but also the Process Monitor tool to understand some complex sequencing techniques

In this chapter, we will assume that several concepts of the App-V architecture and components we reviewed in *Chapter 1, Taking a Deep Dive into App-V*, are clear to the reader.

It is highly important that, before diving into the troubleshooting, we have the chance to review all the official information about App-V regarding installation, sequencing, publishing, and delivery procedures available from Microsoft.

# Troubleshooting App-V implementations

In this quest of troubleshooting and solving problems, our first stop is going to be the App-V implementations, starting with when we install the App-V component, common configurations, and then operating it.

But, as mentioned earlier in the chapter, before we start reviewing logs to understand what could be the problem, we should start checking the Microsoft guides about implementations.

This previous verification is important, since most of the problems we usually have with implementations are regarding prerequisites not completed.

In this section, we will take a look at:

- Troubleshooting the App-V management server: installation and implementation problems
- Troubleshooting the App-V client installation: common problems when we are trying to install the client component

# Troubleshooting the App-V management server implementation

Having problems with the implementation of the App-V management server could be because of a component; we would require detailed analysis to understand the problem. This is mainly because the App-V management server, as we've seen in *Chapter 1, Taking a Deep Dive into App-V*, has several components in its architecture.

As a reminder, the architecture of an App-V management server looks as follows:

If one of the prerequisites of the App-V management server is not in place, we will have problems implementing any of these components. But, of course, the main idea of troubleshooting is to find the prerequisite we are not fulfilling, and then solve the problem.

In the troubleshooting scenario, understanding components and prerequisites is the first half of our job; the second half would be reviewing the log files.

# Solving App-V management server installation problems

As a reminder, the prerequisites we have to be aware of the App-V management server are the following:

- **Active Directory and DNS services**: Remember that, for installing, we will need two groups—one for App-V users and one for App-V administrators

- **SQL instance available locally or remotely**: And sufficient permissions to create a database (APPVIRT)

- **IIS**: Management service in IIS requires:

  ○ ASP.NET and all dependencies

  ○ The Windows Authentication feature

  ○ Complete **Management Tools** section (including the IIS 6 Management Compatibility)

There is no particular prerequisite for the Management Server component.

There is no particular prerequisite for the Management Console component.

If we are planning to use the RTSPS protocol, we are going to need the certificate installed in the server.

Installing the App-V Management Console on a different machine is a possible task but not a simple one. The App-V team designed a configuration guide to achieve this; you can access this guide on the official Microsoft App-V blog at `http://blogs.technet.com/b/ appv/archive/2009/04/21/app-v-4-5-remote-console- configuration-guide.aspx`.

When we are installing the App-V management server, we also receive a particular log file where all the activity is stored — `%temp%\Softgrid-Server-Setup.txt`.

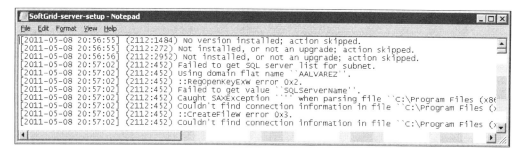

What we've seen so far, in this section, are the common requirements that we must never overlook, if we are planning an App-V management server installation; in those requirements we'll find the root cause of almost any error we might encounter in the installation.

Yes, "almost" is the actual word I'm selecting, because there are some particular scenarios where the prerequisites are in place but the installation still fails.

# Reviewing installation errors "251xx"

If you are an App-V admin and you are in charge of a few App-V management server implementations, you've seen some of these "251xx" errors. Here's a chance to take a look at some common ones and how to solve them:

- When "**Error 25100. An internal error occurred**" appears:
    - **Root cause**: Installing App-V management server on a Windows Server 2008 or Windows Server 2008 R2 server that has either the .NET 4.0 client profile or full installation of the .NET 4.0 framework.
    - **Resolution**: Remove the .NET 4.0 framework prior to server installation and reinstall the .NET 4.0 framework after App-V management server installation. More information is available at http://support.microsoft.com/kb/2212140.

- When "**Error 25109: The installation program could not create the configuration data store**" appears, there are several possible causes:
    - **Root cause 1**: The APPVIRT database (or the name you've selected) was created earlier than the installation.
    - **Resolution**: Do not create the database prior to installation. If it is created, delete it and let the installation wizard create and configure this database.
    - **Root cause 2**: SQL server protocol options **TCP/IP** and **Named Pipes** are not enabled.
    - **Resolution**: Open **Sql Server Configuration Manager | SQL Server Network Configuration**, select the protocols for the database instance, and enable them.

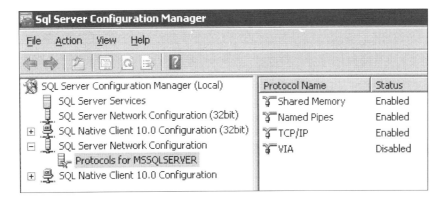

- ° SQL Server also needs particular ports to be open for communication; the default used by the engine is 1433.

- ° If you are using SQL Server Express editions, this option can be found in the **Surface Area Configuration | Services and Connections** under **Remote Connections**.

Using SQL Server Express also requires enabling options **CLR Integration** and **OLE Automation**. More information is available at `http://blog.augustoalvarez.com.ar/2009/07/12/ implementing-app-v-part-ii-choosing-and-preparing- the-environment/`.

Remember that SQL Server Express editions can be used with the App-V management server but are not supported in a production environment.

- ° **Root cause 3**: In the installation wizard of the App-V management server, we've selected, as App-V administrator, the local administrator of the machine.

- ° **Resolution**: Select a domain group that has an administrator profile in the domain (for example, Domain Admins).

- ° **Root cause 4**: The SQL Server is configured to use a Collation that is case-sensitive, such as `SQL_Latin1_General_Cp1_CS_AS_KI_WI` (dictionary order, case-sensitive).

- ° **Resolution**: Change the SQL Collation configuration.

- When "**Error 25120 unable to create the required IIS virtual directory**" appears, these are the possible causes:

  - ° **Root cause 1**: IIS or the section **Management Tools** (complete) is not installed.

  - ° **Resolution**: Install IIS with all the prerequisites named earlier.

  - ° **Root cause 2**: The default website in IIS does not exist.

  - ° **Resolution**: Repair IIS installation to recreate the default website.

- When "**Error 25122. The installation program was unable to register the ASP.NET web service extension**" appears, there are two possible causes:
  - **Root cause 1**: Installing App-V management server on a Windows Server 2008 or Windows Server 2008 R2 server that has either the .NET 4.0 client profile or full installation of the .NET 4.0 framework.
  - **Resolution**: Remove the .NET 4.0 framework prior to installation and reinstall the .NET 4.0 framework after installation. More information here: http://support.microsoft.com/kb/2212140.
  - **Root cause 2**: The default website in IIS was renamed.
  - **Resolution**: Rename the default website to its original name in the IIS console.

The last one covers up most of the errors we could find in the installation process. But, there are other scenarios where we can find ourselves unable to use the App-V management server after the installation seemed to be completed successfully.

## Solving App-V management server implementation problems

Once we've completed the installation, there are a few steps we should consider as "post-installation" tasks, in order to guarantee that the App-V management server has been installed successfully.

As post-installation tasks:

- The content folder must be shared. This is not particularly needed in the installation process, but it will be required later.
- If we are using RTSPS, we need the port 322 open in Windows Firewall.
- If we are using RTSP, the executables sghwdsptr.exe and sghwsvr.exe must be allowed connections in Windows Firewall.

In RTSPS scenarios, adding the program exceptions also works as a valid configuration.

Remember that using RTSP doesn't only require port 554 in the management server, since there are several ports used in this connection. The only supported approach is adding the program exceptions.

# Common validations post installation

There are some tasks we can execute to validate that our App-V management server installation and post-installation tasks have been completed successfully.

For verifying the database connectivity:

1.  Locate the file SftMgmt.udl within the App-V management server installation folder %ProgramFiles%\Microsoft System Center App Virt Management Server\App Virt Management Service.

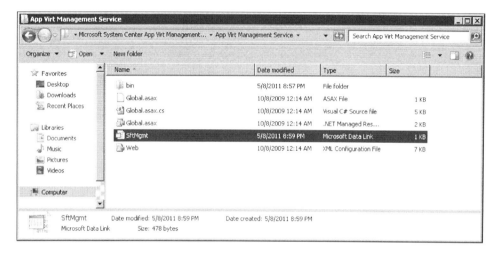

2.  Access the file properties and select the **Connection** tab.
3.  Verify the server name used where the database should be installed, and click on **Test Connection** to validate the connection.

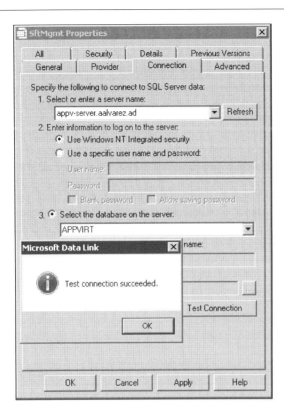

> The App-V team published, on their blog, some detailed information for when we perform low-level troubleshooting for App-V and SQL; take a look, here: *Tips and tricks for troubleshooting App-V and SQL* (http://blogs.technet.com/b/appv/archive/2011/03/21/tips-and-tricks-for-troubleshooting-app-v-and-sql.aspx).

When we need to verify that this server is ready to distribute applications, there are tasks we can execute in order to get this guarantee, but one of the most effective ways is using the **App-V Ping** tool from **Immidio**, available at http://immidio.com/resourcekit/.

With App-V Ping, we can easily verify the communication and configuration from the App-V client to the App-V server, a far more powerful tool than just using **telnet** to port 554 (or the streaming port selected).

 For more information about tools available for App-V, take a look at *Appendix, Reviewing App-V Microsoft and 3rd Party Tools*

1. Install the **Immidio Resource Kit**.

2. In a command prompt, open the installation path for the Immidio Resource Kit. In my case, it is `C:\Program Files\Immidio\Resource Kit`.

3. Type `App-V-Ping.exe –s` *<name of the server>* `-v` and verify the results.

```
Administrator: C:\Windows\system32\cmd.exe

C:\Program Files\Immidio\Resource Kit>App-V-Ping.exe -s appv-server.aalvarez.ad
-v

App-V Ping v1.0.1.0, part of the Immidio Resource Kit.
Copyright (C) 2008 Immidio, http://www.immidio.com

*** Initializing WinSock...                    Success.
*** Resolving server...                        Success.
*** Creating socket...                         Success.
*** Creating socket event...                   Success.
*** Starting connection...                     Success.
*** Waiting for connection to be accepted...   Success.
*** Sending data...                            Success.
*** Shutting down socket for sending...        Success.
*** Waiting for response...                    Success.

Server 'appv-server.aalvarez.ad' is accepting RTSP connections on port 554.

C:\Program Files\Immidio\Resource Kit>
```

Once the server is installed, there is one log where App-V saves all the information: `sft-server.log`. This can be found at the following path: `%ProgramFiles\ Microsoft System Center App Virt Management Server\App Virt Management Server\logs`.

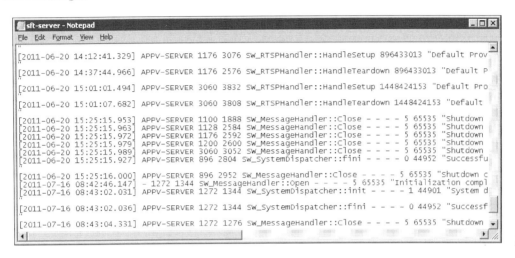

And, of course, prior to starting the App-V management server, we must verify that the **Application Virtualization Management Server** service has been started; we can then open up the App-V Management Console and connect to the server normally.

When we place all App-V management server components in one server, the common behavior of this service is that, whenever the operating system is rebooted, it cannot be started automatically even though the option is set correctly.

Another reason why we could have problems with starting the App-V management server service is if we try to use a certificate that has not been imported correctly, for SSL communications. For more information about this, please see the *Configuring SSL communications* section in *Chapter 3, Deploying Applications in Complex Environments*.

## Understanding sft-server log

Even though, at first glance, this log file can be considered a bit rough to understand or read, Microsoft provides a Knowledge Base article to understand the delimited values; go to `http://support.microsoft.com/kb/930871`.

| Value | Description |
|---|---|
| DateTime | The date and time in the [YYYY-MM-DD HH:MM:SS:MS] format |
| ServerName | The name of the SoftGrid Virtual Application Server that is reporting the message |
| ProcessID | The process ID (PUID/PID) of the process that logged the message |
| ThreadID | The thread ID (UID) of the thread that logged the message |
| Module | The module that reported the message |
| SessionID | The session ID of the request |
| ProviderName | The Provider Policy name to which the request was submitted |
| UserName | The user name of the user that was authenticated |
| ApplicationURL | The application URL of the application that is being requested |
| ErrorLevel | The error level of the message, as follows: |
| | 0: Transactions |
| | 1: Fatal Errors |
| | 2: Errors |
| | 3: Warnings |
| | 4: Informational |
| | 5: Debug (Verbose) |
| | 6: Trace |
| ErrorNumber | Error code |
| ErrorMessage | The error message |

The ErrorLevel setting can be modified by accessing the following registry key:

- x86: HKEY_LOCAL_MACHINE\SOFTWARE\Microsoft\Softgrid\4.5\Server\ SOFTGRID_LOG_LEVEL

- x64: HKEY_LOCAL_MACHINE\SOFTWARE\Wow6432Node\Microsoft\ Softgrid\4.5\Server\SOFTGRID_LOG_LEVEL

But, that's not all; since this log (as for all App-V logs) is using delimited data, we can utilize it in Microsoft Excel to retrieve some interesting statistics and information about our virtual applications usage.

A complete guide can be found in Justin Zarb's blog, on the Microsoft TechNet site: *Getting to Grip with the App-V Server Log File (sft-server.log)* (`http://blogs.technet.com/b/virtualworld/archive/2009/04/10/getting-to-grip-with-the-app-v-server-log-file-sft-server-log.aspx`).

This is an example of an `sft-server` log file rearranged in Excel:

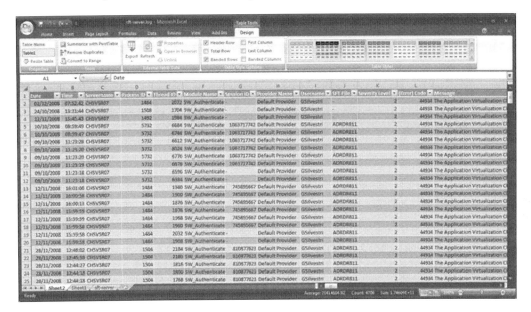

In addition to this arranged table, we can use Excel's pivot chart option to understand a little bit further what we are seeing here.

## Reviewing common implementation problems

As mentioned in the installation errors, when we discussed about most of them being present because of the prerequisites not being fulfilled, the implementation problems appear mostly because the post-installation tasks have not been completed successfully.

In this case, we are going to focus just on the App-V management server implementation, without considering, for now, the process of delivering applications with the server. Using the MMC requires that the App-V web service be healthy, in order to avoid any problems.

The errors we can find here are mostly related to the web service, and the error codes we are going to see are represented by the "0000C8xx" code. Let's take a look at some of them:

- When **Error code: 0000C801** appears:

  ○ **Root cause**: The **Windows Authentication** service is not available in IIS.

  ○ **Resolution**: Install the **Windows Authentication** feature in IIS, using Server Manager.

- When **Error code: 0000C802** appears, there can be more than one root cause associated:

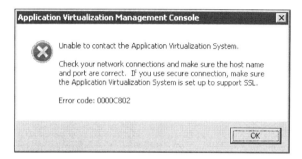

  ○ **Root cause 1**: The port specified for the connection is invalid.

  ○ **Resolution**: Verify the port used by the default website used in IIS console, and modify it when you try to connect in the App-V Management Console.

  ○ **Root cause 2**: The World Wide Web Publishing service is not running.

  ○ **Resolution**: Start the World Wide Web Publishing service.

  ○ **Root cause 3**: The default website is not running.

  ○ **Resolution**: Start the default website in the IIS console.

  ○ **Root cause 4**: The IE browser on the machine is configured to use a proxy server.

  ○ **Resolution**: Remove the proxy server configuration, or set an exception in IE to bypass the proxy for the App-V server connection.

 More information about **Error code: 0000C802** is available in this Microsoft Knowledge Base article: http://support. microsoft.com/kb/930469/en-us.

- When **Error code: 0000C806** appears:
  - **Root cause**: The App-V management server is configured to use SSL for the web service connection, and the certificate is not issued by a trusted root certification authority.
  - **Resolution**: Verify the certificate imported in the operating system. More information can be found in this Microsoft Knowledge Base article: `http://support.microsoft.com/?kbid=930472`.

- When **Error code: 0000C81B** appears:
  - **Root cause**: The ASP.NET feature in IIS is not installed.
  - **Resolution**: Install the ASP.NET feature in IIS, using the Server Manager Console.

- When **Error code: 0000C824** appears:

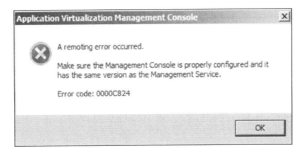

  - **Root cause**: This error is telling us that either our App-V management server service installation did not complete successfully (most likely) or there's something that misconfigured it.
  - We can find in the installation log file (`softgrid-server-setup.txt`) errors regarding `server.conf` and `sftMgmt.udl` indicating "files not found".
  - **Resolution**: Reinstall the App-V management server service.
  - More information about **Error code: 0000C824** can be found on the App-V team blog, which mentions a few more steps to troubleshoot the error, instead of reinstalling the service: *App-V and Console protocol mismatches* (`http://blogs.technet.com/b/mkleef/archive/2011/04/20/app-v-and-console-protocol-mismatches.aspx`).

The **0000C824** error is commonly known to appear also in App-V management server 4.5 scenarios when Service Pack 2 is applied. We can find a detailed step-by-step procedure to solve this particular problem on the App-V team blog, here: *Help! After Upgrading the App-V Management Server to version 4.5 Service Pack 2, I can no longer access the server through the Management Console* (`http://blogs.technet.com/b/appv/archive/2011/06/13/help-after-upgrading-the-app-v-management-server-to-version-4-5-service-pack-2-i-can-now-longer-access-the-server-through-the-management-console.aspx`).

Another common error we can find is the **0000C800**, which actually can be presented with several of the causes we've reviewed recently. For more information about this error code, please visit this Microsoft Knowledge Base article: `http://support.microsoft.com/kb/930565/`.

We can receive a **0000C800** error, or an error indicating that we are unable to start the App-V management server, when there are database connectivity options. If the SQL Server service is stopped and we try to start the App-V service, we should see an error such as this:

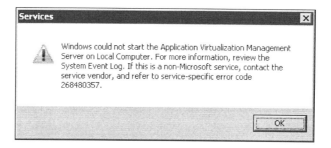

- **Resolution**: In this case, we must always start the SQL Server service prior to starting the App-V management server service.

- If we are using the **Reset Administrators** option in the App-V management server console, we will receive the **0000C833** error.

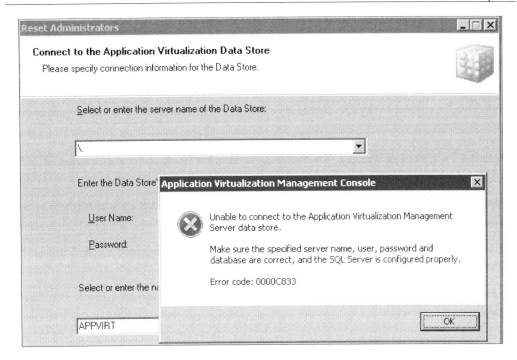

- **Root cause**: The process for resetting administrators using the UI does not work.

- **Resolution**: We must change the database location using the `SftMgmt.udl` file present in the App-V management server installation path, using the following procedure:

    ○ Edit `SftMgmt.udl`: Data source, initial catalog.
    ○ Use `regedit` to locate `HKEY_LOCAL_MACHINE\SOFTWARE\Microsoft\Softgrid\4.5\Server\`.
    ○ Modify the parameters `SQLDatabaseName`, `SQLServerName`, and `SQLServerPort`.
    ○ Edit the database information in **Default Server Group | Logging | Edit SQL Database**.
    ○ Restart the management server service.

Microsoft includes the process we can use to move the SQL database to another SQL Server. Check the following link:

*How to Migrate the App-V SQL Database to a Different SQL Server* (`http://technet.microsoft.com/en-us/library/gg252515.aspx`).

When we are experiencing performance problems in the App-V management server, there are several causes for it. If we are having problems related to some of the App-V components, we should do the following:

1.  Open **Task Manager**.

2.  Look for processes named **sghwsvr.exe**.

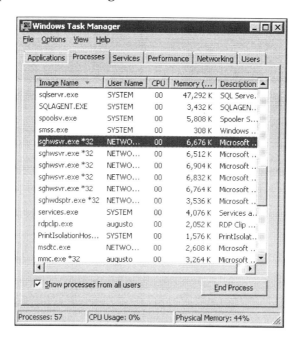

3.  Compare memory capacity with the values shown here.

4.  We can change the amount of memory used for the server file cache by accessing **App-V Server Management Console | Server Groups | Properties**, for the selected server.

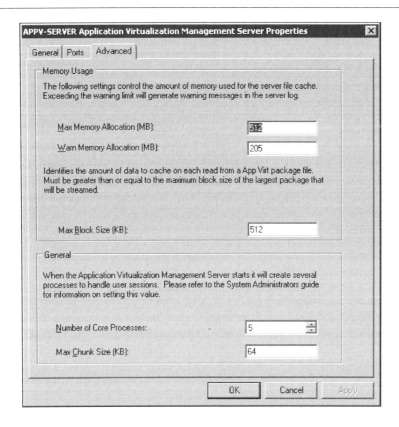

As you can see, we can also set the **Warn Memory Allocation** threshold. This way, if we are monitoring the App-V management server log, we will receive a notification prior to major performance problems.

An interesting approach using these mentioned settings, if we are having **crash dumps**, also known as **BSOD (Blue Screen Of Death)**, is to reduce the value in **Number of Core Processes** to **1**. This will let us analyze only one core process in order to find the problem.

Even though crash dumps appear rarely in an App-V management server, you never know what kind of hardware-drivers-software combined scenario you might find.

# Troubleshooting the App-V client implementation

In this section, we are only going to cover the installation of the App-V client; there are some misconfigurations that can be present once it's installed, but those will be covered in the *Troubleshooting applications delivery* section.

## Solving App-V client installation problems

Regarding App-V client installation, there are no varieties of errors we can find. This is because, in the installation wizard, there is no connection with the App-V management or streaming server; that only occurs when the publishing refresh is triggered.

### Reviewing installation errors "250xx"

These types of errors are pretty much all the varieties we can expect to find, for when there's something wrong with the installation process:

- When **Error 25010. A prerequisite for installation is missing. Installation cannot continue** appears, there's nothing much to explain:
    - **Root cause**: One of the prerequisites is missing. It usually appears when we try to launch the installation using the setup.msi file instead of setup.exe.
    - **Resolution**: Run the installation using the setup.exe file instead of setup.msi. The former always installs all the prerequisites prior to launching the App-V client installation.

- If we are installing App-V Remote Desktop Services Client in our session host, we can also get **Error 25001. Microsoft Application Virtualization Client for Remote Desktop Services requires that Remote Desktop Services is installed on the system**:
    - **Root cause**: Remote Desktop Session Host role is not installed.
    - **Resolution**: Install the Remote Desktop Session Host role using Server Manager.

Handling App-V Client errors rarely involves troubleshooting the installation; this process is not complex. Most of the errors we will be handling in App-V are related to virtual application operations such as publication and delivery.

# Troubleshooting applications delivery

In this section, we are going to review the common errors that appear when handling App-V client connections to the streaming management server, or in the standalone scenario.

Again, to understand where we should start troubleshooting, we must understand the components intervening in the App-V client architecture:

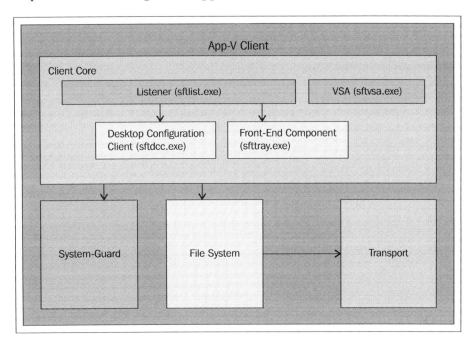

A quick look at the components at work here:

- `Sftlist.exe`: Represents the App-V client service
- `Sftdcc.exe`: In charge of publications refreshes
- `Sfttray.exe`: Handles the notification pop-ups; is placed in the system tray
- `Sftvsa.exe`: In charge of handling the virtual services included by virtual applications
- **System guard**: The isolated environment for the virtual application
- **Transport**: Communicating channel to stream down the application into the client

# Reviewing App-V client log files

Besides the Event Viewer possibilities to monitor and troubleshoot problems with the App-V client components, the component includes a set of logs to be used:

- App-V client log file `sftlog.txt`: This file stores the activity of the App-V clien:

    ◦ Location: `%programData%\Microsoft\Application Virtualization Client\sftlog.txt`

- App-V Client Transport `sftnta.txt` and `sftlist.txt`: This set of logs is not created by default, must be enabled manually, and is in charge of logging information about transport activity. The log that will be used depends on the protocol used (RTSP/S or HTTP/S):

    ◦ `SFTNTA` location: `%programData%\Microsoft\Application Virtualization Client\sftnta.txt`

    ◦ `SFTLIST` location: `%programData%\Microsoft\Application Virtualization Client\sftlist.txt`

## Enabling sftnta.txt and sftlist.txt

These transport logs are not created by default and must be configured manually, prior to generation, by modifying registry values.

The `sftnta.txt` log is used for RTSP/S connections; to enable it, follow these steps:

1. Enter `regedit.exe` in the client machine.
2. Look for the registry path `HKEY_LOCAL_MACHINE\SOFTWARE\SoftGrid\4.5\Client\Configuration`.
3. Create a DWORD value `TRAN`.
4. The values accepted are:

    ◦ **verbose level: FFFFFFFF**
    ◦ **Info: 00030002**
    ◦ **Error: 00020002**
    ◦ **off: 0**

The `sftlist.txt` log is used for HTTP/S connections; to enable it, follow these steps:

1. Enter `regedit.exe` in the client machine.
2. Look for the registry path `HKEY_LOCAL_MACHINE\SOFTWARE\SoftGrid\4.5\Client\Configuration`.

3. Create a DWORD value `NtaLogMask`.

4. The values accepted are from `0` to `6`:

    Log level: 0-6: NEVER-1; ALWAYS-2; FATAL-3; ERROR-4; WARN-5; INFO: VERBOSE

# Understanding error codes in App-V client

Prior to getting specific with common error codes in the applications delivery process, we must be aware of the error codes we can receive. Understanding them could facilitate our work as App-V admins in order to get to a solution effectively and efficiently.

In the error numbers we receive, we always get 22 characters; those are divided into three groups. Even though we see three large numbers of groups, analyzing it we have the following description:

- Characters 1 - 6: Version number
- Characters 7 - 9: File ID where the error occurred
- Characters 10 - 12: Line where the error occurred
- Characters 13 - 14: Error category code
- Characters 15 - 22: Problem code, which can be located in the `sfterr.xml` file available with all App-V clients, and located in `%programFiles%\Microsoft Application Virtualization Client\language\`

Let's take a look at a common example we can find when we are having problems launching an application:

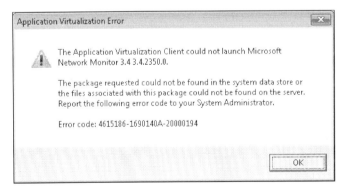

The error code number is **4615186-1690140A-20000194**. Analysing it, we will get the following:

- **4615186**: In this version we have:
  - ° **461**: App-V 4.6 SP1
  - ° **5186**: Build number

- **169014**: File ID and line where the error occurred
- **0A**: Error category code: Net transport agent
- **20000194**: Problem code we can find in `sfterr.xml`

To execute a root cause analysis, we don't actually need the 22 characters, we just need the last 10, that is, the error category plus the problem code.

The following table shows information regarding the error category:

| Number | Identifier | Description |
|--------|-----------|-------------|
| 00 | UNK | Unknown |
| 01 | FEC | Frontend component |
| 02 | SVR | Server |
| 03 | LST | Listener |
| 04 | COR | Client core |
| 05 | XML | XML library |
| 06 | USR | User library |
| 07 | FSL | Core FS interface |
| 08 | FSI | FS Interface |
| 09 | FSD | FS driver |
| 0A | NTA | Net Transport Agent |
| 0B | CDC | Codec |
| 0C | SGL | SystemGuard Library |
| 0D | SGD | SystemGuard Driver |
| 0E | INT | Client interface |
| 0F | VSM | Visual Service Manager |
| 10 | SEQ | Sequencer |
| 11 | SYN | Synchronization manager |
| 12 | DCC | Desktop Config Controller |
| 13 | RPC | Remote Procedure Call |

| Number | Identifier | Description |
|---|---|---|
| 14 | PFM | Platform library |
| 15 | DDE | DDE launcher |
| 16 | MDE | Minidump Exception |
| 17 | MAPI | MAPI |
| 18 | SCR | Script |
| 19-1F | | Reserved |

As we said, the problem code can be found in `sfterr.xml`, so let's look for it in this example.

Quickly using the **Find** option for **20000194**, we get as information, the **String ID='0x00000129'**, which is saying that we should look for **00000129** to find a detailed explanation.

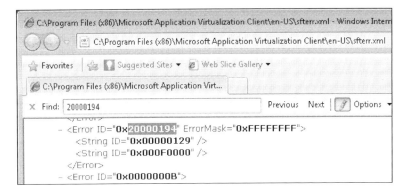

Looking for **00000129**, we get: **The package requested could not be found in the system data store or the files associated with this package could not be found on the server**:

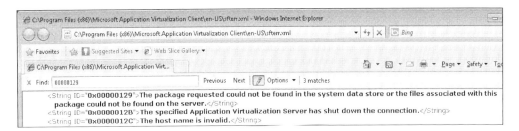

In this case, the root cause is that the SFT file is not located in the referenced place, by the OSD.

But, of course, expecting to solve our problems using the 10 digits of the error code is not sufficient; that's why we are going to analyze a few more of these problems with some specific examples.

# Reviewing common application delivery problems

If we look inside the `sfterr.xml` file, we are going to see an enormous list of error codes, which in most cases are not sufficient to solve the actual problem.

Fortunately, Microsoft also provides a large number of Knowledge Base articles, in order to help us troubleshoot those scenarios. Here, we are going to use some examples:

- When **Error code: xxxxxx-xxxxxx0A-20000194** appears, as used in the example, there are a few possible causes:

    ◦ **Root cause 1**: Trying to use a virtual application that is not added in the App-V Management Console (it is possible that we are trying to access an application that we've removed from the App-V Management Console and that removing the application did not affect the existence of the shortcut).

    ◦ **Resolution**: Verify the existence of the application in the App-V Management Console.

    ◦ In case of an orphaned shortcut, we could also receive the error: **Error code: xxxxxx-xxxxxx04-00000A09**.

    ◦ **Root cause 2**: The SFT file does not exist in the path mentioned by the OSD file or in the **Application Source Root** setting.

    ◦ **Resolution**: Verify the path mentioned in the OSD file in HREF and the **Application Source Root** path applied to retrieve the SFT. For more information about editing OSD files and the **Application Source Root** setting, take a look at *Chapter 2, Sequencing in Complex Environments*, and *Chapter 3, Deploying Applications in Complex Environments*.

    ◦ **Root cause 3**: The Provider Policy does not exist.

- ○ **Resolution**: Verify, in the OSD file, the Provider Policy applied; we can review it in the HREF section, for example, `HREF="RTSPS://%SFT_SOFTGRIDSERVER%:554/MyApp/MyApp.sft?Customer=MyProviderPolicy"`.

- ○ For more information about Providers Policies, see *Chapter 3, Deploying Applications in Complex Environments*.

Take note that, in the App-V management server log file (`sft-server.log`), we can find a specification of this error and the particular root cause. For example: "Unable to locate <provider_policy>" or "Unable to open <path>\<file name>.sft".

- Related to this last error, is **Error code: xxxxxx-xxxxxx64-00000002**, which is related to not finding the OSD file in the right path. For more information, take a look at this Microsoft Knowledge Base article: `http://support.microsoft.com/kb/931124`.

- When **Error code: xxxxxx-xxxxxx0C-0000003C** appears:

  - ○ **Root cause 1**: The `Settings.cp` file (user's specific data for App-V applications) is corrupted.

  - ○ **Resolution**: We need to regenerate this file in order to run the application again. More information can be found in this Microsoft Knowledge Base article: `http://support.microsoft.com/kb/930829`.

  - ○ **Root cause 2**: Antivirus scanner running in the *Q* drive.

  - ○ **Resolution**: Disable antivirus or add the *Q* drive as an exception in your antivirus.

The error **0C-0000003C** was also known to appear in older versions of App-V, when the server had Page Pool memory starvation or fragmentation. More information is available at `http://support.microsoft.com/kb/312362`.

- One of the most common errors we can receive in the App-V client is **Error code: xxxxxx-xxxxxx0A-10000004**:

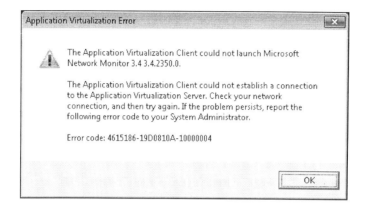

- ○ **Root cause**: The App-V management server service is stopped or the App-V management server is not available.

- ○ **Resolution**: Verify the connection to the App-V management server using the Immidio tool shown previously, and verify whether the service is started.

- ○ There could also be a connectivity problem based on a firewall misconfiguration; using the Immidio tool will show us whether we have any problem in this area.

- Based on the same root cause as this last error, the **Error code: xxxxxx-xxxxxx2A-0000274D** could also appear; in this case, we should also check the App-V management server service and restart it, if need be, or verify the firewall exceptions (mentioned earlier in this chapter).

- We find **Error code: xxxxxx-xxxxxx0A-10000002** messages, when we try to run an application that has been misconfigured, for example:

- ○ **Root cause**: The OSD reference is using the `%SFT_SOFTGRIDSERVER%` variable, which is not present in the App-V client.

- ○ **Resolution**: Verify the `%SFT_SOFTGRIDSERVER%` variable in the client machine, or use an accessible FQDN or IP in the OSD file for that application.

- ○ Use the **Application Source Root** configuration (changing the registry value or using the App-V ADM Template) to override the value presented by the OSD file.

- When **Error code xxxxx-xxxxx 0A-10000005** appears, there are a number of reasons causing this issue:

  ○ **Root cause**: If we take a look at the Microsoft Knowledge Base article available at `http://support.microsoft.com/kb/930697`, we will see that there are a number of reasons associated: the HREF path in the `.osd` file contains a space, the `?Customer=` element in the OSD file does not contain the question mark (?) or the equal-to sign (=) characters, or the App-V client times out.

  But there are also other known factors that could be causing this issue: network traffic being filtered (for example, in a VPN connection), and the possibility of the user belonging to a large number of groups.

  ○ **Resolution**: Verify the OSD file checking for errors mentioned in the Knowledge Base.

  In case of traffic being filtered, we need to disable RTSP inspection in the communication.

For the large number of groups involved, we can also modify the `MAX_RTSP_HEADER_BYTES` registry in the App-V management server. For more information, check the article **Error: 0A-10000005**, at `http://blogs.technet.com/b/virtualworld/archive/2010/02/07/error-0a-10000005.aspx`.

For inspection problems in RTSP, another error appearing could be **xxxxx-xxxxx 0A-10000009**. We must disable RTSP inspection in order to solve this.

Also, regarding connectivity and security problems between client and server, one of the errors appearing is **xxxxx-xxxxx 2A-80090322**; this is related to a mismatch in certificate configuration using the RTSPS protocol. For more information about problems using certificates and RTSPS, review the following article in Microsoft Technet:

*Troubleshooting Common RTSPS Issues with App-V* (`http://blogs.technet.com/b/appv/archive/2010/03/09/troubleshooting-common-rtsps-issues-with-app-v.aspx`).

Regarding performance problems, we can also find **Error code: xxxxx-xxxxxx0A-00000193**, when for example, the server has limited connectivity or the streaming process is interrupted. Good advice regarding this error is to use the preload option for all virtual applications.

If we use the standalone mode and place the MSI and/or the SFT file in a network share, we could sometimes have permission problems. With those problems, we receive errors such as **Error code: xxxxxx-xxxxxx0A-000001D1** or **Error code: xxxxxx-xxxxxx2A-00000005**; mitigation in these cases would be to grant the network share the read permission to the client computer object (`Domain\ClientComputerName$`).

Misconfigurations in the standalone mode could generate several error codes, for example:

- **Error code: xxxxxx-xxxxxx00-00000000 Unspecified Error Message**

- **Error code: xxxxxx-xxxxxx0A-1000000D The hostname is invalid**

- **Error code: xxxxxx-xxxxxx0A-1000000B The Application Virtualization Service could not be contacted**

To mitigate all of these, please review *Chapter 3, Deploying Applications in Complex Environments*, for the configurations necessary when using the standalone mode.

In this section, we've covered just a few errors, but there are several more that are already registered by Microsoft. All of those are available at the Microsoft Support Center: `http://support.microsoft.com/`.

Tim Mangan has also created a very intuitive and interesting web application for detecting and identifying errors in application publishing and launching. You can access it at `http://www.tmurgent.com/AppVirt/FTL/Ftl.aspx`.

# About application client log parser

The information we can retrieve from the App-V client log is huge, but to actually use it, we need to understand and read the client log in an effective way. **Application Client Log Parser** is the definitive tool to do that.

This free tool (available at Microsoft Download Center, `http://www.microsoft.com/download/en/default.aspx`) provides us with a simpler way to retrieve the information generated by the log file. The main task is to parse this information and generate the following fields for each event: `system`, `operating system`, `build`, `date`, `time`, `module`, `log level`, `hApp`, `app`, `user`, `thread`, and `message`.

Since the output file is delimited, we can use Microsoft Excel to generate a complete file where we can understand, in a few clicks, for example, how to retrieve all the error codes generated in the client, the average launch time of an application (which we can compare to the non-virtualized version of that application), and so on.

The Virtual blog team, at Microsoft, developed two complete guides to use this tool and has some great examples of using Microsoft Excel to generate some neat reports:

- *Getting to Grips with the App-V Client Log Parser Utility (Error Codes)* `http://blogs.technet.com/b/virtualworld/archive/2009/04/20/getting-to-grips-with-the-app-v-client-log-parser-utility-error-codes.aspx`

- *Getting to Grips with the App-V Client Log Parser Utility (Launch Times)* `http://blogs.technet.com/b/virtualworld/archive/2009/04/20/getting-to-grips-with-the-app-v-client-log-parser-utility-launch-times.aspx`

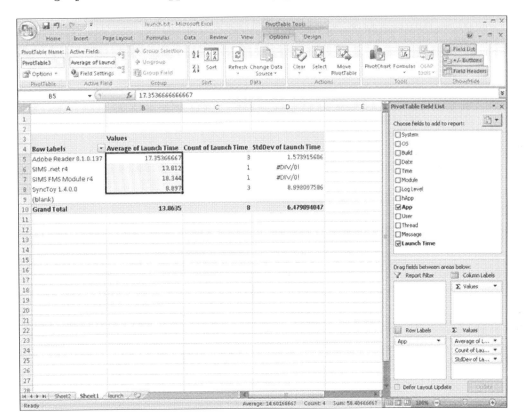

This example, appearing on the App-V TechNet blog (`http://blogs.technet.com/b/appv/`), has a pivot table with the average launch time of some applications plus the Standard Deviation function that applies to each of them.

This last function tells us that if we retrieve a low value, the launch times are pretty much the same; if we have a high value, then there's at least one value in the sample which is incredibly high that is affecting our average time (`#DIV/0!` just implies that there are not many launches of that application to retrieve a value).

# Reviewing common problems with virtual application usage

So far, we've covered the scenarios where we are having problems: while installing the App-V platform, when we try to launch an application, and when we cannot use an App-V management server already installed. But, what we haven't covered so far is a scenario in which we launch an application but it is not functioning properly.

Those cases are not particularly simple to troubleshoot, since most of the scenarios are related to problems in the sequencing phase or incompatibilities of the application in the virtual environment. We've covered these matters in *Chapter 2, Sequencing in Complex Environments* (including some unsupported cases with App-V).

Also, Microsoft already has some reported issues with some applications working as virtual, for example:

- *Sequencing AutoCAD 2008 on Windows 7 x86 computer fails when installing to Q:\*: http://support.microsoft.com/kb/2496653
- *Known issues and limitations when using virtualized Office 2010 applications on App-V 4.6 and App-V 4.5 SP2 clients*: http://support.microsoft.com/kb/2481474

What we are going to cover in this section are those particular scenarios that could involve some tweaking in the App-V platform in order to make our applications work normally.

# Working with applications that require elevation

Microsoft User Access Control (UAC) changed significantly the use of the Operating System tasks, including for applications. There are several applications that require elevated privileges in order to work as virtual; otherwise we receive a message such as this:

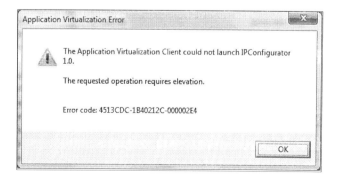

This problem is simply avoided by right-clicking the shortcut and selecting **Run as Administrator**, but of course, it is not the best approach to ask end users to perform this task.

We can solve this problem directly by modifying the OSD file of the application, adding an environment variable. To do so, we must work within the `<ENVLIST>` section of the OSD, adding the `__COMPAT_LAYER` variable as `RunAsInvoker`:

```
<ENVLIST>
  <ENVIRONMENT VARIABLE="__COMPAT_LAYER">RunAsInvoker</ENVIRONMENT>
</ENVLIST>
<DEPENDENCIES />
```

For more information about *RunAsInvoker*, check this article from MSDN blogs: *How to Run Applications Manifested as Highest Available With a Logon Script Without Elevation for Members of the Administrators Group* (`http://blogs.msdn.com/b/cjacks/archive/2009/09/13/how-to-run-applications-manifested-as-highestavailable-with-a-logon-script-without-elevation-for-members-of-the-administrators-group.aspx`).

# Using workarounds to analyze application problems

Every application has a singular behavior regarding interaction between the operating system and other components; this means that the troubleshooting needed for a particular error (which did not appear in the sequencing process) could be a real challenge.

But, there are some ways, which we can introduce in order to understand a little bit more about how the application works and, of course, how it is being captured by App-V.

## Using CMD inside the virtual environment

A good example of that is to get inside this virtual environment to analyze the data available within and retrieve some valuable information. To accomplish that, we can use the `cmd` executable inside the virtual environment.

There are three basic ways to do it:

- Including `cmd` while we are sequencing the application
- Modifying the OSD file of the application
- Using `SFTTRAY`, this last one being the simplest way

To include the `cmd` app within the package, we only need to add it as an application in the sequencing wizard.

Using cmd, the steps involved would be:

1.  Access the OSD file of the application we would like to troubleshoot.

2.  Insert the following <HREF> script:

    ```
    <DEPENDENCY>
      <SCRIPT TIMING="PRE" EVENT="LAUNCH" WAIT="TRUE" PROTECT="TRUE">
        <HREF>C:\Windows\System32\cmd.exe</HREF>
      </SCRIPT>
    </DEPENDENCY>
    ```

3.  Save and close the OSD file.

Since we are using the pre-launch timing when we run this application, the application executable will start as soon as we close down cmd.

Using SFTTRAY it is the simplest way to do it since we don't need to modify the OSD file. Using this command, we force the loading of the application in the virtual environment, but instead of using the application's executable, cmd is used:

1.  Launch cmd in the App-V client.

2.  Run the following command:

    ```
    SFTTRAY /EXE cmd.exe /LAUNCH <Application Name>
    ```

Once we press *Enter*, a new command prompt window will open, but in this case, the location will be in the mounted drive.

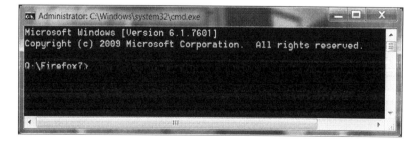

In this case, when we close the `cmd` window, the application will not start. This is an interesting approach, since we can run any executable file and not just the command line.

 For more information about including scripts in OSD and command lines in App-V, refer to *Chapter 4, Handling Scripting and App-V Command Lines.*

# Changing the virtual environment for troubleshooting

There are some cases in which we just can't find the reason why our application is not working properly; for that, we need to start trying some workaround methods in order to solve our problem.

There are four variables we can change in the virtual environment, to experiment and find out the real problem: application isolation, virtual services, virtual registry, and virtual file system.

Enabling/disabling these options could help us to understand the real problem of our virtual application. For example, there are some particular cases that require the ability to interact with the operating system, outside the virtual environment.

To change application isolation (letting our virtual application interact with the operating system) we use the `LOCAL_INTERACTION_ALLOWED` option; we can modify it in the OSD file of the application:

```
<VIRTUALENV>
  <POLICIES>
    <LOCAL_INTERACTION_ALLOWED>TRUE</LOCAL_INTERACTION_ALLOWED>
  </POLICIES>
</VIRTUALENV>
```

In case we are having problems related to the virtual services installed by the application, we can easily edit this option, also within the OSD file:

```
<VIRTUALENV>
  <POLICIES>
    <VIRTUAL_SERVICES_DISABLED>TRUE</VIRTUAL_SERVICES_DISABLED>
  </POLICIES>
</VIRTUALENV>
```

The virtual registry option can also be disabled in order to find out whether there's an incompatibility in any of its components:

```
<VIRTUALENV>
  <POLICIES>
    <VIRTUAL_REGISTRY_DISABLED>TRUE</VIRTUAL_REGISTRY_DISABLED>
  </POLICIES>
</VIRTUALENV>
```

To disable the virtual file system, the procedure is the same:

```
<VIRTUALENV>
  <POLICIES>
    <VIRTUAL_FILE_SYSTEM_DISABLED>TRUE</VIRTUAL_FILE_SYSTEM_DISABLED>
  </POLICIES>
</VIRTUALENV>
```

> Remember also, that we can use the App-V sequencer **OSD** tab to modify these values, using a GUI.
>
> For more information about setting virtual environment policies, refer to *Chapter 2, Sequencing in Complex Environments*.

This is an example of adding the Policy using the **OSD** editor in App-V sequencer:

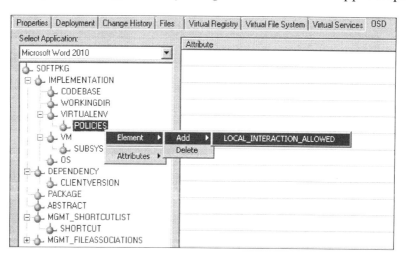

As we mentioned earlier, modifying these parameters is not recommended for most production environments. We should experiment with these changes in order to find the root cause of a particular problem, but we must try to avoid maintaining those in our environment.

Once we have the application sequenced, there are not many cases where we can find erratic functionalities in a virtualized application. But, of course, if we follow the best practices to sequence an application, we could find some problems in that phase.

# Analyzing performance problems in applications

It is not an easy task to troubleshoot performance issues in a virtual application, when a normal installation in the same environment does not present any issue.

The truth is that we won't find many of these situations using App-V; pretty much all the applications that work normally in the operating system, and that are not categorized as "incompatible" applications for App-V, will work with the same parameters as virtual.

Here are some considerations to help analyze this performance situation, bearing in mind also some examples about App-V client cache issues:

- **Applications taking a long time to load into cache**: There are some cases when the App-V client takes too much time to load into cache when an application is being launched for the first time.

  For those situations, there are some known issues using Windows Server 2003 and the TCP Chimney configuration. To solve this, modify the EnableTCPChimney registry with the value 1 (can be located in HKEY_LOCAL_MACHINE\SYSTEM\CurrentControlSet\Services\Tcpip\Parameters).

- **Applications working with poor performance using a "shared cache"**: The shared cache feature is commonly used in VDI scenarios where several clients can use the same App-V client cache, in order to optimize storage utilization. This configuration is only supported in the Full Infrastructure model.

  If we are using the shared cache feature, we must keep in mind that the location for this cache file must be accessible to the client, where we can guarantee an acceptable "read" performance, as in, say a hard drive.

  A good tip for handling a shared cache in a VDI environment is to modify the AutoLoad Target and AutoLoad Triggers options of the App-V client. Since the shared cache is a static file and does not require any streaming, we can disable those two options to improve the response time.

 For more information about shared cache and VDI environments, take a look at *Chapter 7, Integrating App-V with Virtual Desktop Infrastructure (VDI)*.

- **Applications working erratically or showing poor performance when we use an antivirus**: App-V, as with any platform, requires setting antivirus exclusions for several files and folders, otherwise we will experience some problems. The exclusions we need to set are the following:

  ○ For Windows Vista, Windows Server 2008 or later:

    ○ `%USERPROFILE%\AppData\Local\SoftGrid Client`

    ○ `%USERPROFILE%\AppData\Roaming\SoftGrid Client`

    ○ `%PROGRAMDATA%\Microsoft\Application Virtualization Client\SoftGrid Client`

  ○ For Windows XP or Windows Server 2003:

    ○ `%USERPROFILE%\Application Data\SoftGrid Client`

    ○ `%ALLUSERSPROFILE%\Application Data\Microsoft\ Application Virtualization Client\`

    ○ `%ALLUSERSPROFILE%\Documents\SoftGrid Client`

For more information about antivirus exclusions, please refer to the following Microsoft Knowledge Base article:

*Recommended antivirus or antimalware exclusions when troubleshooting Application Virtualization (App-V) client issues* (`http://support.microsoft.com/kb/2576031`).

# Troubleshooting application sequencing/launching

There are several scenarios for which we might need a little help when we are trying to sequence an application. We've learnt earlier, in *Chapter 2, Sequencing in Complex Environments*, about complex and even unsupported applications that require some tweaking.

In those cases, when we need some deep troubleshooting to make our application work, we can use Microsoft Sysinternal's Process Monitor.

We are going to focus, in this section, on how to use Process Monitor for troubleshooting virtual applications, but it is not necessary for us to do this with the sequencing process. There are some cases for which we will not need to resequence the application, after this troubleshooting.

# Using Process Monitor for troubleshooting

Process Monitor is probably the best collection tool for monitoring process activity in an operating system; it is not used only by IT admins; Microsoft Support engineers also work with this tool in order to find the root cause of a problem.

Process Monitor also works when we need to obtain data about a particular error in a virtual application, but this capturing tool will not magically find the problem for us; we need to parameterize it correctly.

Using Process Monitor for troubleshooting has the following phases:

* Understanding the application problem
* Monitoring the activity with Process Monitor
* Using **Filter** options to research for the problem

The new version included in Process Monitor already includes one important feature regarding virtual applications: using the `ExternalCapture` parameter includes the virtual environment in the monitoring process.

Earlier versions of Process Monitor could not complete any capture within the virtual environment, and we were forced to use Process Monitor inside the bubble. To achieve that, we had to follow the instructions covered earlier, in the *Using CMD inside the virtual environment* section.

For more information about that process, take a look at the Microsoft Knowledge Base article, *How to use the Process Monitor tool to generate a log file for an application in the App-V (SoftGrid) virtual environment*, at `http://support.microsoft.com/kb/939896`.

## Understanding the application problem

Even though this could seem like a simple step, we must first understand the scenario from which we are receiving the error. Depending on this, our Process Monitor capture and analysis can significantly change.

Let's review some guidelines to understand the application problem:

* If there's a problem in the installation phase:
    ° We must be aware that the Process Monitor capturing process must be executed in the App-V sequencer machine and in the sequencing process.

*Troubleshooting App-V*

- When the error appears, we must look for keywords related to the problem. If the error pop-up is not enough, we can always look for the application log and/or the Event Viewer.
- Common problems that could actually be solved with a workaround are: **Cannot access the folder**, **Registry path not found**, and so on

- If there's a problem while the application is running in the App-V client:
  - The Process Monitor must be executed in the App-V client machine
  - We are assuming, in this case, that the problem did not appear in the App-V sequencer, where the application was installed normally

- If the problem appears while the application is running and we receive an error such as **File not found**:
  - Once we retrieve this error in the App-V client, we must reproduce the error while we are performing a capture with Process Monitor

- If the problem seems related to a missing component or driver:
  - If we don't know and cannot determine the missing component or driver, we should capture a normal installation of the application, with Process Monitor

- If the problem is related to file or registry permissions:
  - Once we retrieve this error in the App-V client, we must reproduce the error while we are capturing with Process Monitor

# Monitoring the activity with Process Monitor

We could divide in two, the scenarios where we need to run Process Monitor with failing applications: applications that cannot be sequenced and virtual applications already sequenced but failing in the launching process.

Let's review each scenario before jumping into Process Monitor.

## Monitoring in the sequencing process

If we are having a problem in the sequencing phase of the application, the recommended process is the following:

- Ensure that the application, without running the capturing process in the App-V sequencer, can actually complete its installation.

  If the application does not complete a normal installation, then we can be certain that App-V is not the problem. We should review the application requirements and the compatibility considerations with our environment.

- If the application completes its installation normally, but the result is not the expected when we are sequencing it, we must use Process Monitor while the capturing process is executing it.

- We don't need to run Process Monitor with any parameter; running it normally while we are reproducing the error will give us all the information we need.

One of the applications that cannot be sequenced normally is Google Chrome. Aaron Parker developed a complete article about troubleshooting the sequencing process of Google Chrome using Process Monitor. Review Aaron's article at `http://blog.stealthpuppy.com/virtualisation/the-case-of-the-disappearing-application-during-sequencing/`.

In the Google Chrome example, by monitoring the sequencing process with Process Monitor, the result that appears, reveals that there is a registry file causing the deletion of a subfolder containing the application executable.

 If our application or the App-V sequencer is crashing during the sequencing process, remember that a possible cause could be insufficient resources in the operating system. The capturing process of the App-V sequencer is memory-intensive, so adding more RAM to the sequencer could solve this kind of problem.

## Monitoring in the launching process

If we have an application that installs and runs normally in a non-virtual environment but receive several problems once we virtualize it, we will need to monitor it using Process Monitor in an App-V client machine.

Let's review the process:

1. Prior to launching the application, execute Process Monitor from an elevated command prompt using the following example:

   ```
   Procmon /ExternalCapture /NoConnect /BackingFile <filename>.pml
   ```

   Here's a little explanation of these parameters:

   - `ExternalCapture`: Includes the virtual environment in the monitoring process
   - `NoConnect`: Does not start to monitor as soon as we run the program; waits for the manual instruction
   - `BackingFile`: Saves the captured data in the given PML file

2. Click on the **Capture** icon in Process Monitor.

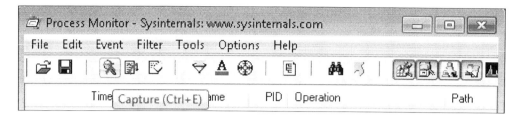

As soon as we click **Capture**, thousands of events will be captured within just a few seconds:

- ° Launch the application and reproduce the error
- ° Once the error is reproduced, stop the capture in Process Monitor

As a result, we'll have a considerable number of events captured by the tool. But don't panic, using this raw data directly can rarely be helpful when we are troubleshooting; the **Filter** options presented by Process Monitor will facilitate our job.

# Using Filter options to research the problem

Once we've reproduced the problem and captured the data, we will see that the number of activities registered by Process Monitor is enormous. Trying to find the root cause of the problem with that could be a real pain; we will need to use the **Filter** options.

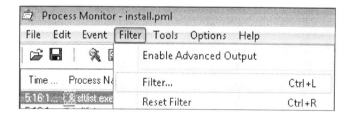

The parameters we need to filter down will depend directly on the error we receive. Let's take a look at some of the scenarios we've discussed:

- If the problem appears while the application is running and we receive a **File not found** error:
  - ° Start Process Monitor within the virtual environment and create a capture, prior to running the virtual application

- Run the application and, as soon as the error appears, stop the capture
- Filter the activity looking for results such as **NOT FOUND** in Process Monitor. Use the **Add** option once we've selected the filter.

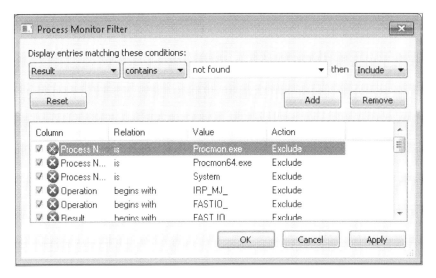

- Apply the filter, and we should see a reduced number of activities
- We can also narrow down some results by selecting only the category of activity we are looking for: registry, file, network, or process

- Once we have found the exact path that is causing the problem, we can verify whether the missing file/folder was possibly ignored in the sequencing process

In the example that we reviewed in *Chapter 2, Sequencing in Complex Environments,* the first problem we received was regarding **Failed to load NPL script**.

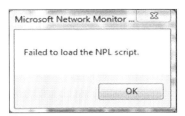

Filtering **NPL** in the Process Monitor capture, we can find some activity with the **NOT FOUND** result and also the exact path where the application is.

The missing NPL scripts are all located in C:\Users\username\AppData\Local, which is included in the App-V sequencer **Exclusion Items**. To solve it, we need to remove this defined exclusion (**%CSIDL_LOCAL_APPDATA%**) prior to capturing the application.

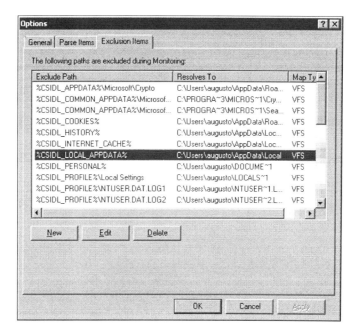

- If the problem seems related to a missing component or driver:

  The following is the error retrieved when we try to run the virtualized Network Monitor: **None of the network adapters are bound to the netmon driver**:

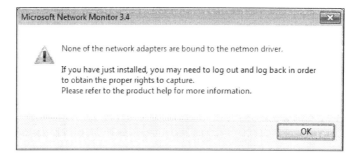

- ○ Run the normal installation process for the application (without using App-V sequencer), and capture it with Process Monitor

- ○ Once the installation is complete, stop the Process Monitor capture

- ○ Filter the activity looking for results such as:

    - ○ Path containing `C:\windows\system32\drivers` (this is the folder used by Windows to store drivers)

- ○ **Operation** containing **write**: Will look for write operations; and if we combine it with the Path filter, it will show only the files added into the drivers folder

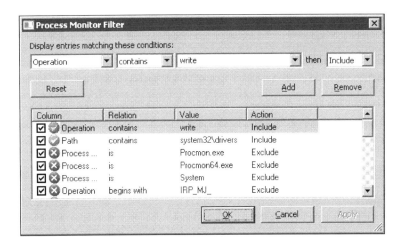

- ○ Apply the filter, and we should see a reduced number of activities:

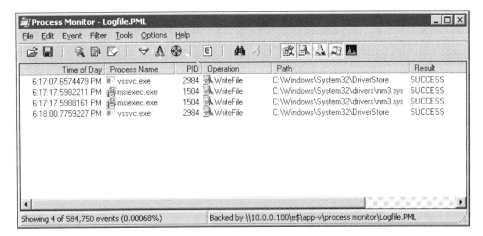

- ○ We can also narrow down some results by selecting only the category of activity we are looking at: registry, file, network, or process
- ○ If we are dealing with drivers, we can apply only to look for files (drivers are usually presented with the .sys extension)
- ○ In the Network Monitor example, the missing driver is represented by the nm3.sys file

Once we find the file+, we can manually deploy it within App-V clients, prior to delivering the application (reviewed in *Chapter 2, Sequencing in Complex Environments*).

- If the problem is related to file or registry permissions:

  - ○ Start Process Monitor within the virtual environment and create a capture, prior to running the virtual application
  - ○ Run the application and, as soon as the error appears, stop the capture
  - ○ Filter the activity looking for results such as **ACCESS DENIED** in Process Monitor

- ○ Verify the file, folder, or registry implied in this error
- ○ To solve this kind of problem, re-sequence the application, applying the necessary permission changes while we are capturing it, and make sure that **Enforce Security Descriptors** is enabled (this option captures the file permissions modified)

Most of the problems related to this stage usually require the "trial and error" approach. So, don't expect to find every solution immediately; it would most likely take a few captures and analysis to detect the root cause and solve it.

Also, using Process Monitor will help us troubleshoot, but do not try to use this tool to solve the problems that we can get with applications not compatible or unsupported for virtualization.

The App-V team blog includes two complete articles about the Process Monitor approach; take a look (please note that the following articles are using an older version of Process Monitor, which did not support the `ExternalCapture` parameter explained earlier):

- Troubleshooting SoftGrid with Process Monitor: `http://blogs.technet.com/b/appv/archive/2007/08/13/troubleshooting-softgrid-with-process-monitor.aspx`

- *Process Monitor – Hands-On Labs and Examples:* `http://blogs.technet.com/b/appv/archive/2008/01/24/process-monitor-hands-on-labs-and-examples.aspx`

# Summary

In this chapter, we've made a large review of pretty much all the possibilities and variables we have to troubleshoot App-V problems.

When we discussed App-V implementations, we saw, regarding installation and implementations, that the App-V management server has several variables that could require some troubleshooting and analysis in order to complete the implementation.

The App-V management server contains a complex architecture (database, web service, management console, Active Directory, and so on) with several pre-requisites and post-installation tasks that must be completed, in order to get a proper functionality. The App-V client on the other hand, to complete its installation, does not offer us much complexity.

The real work regarding the App-V client resides in the application's delivery and usage. When the client retrieves the application from the streaming or management server, there are several aspects of the environment that must be in place for the process to complete.

Virtual application sequencing and usage also offers some complexity, since the isolated environment can present us with some interesting challenges: analyzing virtual services included, components inside and outside the virtual environment, and so on.

Fortunately, App-V provides all the necessary log files and alternatives to analyze the environment and quickly find a solution; but of course, we need all the background information to understand the information generated.

In the next chapter, we are going to review how to scale up our App-V implementations by publishing our App-V infrastructure outside our organization or generating "high-availability" solutions for virtual applications.

# 6
# Scaling Up App-V Implementations

Microsoft Application Virtualization has had important improvements throughout its lifecycle; gaining security, facilitating normal processes for virtualizing and distributing applications, user interface improvements, and scalability, to name a few.

Natively, App-V has some advantages over other platforms when we talk about agility and scalability. Examples of this include MSI deployments to ease up the deployment, Dynamic Suite Composition (DSC) for the virtual applications interaction, HTTP/S streaming as an alternative to deploying applications, and so on.

For all those of us in charge of designing solutions for our infrastructure however, we always try to evaluate far more than just how to deploy applications. We want to customize the platform that we are deploying to adhere to the company's policies and Service Level Agreements (SLAs), and of course configure it to optimize costs.

It's while using these last few concepts that we start thinking in terms of providing our platform with 'high availability' and 'load balancing' capabilities. App-V does provide both of these options, but not for all of its components; the ones supported for Load Balancing are the App-V Management Server and Streaming Server but not the Management Server service (for the Management Console). Still, this last one can be configured if we configure **Service Principal Names (SPN)** correctly.

Regarding Failover Cluster, the only component supported is SQL Server for the App-V data store.

Extensibility in App-V is also another important topic for most organizations. Whether we can extend our implementation beyond the company's network is one of the most common questions we would encounter.

In this chapter, we will learn about:

- General guidelines for achieving a correct design in App-V
- Reviewing the possibilities for fault tolerance in App-V
- Implementing Network Load Balancing (NLB) in App-V
- Implementing database mirroring for the App-V data store
- Implementing Distributed File System (DFS) for the content folder in App-V
- Extending App-V implementations and reviewing necessary configurations needed for implementing App-V across firewalls

# Reviewing general guidelines for the right design

When we think in terms of scenarios with high availability or load balancing, it must begin with the correct platform design.

In this section, we will name just a few of the considerations and concepts that you should take into account when designing the right 'high availability' and 'load balanced' solution:

- *There's no golden rule*: We should never try to apply a previous design to our implementation; every organization, with its requirements, policies, applications, users, and so on, is unique. Get references and investigate, but do not try to implement a previous design.

  In my previous book, *Getting Started with Microsoft Application Virtualization 4.6* (http://www.packtpub.com/getting-started-microsoft-application-virtualization-46/book), we had a good look at the "right questions" that we should be asking in order to achieve a proper design.

- *Start with the "Infrastructure Planning and Design" guides from Microsoft*: This complete set of guides will guide us as we achieve a well-fitted design on every Microsoft platform. The papers are available at Microsoft TechNet (including for App-V 4.6)—http://technet.microsoft.com/en-us/library/cc196387.aspx.

- *Start with high availability and load balancing*: High availability and load balancing scenarios must be introduced when we are designing the solution for the first time; do not deploy a solution and then think about high availability or load balancing after it's stabilized.

- *Think about Service Level Agreements in your organization*: Your IT department could already have an SLA; we should consider reviewing it in order to evaluate high availability for App-V.

- *Not all roles and services in App-V can be clustered*: When we start designing, we should be aware that not all roles and services in App-V can be clustered with high availability or load balancing. We'll review that in the upcoming section.

- *Not all roles and services in App-V could require fault tolerance or load balancing*: Always analyze the cost-benefit equation of applying fault tolerance in your implementation; those do not come cheap and should be discarded if not required by the business.

- *Always think of the backup solution*: High availability solutions should not be implemented in order to replace backup solutions; they should always be implemented as a complement. Having a **Disaster Recovery Plan** (DRP) is always required for every well-designed implementation.

- *Load balancer possibilities*: Regarding load balancing, there are two ways that we could implement it—hardware or software. NLB by software is cheaper and more effective, and hardware possibilities are preferred by several organizations, but it costs more.

# Reviewing fault tolerance possibilities in App-V

When we think about fault tolerance and high availability, we must also know that there are several possibilities that we could use and also some considerations and restrictions that we must be aware of.

Regarding App-V roles and possibilities, and using them in high availability and load balancing, here's a quick review about each role and availability of NLB and high availability:

| Role | NLB | High availability | Minimum servers |
| --- | --- | --- | --- |
| SQL Server | Not supported | √ | 2 |
| Streaming Server | √ | Not supported | 2 |
| Management Server | √ | Not supported | 2 |
| Management Server service | Not supported | Not supported | Not supported |

When we mention high availability, we are referring to Windows Server Failover Clusters; this of course, only points to failover and not load balancing.

Regarding high availability, as we have seen, it only applies to SQL Server roles, and the possibilities referring to this stage are the following:

- **Windows Server Failover Cluster**: This is an effective solution for high availability, broadly used in other Windows platforms, such as Hyper-V, Remote Desktop Services (RDS), DHCP, and so on.

  It is not a cheap solution, since it requires shared storage (using iSCSI, Fiber Channel, or SAS connectors) for all nodes in the cluster.

  For more information about Windows Server Failover Clusters, visit the following link on Microsoft TechNet: *Failover Clusters in Windows Server 2008 R2* (`http://technet.microsoft.com/en-us/library/ff182338(WS.10).aspx`).

- **SQL Server Database Mirroring**: This solution is also effective and does not require shared storage to set up. It depends on (at least) a second SQL Server instance where the App-V data store can be replicated.

  There's also the possibility of automatic failover for the database by using a third SQL Server instance that works as a "witness", monitoring the availability of the "primary" instance with the active database.

  For more information about SQL Server database mirroring, please check out the page *Database Mirroring Overview* — `http://msdn.microsoft.com/en-us/library/ms189852.aspx`.

 SQL Server load balancing, also known as active-active cluster, is not supported by Microsoft.

Within this chapter, we will also evaluate a solution for the `content` folder in App-V; using a great and cheap Microsoft solution, largely implemented in File Servers scenarios, called **Distributed File System**.

DFS provides a unified namespace, behind which several file servers distributed across data centers can be used to host replicated content. This allows the same network location to be accessed, regardless of physical location. DFS provides the use of these namespaces across our Active Directory domain; namespaces have attached several synchronized file servers and shared folders. This transforms the file server service into being completely agnostic of the server we are connecting to or even the location (Active Directory Site) we are using.

In App-V, it's quite useful to achieve a high availability solution for the application's files (SFT, icons, and OSD) which are as necessary for services in charge of publications and streaming.

# Implementing Network Load Balancing in App-V

There are five different tasks that we need to perform in order to complete the implementation:

1. Prepare accounts for delegation in Active Directory.
2. Create a Network Load Balancing cluster.
3. Add Service Principal Names.
4. Install/configure App-V Management Server services in NLB.
5. Configure App-V Clients.

We are going to review a basic example of configuring the App-V services in Network Load Balancing with the following scenarios:

- Active Directory working (necessary for the App-V Management Server scenario)
- Two Windows Server 2008 R2 servers with IIS role installed with all prerequisites for the App-V Management Server
- One Windows Server 2008 R2 server hosting the App-V data store

# Preparing accounts for delegation in Active Directory

This step is necessary to configure the Service Principal Names in Active Directory for the services we would like to load balance (HTTP and App-V services, in this case).

When we trust delegated accounts in Active Directory, we are allowing a service to impersonate a user account or computer account in order to access resources throughout the network. We need this because our NLB cluster must be allowed to be impersonated to access the App-V services.

You can accomplish this with the following steps:

1. Access the **Active Directory Users and Computers** console and locate the computer objects for the two servers with the App-V services to be load balanced.

2. Access the computer's properties and click on the **Delegation** pane.

3. Select **Trust this computer for delegation to any service (Kerberos only)** and click on **OK**.

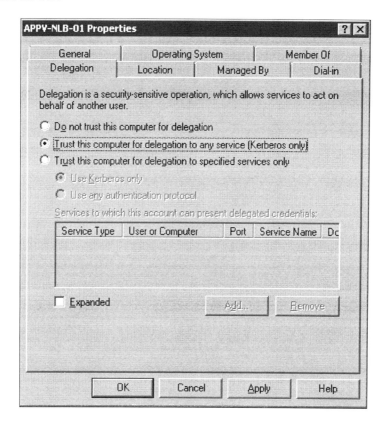

If we are using an Active Directory user account for the App-V Management Service instead of the default configured option (**NETWORK SERVICE** is used in a default installation), we must also verify that the account is enabled for delegation.

To do that, we must access the user account properties in **Active Directory User and Computers**, and ensure that the option **Account is sensitive and cannot be delegated** is NOT marked in the **Account** tab.

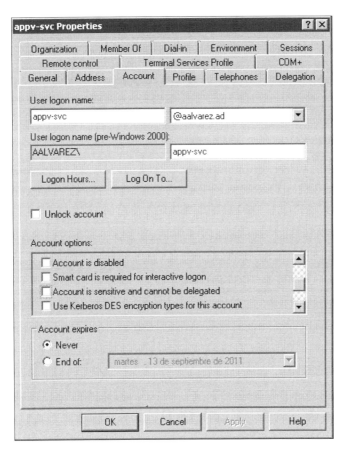

# Creating a Network Load Balancing cluster

The steps and even the console used to create the NLB cluster has not changed since Windows Server 2003.

Let's review the steps for creating the NLB:

1.  The **Network Load Balancing** feature can be found in **Server Manager**; we must add this feature for all servers that will be included in the cluster.

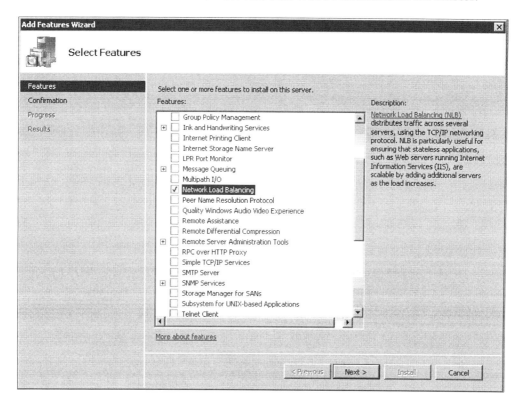

2.  Once installed using the NLB console, we simply use the **New Cluster** option to start with the creation.

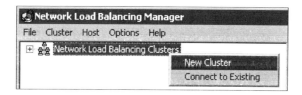

3.  In the next step, we must connect to one of the hosts and select the interface with which we want to load balance the requests.

    As we are using each node with two network cards, in the first option, we must select the interface that will receive all requests (the other one is dedicated for the cluster heartbeat).

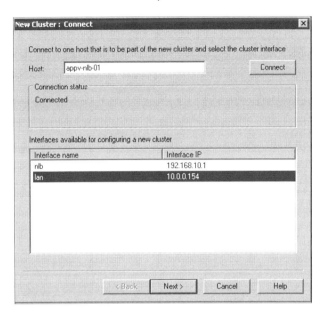

4.  The host **Priority** is set to **1**, in this case, since it is the first node.

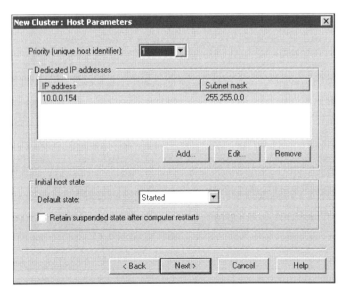

5. We need to set a cluster virtual IP. This virtual address is shared by all hosts, and the NLB driver installed on each host (applied when we add a host to the cluster) is the one in charge of load balancing and directing each request to a specific node.

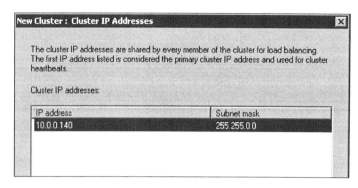

6. In the next option, we must select the cluster name from which clients will try to connect to the load balance instance. In this case, we will be using **appv-nlb-clstr**. We must also select the type for **Cluster operation mode**.

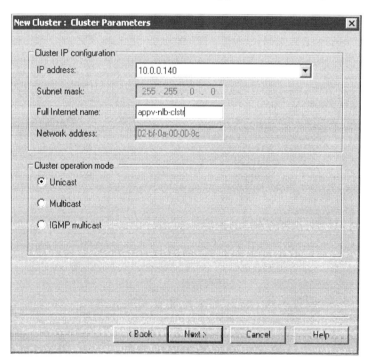

In order to understand which option we should be using, we must have a deep understanding of the difference between the requirements and benefits of each of these. To do so, please review the links to *Network Load Balancing parameters*—http://technet.microsoft.com/en-us/library/cc778263(WS.10).aspx and *Configure Network Load Balancing Cluster Operation Mode*—http://technet.microsoft.com/en-us/library/cc731616.aspx.

7.  In the next window, we must add some rules for the NLB cluster. These rules will basically define the NLB cluster behavior in the clients' request handling (ports used for load balancing, the filtering mode, and the affinity level).

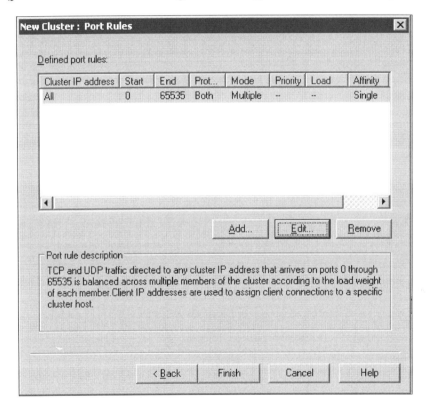

When we are using App-V for load balancing, we must remember that the only chance to set one port for NLB is when we use SSL connections; in App-V, the default port for secure communication is 322. If we are not using SSL, App-V uses port 554 or other higher ports that we cannot predefine.

The **Filtering Mode** will define whether the rule that we are applying affects all nodes or just one. Using **Multiple hosts** expresses that port handling will include all nodes in the cluster.

**Affinity** sets the preference that will apply when several requests from the same client appear. In the **Single** option (default in NLB), when we receive multiple requests from the same client IP, all those will be redirected to the same node in the cluster.

For more information regarding these options, review the **Network Load Balancing parameters** page, available at `http://technet.microsoft.com/en-us/library/cc778263(WS.10).aspx`.

8. Click on **Finish** and the cluster will be created with one node.

9. To add a second one, use the **Add node** option in the NLB console and close the wizard.

Your scenario completed with an NLB cluster using two nodes should look like this:

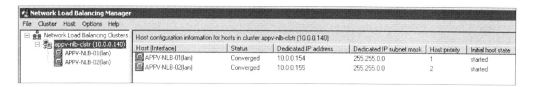

In order to validate that the cluster was successfully created, we should check whether the **Initial host state** field has the value **started** for each node in the NLB console. And the basic test we can execute is from a third host in the network — the **ping** command to the cluster virtual IP address when the principal node goes down.

# Adding Service Principal Names

A **Service Principal Name** is the name by which a client uniquely identifies an instance of a service. The SPN is a necessary component when we are configuring App-V in NLB, since it will allow the App-V services to be identified as a clustered instance.

Registering SPN requires a command-line tool — **setspn** — included in Windows Server 2008 R2, natively (for Windows Server 2003, we need the Support Tools CD). The services to be registered in Active Directory are: Computer names involved in the cluster, the SQL Server storing the App-V data store, and the `HTTP` and `SOFTGRID` services.

Let's take a look at the procedure:

1. Open the command prompt and execute the following command:
   ```
   setspn -R computername
   ```

```
Command Prompt                                              _ □ X

C:\Users\augusto>setspn -R appv-nlb-01
Registering ServicePrincipalNames for CN=APPV-NLB-01,CN=Computers,DC=aalvarez,DC
=ad
        HOST/appv-nlb-01.aalvarez.ad
        HOST/appv-nlb-01
Updated object

C:\Users\augusto>_
```

This command will reset the default SPN registrations for the host names for `computername`.

And, as we can see in the result shown in the command prompt, the SPNs registered are: *HOST/computername* and *HOST/{DNS of computername}*.

2. Repeat the previous step for all nodes in the cluster.

3. In the same command prompt, register the SQL service where the App-V data store will be stored (or is stored, in case we already have the platform deployed):

   **Setspn -A MSSQLSvc/**computername**:sqlport** computername

```
Command Prompt                                              _ □ X

C:\Users\augusto>setspn -A MSSQLSvc/appv-datastore.aalvarez.ad:1433 appv-datasto
re
Registering ServicePrincipalNames for CN=APPV-DATASTORE,CN=Computers,DC=aalvarez
,DC=ad
        MSSQLSvc/appv-datastore.aalvarez.ad:1433
Updated object

C:\Users\augusto>_
```

To register a service, we must use the `-A` parameter; `MSSQLSvc` represents the name that the SQL service will be identified as, and, of course, `1433` is the default port associated with the installed SQL Server.

Registering the SPN for the SQL Server is not a requirement for the NLB scenario, but is a recommended option.

We will need an SPN in case of Database Mirroring, to be reviewed later in this chapter.

4. The same procedure applies to the HTTP and SOFTGRID services, but this time the object associated will be the cluster name and one service account.

We need to configure a user account instead of a computer account, as shown in the SQL Server service, since the HTTP and SOFTGRID identities on each node must be configured to use the same domain user account.

Prior to executing this command; ensure that the cluster name is accessible using DNS resolution:

Setspn -A HTTP/*clustername useraccount*

This is the example used for the HTTP account:

This is the example used for the SOFTGRID account:

 To review SPNs registered by a server in our domain, we can use the following command, which will retrieve the Service Principal Names for the selected server:

Setspn -L computername

For more information about Service Principal Names and the setspn command, please review the following link in Microsoft TechNet: **Setspn**—http://technet. microsoft.com/en-us/library/cc731241(WS.10).aspx.

# Installing or configuring App-V Management Server services in NLB

Even though this step could appear tricky, there aren't any particular considerations regarding the installation of the App-V Management Server.

Since we've omitted the installation steps after the configuration of the NLB cluster in the previous example, we only need to install the App-V Management Server services in both nodes, using the same options.

In the explained case, the SQL Server instance where the database will be stored is placed on a third server. When we install the first node, we can complete the installation steps normally, as for any Management Server, from scratch; in the second node, we must select **Existing database** in the database options, using the database created when we installed the first node.

This is an example of a scenario, as we described in the example: two App-V Management Servers configured in NLB, one App-V SQL data store, and one common database for the environment:

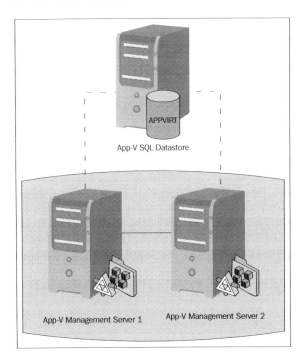

# Configuring App-V Clients

Once we have our NLB cluster in place with the Service Principal Names added successfully and the App-V Management Server services installed correctly in all nodes, all we have left is to configure our App-V Clients to retrieve publishing information from the cluster name instead of just one server.

The procedure is the same as for configuring any App-V publishing server:

1. Access the **Application Virtualization Client** console and select **Publishing Servers**.
2. Right-click and select **New Server**.
3. Select the **Display Name** and the type of publishing server.
4. In **Host Name**, introduce the cluster name with the port used and click on **Finish**.

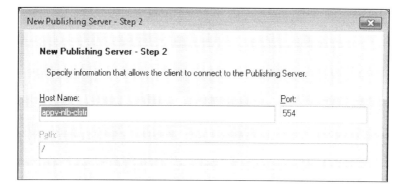

5. Once added, we can test our **Refresh** options when the priority node is up or down, in order to validate the fault tolerance.

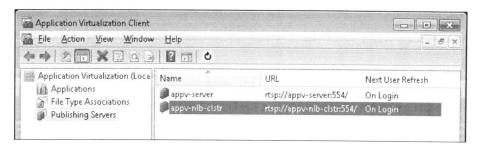

# Troubleshooting App-V Clients in the NLB scenario

With the App-V Client installed and configured to retrieve the applications from an NLB cluster, there are some cases that might appear problematic when we do not complete the normal configurations shown earlier.

The most common problem is related to Service Principal Names; if we don't complete the proper registrations, we will receive the following message:

**Error code: xxxxxxx-xxxxxx0A-200001F4**

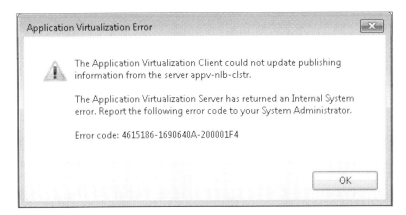

To solve this, we must verify whether the Service Principal Names registered for each service and account were added with the correct parameters, as we've discussed earlier. We can use the `setspn` command to verify it thus:

`setspn -l` *accountname*

And, in case there is an error registering these names, we can always delete them, also by using the setspn command, for example, for the HTTP service, use:

`setspn -D HTTP/`*computername username*

# Considerations about using the Management Console in NLB

If we have clustered and load balanced our App-V Management Server, we most likely would like to see how our App-V Management Server service (in charge of the Management Console) works. This configuration is viable but not yet supported.

If we try using the cluster name when we connect to the Management Console, we will get the `0000C801` error with the **Invalid user name or password** warning.

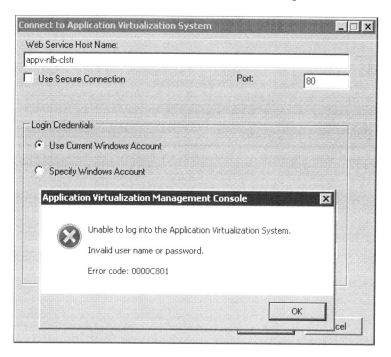

On the other hand, we can use the cluster virtual address to connect to the console, but again, this does not support failover or load balancing.

# Implementing database mirroring for the App-V data store

As you probably know already, the App-V Management Service controls the read/write access in the App-V database, when we are using the App-V Management Server, and that if the database is not available, this Management Server won't be able to answer client requests or requests from Management Console access.

Providing high availability to this component in App-V should be considered in every scenario. One of the methods available to do so is mirroring the database to a separate SQL Server; this is supported by App-V.

The procedure to implement it consists of the following steps:

- Preparing the database for mirroring
- Configuring SQL database mirroring
- Configuring the App-V Management Server for database mirroring

For more information regarding the functionalities in SQL Server 2008 R2 and database mirroring, please visit the *Database Mirroring Overview* page at `http://msdn.microsoft.com/en-us/library/ms189852.aspx`.

# Preparing a database for mirroring

In order to complete the prerequisites of the App-V database, to achieve mirroring, we must change some of the default values included in the installation.

To check the complete guide about database mirroring preparation, check the **How to: Prepare a Mirror Database for Mirroring** page at `http://msdn.microsoft.com/en-us/library/ms189047(v=SQL.105).aspx` (SQL Server 2008 R2):

1. Open **SQL Server Management Studio** and connect to the instance where the App-V database is located.

2. Expand **Databases** and access **APPVIRT** (or the selected name for the App-V database) properties.

3. Select **Options**, and in **Recovery model**, select **Full** and click on **OK**.

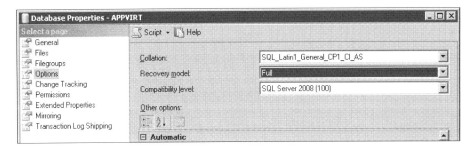

4. In the SQL Server Management Studio, right-click on **APPVIRT**, and select the option **Tasks | Backup**, using the **Full** option.

5. Once the database is backed up, we need to restore it in the second SQL Server instance where the mirror database will be located.

6. Access the second instance of the SQL Server using SQL Server Management Studio.

7. Right-click on **Databases**, select **Tasks**, and select **Restore database**.

8. Select the file from the previously made backup of APPVIRT, and in **Options**, select the option **RESTORE WITH NORECOVERY** and click on **OK**.

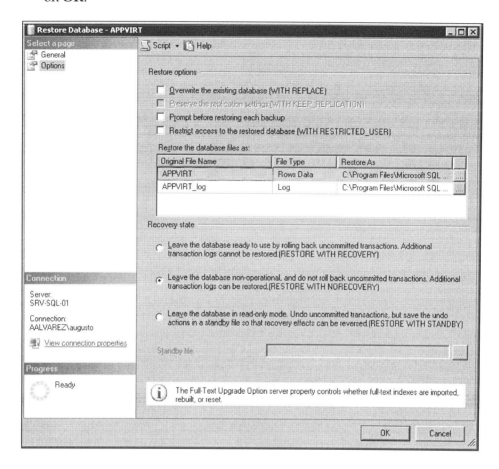

Also, a recommended best practice, if possible: the path (including the drive letter) of the mirror database should be identical to the path of the principal database.

Once the second APPVIRT database is located and restored successfully, we can now proceed to create a mirror in the principal SQL Server instance.

# Configuring SQL database mirroring

Configuring database mirroring in the SQL Server is a simple procedure once we complete the prerequisites mentioned earlier. This process only requires completing a wizard that we can access from the SQL Server Management Studio.

Database mirroring, here, includes the possibility of using an automatic failover option by including a SQL Server witness instance. This is a normal SQL Server instance that we can configure in the mirroring procedure as the witness in charge of monitoring the availability of the active database; in case this goes down, the mirror database automatically starts working as active without requiring user intervention.

The procedure is as follows:

1. Access SQL Server Management Studio and connect to the SQL Server instance where the active App-V database is stored.

2. Expand **Databases**, right-click on **APPVIRT**, select **Tasks**, and then select **Mirror**.

3. In the new window, select **Configure Security**.

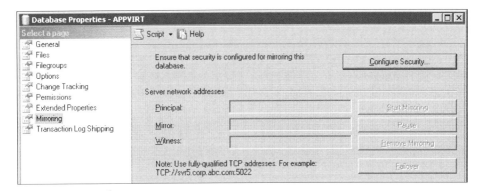

4. When we start the wizard, we will be prompted to use a **Witness Server** instance. If so, remember that all instances must be accessible from the server with the proper ports opened.

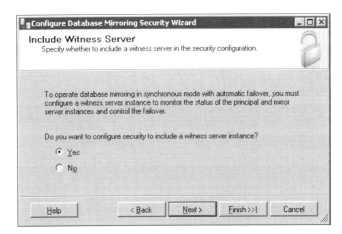

5. In the **Principal server instance** field, we should see the server name for the current instance grayed-out. We can also configure the **Listener port** used for the mirroring communication.

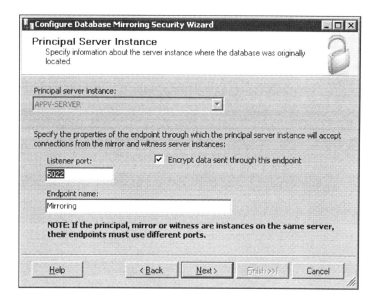

6. In the **Mirror server instance** drop-down list, we must select and connect to the second SQL Server instance. In this example, we are using **SRV-SQL-01** as the secondary server.

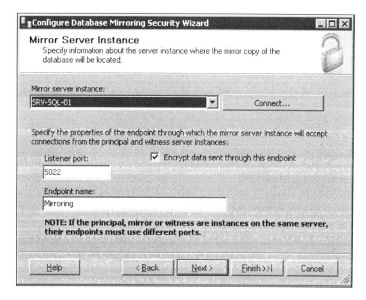

7. If we decided to use a witness server, we will be asked to select and connect to that instance.

8. Next, we will be required to introduce service accounts for connecting to the SQL Server instances configured.

   When using Windows Authentication, if the server instances use different accounts, specify the service accounts for the SQL Server. These service accounts must all be domain accounts (in the same or trusted domains).

   If all the server instances use the same domain account or use certificate-based authentication, leave the fields blank.

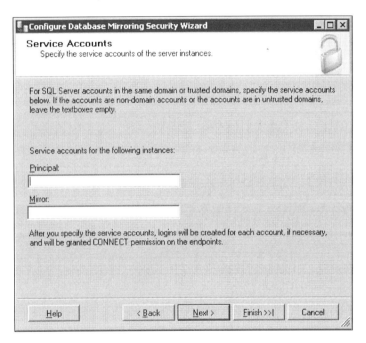

9. In the last window, we can click on **Finish**, and we should verify that the endpoints are successfully configured.

10. In the database properties, we can now check the two instances configured for the mirroring database. We can also configure the following operating modes available in mirroring:

    ○ **High performance, asynchronous**: The mirror database always lags somewhat behind the principal database, never quite catching up.

    ○ **High safety without automatic failover, synchronous**: All committed transactions are guaranteed to be written to disk on the mirror server.

- ° **High safety with automatic failover, synchronous**: All committed transactions are guaranteed to be written to disk on the mirror server. Witness server is necessary to provide automatic failover.

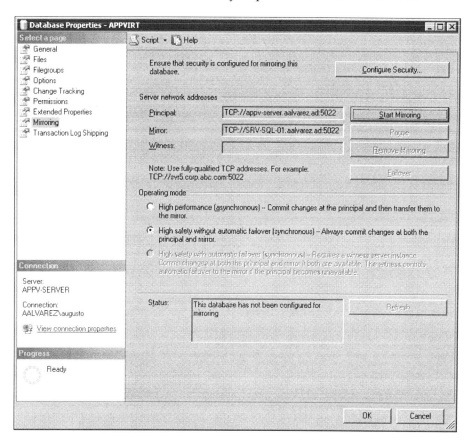

11. Once we've completed the wizard correctly and validated that the **Server network address** information shown here is correct and all servers are accessible using that configuration, we can click on **Start Mirroring**.

There are several ways to verify the status of this procedure; visit the *Monitoring Mirroring Status* page on Microsoft MSDN — http://msdn.microsoft.com/en-us/library/ms365781.aspx (SQL Server 2008 R2).

# Configuring the App-V Management Server for database mirroring

In order to complete the mirroring configurations of the database, App-V requires some particular changes in the platform to get this configuration finished successfully.

The complete guide for this procedure can be found on the following page from Microsoft TechNet: **How to Configure Microsoft SQL Server Mirroring Support for App-V** — `http://technet.microsoft.com/en-us/library/ff660790.aspx`.

Let's take a look at the process:

1. Verify that both servers have their SPN registered in the domain. The process is mentioned earlier in this chapter in the *Adding Service Principal Names* section.

2. Verify that the options for **TCP/IP** connections and **Named Pipes** are enabled in both servers.

3. In the secondary SQL Server instance holding the mirrored database, create the SQL Server Login for the network service account of the App-V Management Server by using the account name `<domain>\<ManagementServerHostName>$`.

> For more information about how to add SQL logins, review the following article: `http://technet.microsoft.com/en-us/library/ms178029.aspx`.
>
> In the example mentioned in the Microsoft article, a user is referred to as a new SQL login. We can still use a computer account for this, for example:
>
> CREATE LOGIN AALVAREZ\APPV-SERVER$ FROM WINDOWS
>
> AALVAREZ is the **Domain Name** and APPV-SERVER is the **Computer Name**.

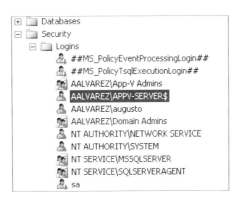

4. In the **Properties** of this new SQL login, access **User Mappings**, and add the **SFT admin** role for the **APPVIRT** database (or the selected name for the App-V data store).

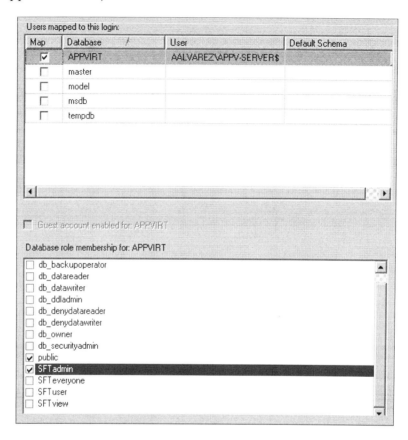

5. Repeat the process in the primary server, adding the SQL login and **SFT admin** to the secondary server.

6. In both servers, grant **connect permissions** for the logins that we've just created:

```
USE master;
GRANT CONNECT ON ENDPOINT::Mirroring TO "DOMAIN\SERVERNAME$"
    WITH GRANT OPTION;
GO
```

7. In the primary server, access **regedit** and locate the HKEY_LOCAL_MACHINE\ SOFTWARE\Wow6432Node\Microsoft\Softgrid\4.5\Server path (for x64 installations).

8. Create the registry key `SQLFailoverServerName` as `REG_SZ` (string), and then set the value to the host name of the SQL Server that hosts the mirror.

9. In the same path, create **SQLFailoverServerPort** as **REG_DWORD** and then set the value to the port number that is used for SQL on the computer that is running the SQL Server to host the mirror.

   If you are using a named instance for the mirror, this key value must be set to the port number that is used for the named instance.

| Name | Type | Data |
|---|---|---|
| (Default) | REG_SZ | (value not set) |
| MaxDcRefreshSize | REG_DWORD | 0x00100000 (1048576) |
| ProductCode | REG_SZ | {1E49B00F-C347-4C51-9BE1-550124CC43C3} |
| SOFTGRID_CONF_DIR | REG_SZ | C:\Program Files (x86)\Microsoft System Center App Vi... |
| SOFTGRID_CONTENT_DIR | REG_SZ | E:\App-V\content\ |
| SOFTGRID_LOG_FILE | REG_SZ | C:\Program Files (x86)\Microsoft System Center App Vi... |
| SOFTGRID_LOG_LEVEL | REG_SZ | 3 |
| SOFTGRID_MODULES_DIR | REG_SZ | C:\Program Files (x86)\Microsoft System Center App Vi... |
| SQLDatabaseName | REG_SZ | APPVIRT |
| SQLServerName | REG_SZ | APPV-SERVER |
| SQLServerPort | REG_DWORD | 0x00000599 (1433) |
| UNAUTHENTICATED_TIMEOUT_SEC | REG_DWORD | 0x0000000a (10) |
| Version | REG_SZ | 4.5.3.19480 |
| SQLFailoverServerName | REG_SZ | SRV-SQL-01 |
| SQLFailoverServerPort | REG_DWORD | 0x00000599 (1433) |

In this example, the SQL Server hosting the mirror database is **SRV-SQL-01**, and the port used by the instance is **1433**.

10. We must also configure the App-V Management web service to understand the failover possibilities of using the mirrored database; to do that, we must locate the `SftMgmt.udl` file placed in the App-V Management Server installation folder (default location: `C:\Program Files (x86)\Microsoft System Center App Virt Management Server\App Virt Management Service`).

11. In the **Provider** tab, select the OLE DB provider **SQL Server Native Client 10.0** and click on **Next**.

12. In the **Connection** tab's **Server Name** box, enter the server name of the SQL Server. Select **Use Windows NT Integrated Security**. Finally, click on the list **Select the database**, and then select the App-V database name.

13. Click on the **All** tab, and then select the entry **Failover Partner**. Click on **Edit Value**, and then enter the server name of the failover SQL Server. Then, click on **OK**.

With that, we've completed the mirroring procedure for the App-V database. We can verify the high availability options by testing the failover between the primary and secondary instances.

# Implementing Distributed File System

As we discussed earlier, Distributed File System provides a way to optimize the use of file servers in our organization by using namespaces in our domain.

These namespaces are associated with file servers and shared folders implemented across our organization, and achieve not only centralized management but also improve the users' accessibility to these resources. This makes the file server service highly available as well as efficiently implemented.

It is beyond the scope of this chapter to explain all the components, requirements, and considerations about Distributed File System; for more information, please visit the following links on Microsoft TechNet:

- **Distributed File System**—`http://technet.microsoft.com/en-us/library/cc753479(WS.10).aspx`

- **The Basics of the Windows Server 2008 Distributed File System (DFS)**—`http://blogs.technet.com/b/josebda/archive/2009/03/09/the-basics-of-the-windows-server-2008-distributed-file-system-dfs.aspx`

- **DFS Step-by-Step Guide for Windows Server 2008**—`http://technet.microsoft.com/en-us/library/cc732863(WS.10).aspx`

Let's take a look at how to configure DFS, step-by-step:

1. Access the **Add Roles** wizard in one of the file servers that will be included in the DFS namespace.

2. The role to install is **File Services** and their services should be **Distributed File System**, including **DFS Namespaces** and **DFS Replication**.

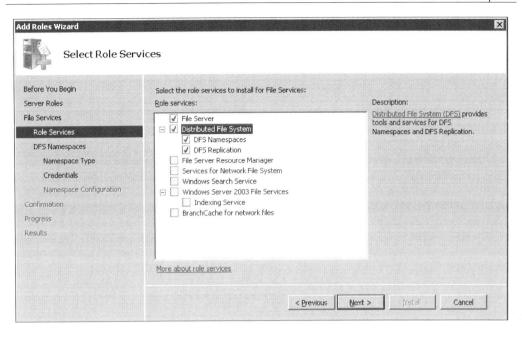

3. We can complete the wizard by creating the first namespace within this process, or we can create the namespace later by using the DFS management console.

4. Run the same **Add Role** procedure to all servers that we would like to add in the namespace we are creating.

5. In my case, I'll be creating the DFS namespace by using the Management Console. Right-click on **Namespaces** and click on **New Namespace**.

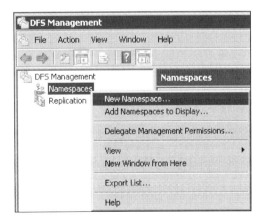

6. A new wizard will appear, select the name of the first server to be included. In my case, I'm using the local server **SRV-DFS-01**.

7. Insert the name for the namespace (I'm using **apps**) that we are creating and click on **Next**.

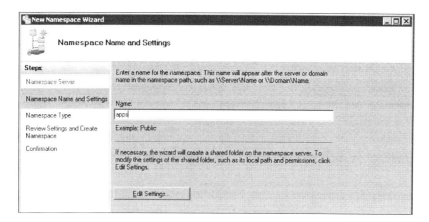

8. Select the type of namespace that we would like to create. The **Domain-based namespace** represents one of the most commonly used namespaces when we are using Active Directory environments.

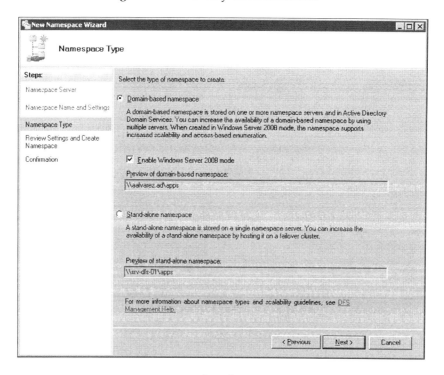

9.  Complete the wizard and we should get a confirmation about the namespace that has been created successfully.

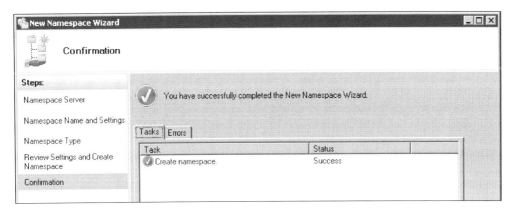

To provide high availability in this namespace, the next step is adding a namespace server.

10. In the DFS console, right-click on the namespace name, select **Add Namespace Server**, and then select the name of the new server to be added.

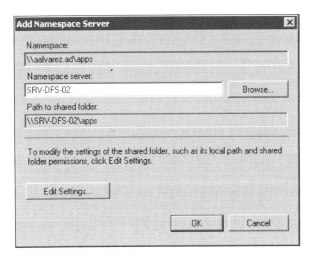

11. Once the server is added to the namespace, we can verify their status in the DFS console.

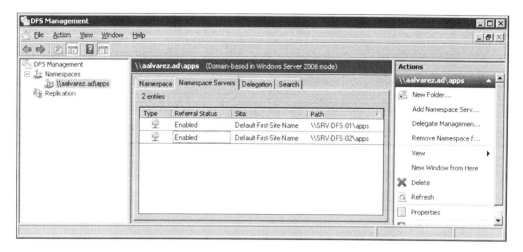

With the namespace created, we can start adding shared folders.

12. Right-click on the namespace and select **New Folder**. Within the options available, select the **content** folder in the DFS namespace server containing the virtual applications.

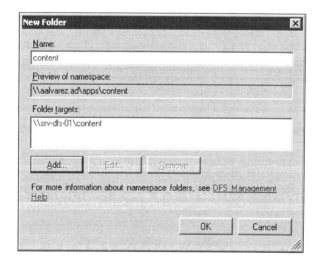

13. Verify that the folder was added successfully in the namespace; we should see it as **Enabled**.

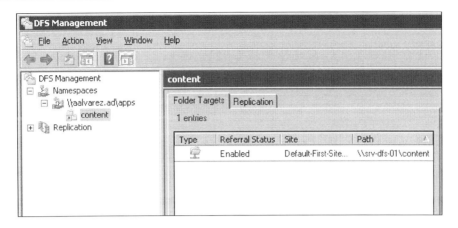

With that, we have the content folder added to the namespace, and we can verify it by accessing the namespace path shown in the console; in my case that will be \\aalvarez.ad\apps\content.

14. To add the second server as a target within this folder, right-click on the **content** folder in the DFS console and select **Add folder target**.

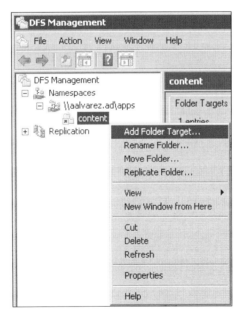

15. Select the new path for the `content` folder. It is not necessary to have this folder already shared on the new server; we can create it within this process.

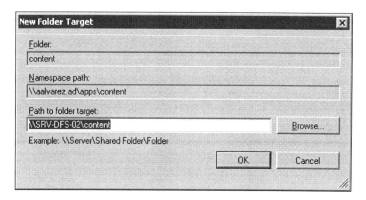

16. Once we complete the steps for the new target, a new pop-up will appear to remind us to keep these targets synchronized. To do that, we can configure a **Replication group**.

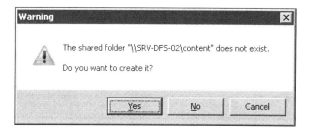

Click on **Yes** to start configuring immediately.

This replication group will define the replication topology as well as particular configurations of the replication, such as the bandwidth to be used.

17. A new wizard will appear; complete the initial names to be used in the **Replication group** and click on **Next**.

18. Select **Primary Member** and click on **Next**. The replications will start on this server and will include any other folders included in this group.

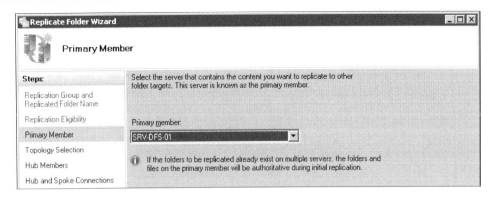

19. Select the topology to be used in this replication group. When we have a few members in this group, the recommended option is **Full mesh**, where each member replicates with all the other members.

    Using a few servers (less than 10 is recommended by Microsoft) and the **Full mesh** replication, we can guarantee that all servers will maintain consistency in information, with low bandwidth cost.

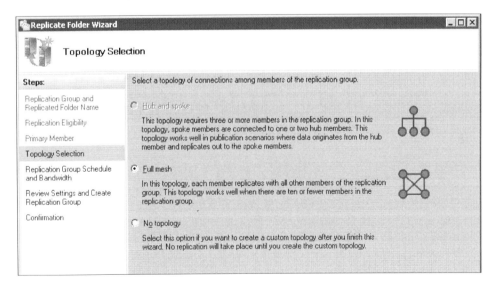

20. Select the Replication Group bandwidth usage during the synchronizations and the schedule on which these will occur.

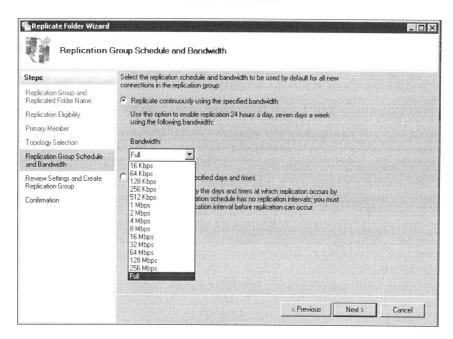

21. Close the wizard and verify that there are no errors in the creation of the replication group.

    We can run the normal tests in the environment by shutting down nodes included in the DFS namespace and verifying that the content folder remains available.

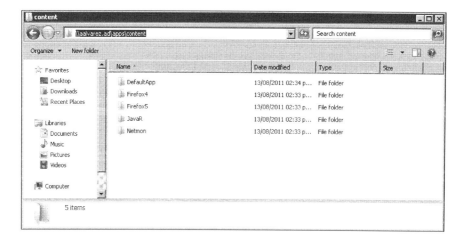

We also have some interesting reporting options within the DFS console using **Create Diagnostic Report**.

What remains is to configure App-V Clients to retrieve the applications using the new namespace in the domain. And of course, we can use the registry settings or Group Policy to accomplish this.

We can access the Group Policy options by downloading the **Microsoft Application Virtualization Administrative Template (ADM Template)**.

It's available on the **Microsoft Download Center**—http://www.microsoft.com/downloads/en/default.aspx.

Once the Administrative Templates are imported, we can start working on the App-V group policies.

22. Create a Group Policy, link it in the Organizational Unit where App-V Clients are located, and click on **Edit**.

23. Expand **Computer Configuration | Policies | Administrative Templates | Classic Administrative Templates (ADM) | Microsoft Application Virtualization Client** (or **Microsoft Application Virtualization Client (64-bit** where applicable).

24. Select **Communication** and modify the following Group Policy values:

   ○ **Application Source Root**: Select **Enabled**, and then set the **Application Source Root Path** to the namespace that we've just created, in my case \\aalvarez.ad\apps\content\.

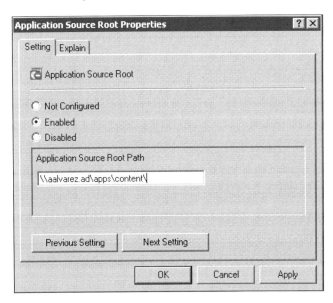

# Extending App-V implementations

Extending the App-V platform using the Internet is possible and does not introduce vast complexity, since the protocols and the communications established between clients and servers can be identified and therefore published to the Internet.

In the *App-V Security Operations Guide* document provided by Microsoft (available at the Microsoft Download Center — `http://www.microsoft.com/downloads/en/default.aspx`), there are examples about some of the most common scenarios associated with publishing the App-V platform to the Internet and also considerations about using domain and non-domain joined clients.

# Publishing App-V in your firewalls

Depending on network complexity and the App-V model selected, the scenarios available to publish App-V are indeed too many to describe each one. We can however, describe two of the most common scenarios: publishing App-V servers located on the internal network and publishing App-V servers located in the DMZ.

## Using App-V servers on the internal network

In this example, all the App-V components are placed on the internal network and are behind a firewall server.

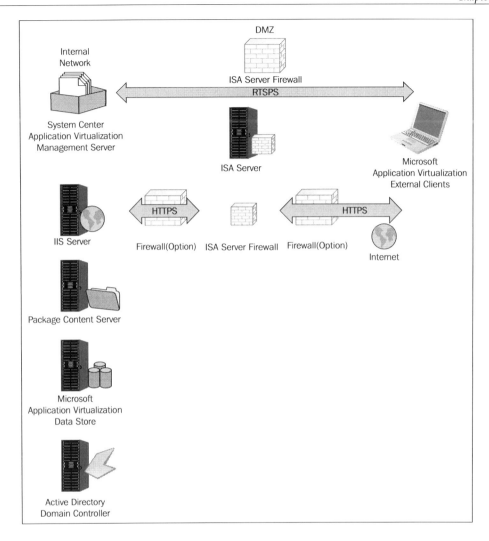

We need to configure two rules in the firewall (for example ISA or Forefront TMG) to correctly publish the App-V services:

1.  Web Publishing rule for the server hosting the virtual packages. More information can be found at Microsoft TechNet—`http://technet.microsoft.com/en-us/library/cc723324.aspx`.

2.  Server publishing rule for the App-V Server (using the RTSPS protocol). More information can be found at Microsoft TechNet—`http://technet.microsoft.com/en-us/library/cc441512.aspx`.

# Using App-V servers in the DMZ

In this scenario we can have several possibilities according to the components that we would like to use on the DMZ network and which ones are to be used in the internal network.

As for a common recommendation in other environments, the servers to be used in the DMZ should be those in charge of communication with the clients and nothing more; in this case, they are the App-V Management Server (if applicable) and the IIS for publishing and streaming.

In this scenario, we are placing the following components in the internal network: *Content server*, *SQL server*, and *Domain Controllers*.

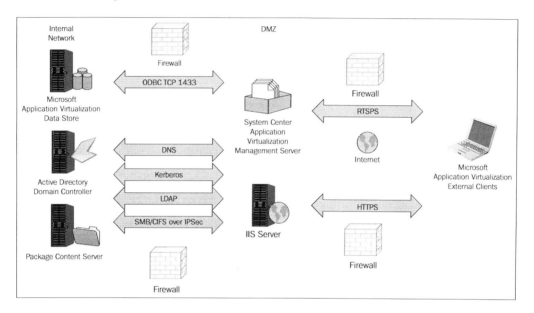

In this example, these are the communications that should be allowed between the different networks.

The following ports are open between the Internet and DMZ:

- **RTSPS** (Publishing Refresh and Streaming packages):
  - ° TCP 322 by default, this can be changed in the App-V Management Server

- **HTTPS** (Publishing ICO and OSD files, and Streaming packages):
  - ○ TCP 443 by default, this can be changed in IIS configuration

- **DMZ to Internal** SQL Server (for communication with the App-V database):
  - ○ TCP 1433 is the default but can be configured in the SQL Server

- **SMB/CIFS** if the content directory is located remotely from the Management Server or IIS server (to retrieve files for the virtual package):
  - ○ **Microsoft File Sharing SMB** requires TCP ports 135 thru 139
  - ○ **Direct Hosted SMB** requires both TCP and UPD port 445 (preferred choice)

- **Kerberos** and **LDAP** (for Active Directory):
  - ○ TCP and UDP 88
  - ○ TCP and UDP 389

- **DNS** for name resolution of internal resources (this could be eliminated with the use of host files on DMZ servers)

If we are using an Internet-based scenario, we would probably want to evaluate the possibilities to include non-domain joined clients, since in that case, we won't need a persistent VPN connection with machines joined in the domain to retrieve virtual applications.

In order for App-V to function properly on the scenario for non-domain joined clients, we will need some extra configuration, since the authentication phase must be completed in any case.

We will need to store the users' information about the App-V platform (App-V Server and a valid domain user account) in the App-V Client. We can do this in **Control Panel | User Accounts | Manage your credentials**.

For more information about the process, check the Microsoft document *App-V Security Operations Guide*, available at the Microsoft Download Center—http://www.microsoft.com/downloads/en/default.aspx.

# Summary

In this chapter, we learnt about high availability and load balancing possibilities in Microsoft Application Virtualization as well as the requirements for extending our implementation outside the organization.

We've learned that the success of a highly available implementation starts with the correct analysis and design. This is an important matter to review since not all roles and services are available to use in a Failover Cluster or in NLB.

We've also reviewed all the necessary steps to accomplish a load balanced solution using Microsoft's NLB role. Even though it could appear as a simple procedure, there are several requirements that we can't avoid, such as Service Principal Names and accounts delegation in Active Directory.

Database mirroring is another feature in high availability for App-V, in this case for the SQL data store. Database mirroring is widely used in several scenarios for its simplicity and effectiveness, but in App-V, we must consider that there are some tasks necessary for this feature to work normally.

Distributed File System appears as the best solution to gain high availability in the content folder of App-V and guarantees an effective use of this shared folder, when we have branch offices and other large implementations.

In the next chapter, we will look at Virtual Desktop Infrastructure (VDI), another great option for scalability in most organizations, and discuss combining it with App-V.

# 7
# Integrating App-V with Virtual Desktop Infrastructure (VDI)

Most organizations today are continuously trying to adapt to a world where agility and resource optimization are some of the main goals. Handling the user's work environment (defined mostly by desktop, applications, and profile data) more efficiently has a direct impact on how we can achieve those goals.

**Virtual Desktop Infrastructure (VDI)** appears as a new approach to how organizations can centralize the management of that work environment. With VDI, not only do we receive benefits specific to hardware optimization but, we also gain agility in the deployment and maintenance of the user's environment by using consistent settings, thus minimizing the impact in support hours.

But VDI does not apply to all organizations; there are several considerations we should evaluate carefully before making any decision on selecting the infrastructure to be used. As with any big implementation, most of the challenges we'll receive are going to be regarding companies' and users' expectations, costs associated, and the new operations for the new infrastructure, considering that the most important actives in our organization will be located in the datacenter.

Regarding optimizing hardware resources, App-V appears as probably the best possible integration with VDI. App-V 4.6 introduced the shared cache feature, which permits administrators to define one common place on the network for the storage of virtual applications and virtual desktops defined in VDI. This saves storage space for the considerable amount of data that needs to be stored in the datacenter.

A VDI approach using the Microsoft platform depends on **Remote Desktop Services (RDS)**; which also provides, as App-V, a method for delivering remote applications using **RemoteApp**. We should evaluate App-V plus RemoteApp as combined technologies if we want to complement our existing infrastructure.

In this chapter, we are going to go through the following topics:

- Understanding what Virtual Desktop Infrastructure is—the components, architecture, and considerations
- How to create our own VDI environment using basic components
- How to integrate VDI with App-V and how to we can configure the shared cache feature in App-V clients
- Review Remote Desktop Services and RemoteApp possibilities, and how to integrate RemoteApp with App-V

# Virtual Desktop Infrastructure (VDI)

Virtual Desktop Infrastructure appeared a few years ago as a response to new challenges being faced by several organizations. VDI offers the way to move the regular users' desktops to the datacenter; a user no longer needs hardware that supports the operating system and their applications. By simply using a thin client PC or other mobile devices, users can access their virtual desktop using a common network protocol (such as RDP).

This, of course, has several important benefits:

- **Centralized management of user data and desktop**: Having the desktop and data in the datacenter lets administrators guarantee several critical matters, for example, backing up users' data.

  This aspect also minimizes several hours that could require not only recovering information from a backup more efficiently. And, also optimize the time we cover providing other support tasks with on-site assistance (such as computer freezing).

- **Agile deployment and maintenance of the user's work environment**: VDI integrated with **System Center Virtual Machine Manager (SCVMM)** optimizes several normal tasks in the provisioning of virtual desktops.

  Also, the definition itself of VDI, detaches operating systems, user data, and applications (when we have App-V integrated) from a physical resource such as a desktop computer. We can have an entire desktop available in an internet browser without major disruption.

- **Consistent configurations in the work environment**: VDI possibilities include the chance to use virtual desktops with a static operating system every time the machine boots (assuming that applications and profiles exist in a different location).

  Guaranteeing stability and consistency in the user's desktop avoids several support hours when we have users that require recurrent modifications in the operating system.

- **Optimizing hardware resources available**: Consolidating all desktops into the datacenter could provide us with a simple way to optimize the hardware. Users that require large resources, such as RAM, on some occasions, can be provisioned dynamically.

  On the other hand, when we have users that do not require large resources with dynamic use, we can provide these resources using our hardware in the datacenter. This would mean saving a lot of money that we should be spending on desktop hardware.

# Understanding VDI components and architecture

In order to understand a little bit more about VDI, let's take a look at the components and architecture involved in this platform.

Even though we are going to discuss the components of the Microsoft platform, using VDI with other vendors can be presented in the very same way including similar components in several cases.

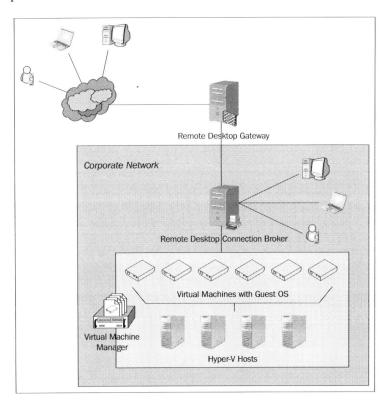

- **Remote Desktop Connection Broker**: This role is in charge of directing the client to the right application or desktop and basically includes the following:

  ° Identifying the virtual machine for the user to make a remote connection.

  ° Preparing the virtual machine for remote connections by communicating with the **Remote Desktop Virtualization Host** server (this can include starting the virtual machine in case it is in a saved state).

  ° Retrieving the IP address assigned to the virtual machine. This address is used by the RD Session Host, which executes the redirection.

  ° Guaranteeing that a user with an existing session in a pool is redirected to the appropriate host virtual machine.

- **Remote Desktop Virtualization Host**: This is our Hyper-V role that is in charge of providing the virtual machines when the RD Connection Broker makes a request.

- **Remote Desktop Session Host**: This server works in "redirection mode", which basically guarantees a secure connection from the client to a virtual machine.

  ° This server queries **RD Connection Broker**, which returns the IP address of the virtual machine available for the connection, and then the client is redirected to this virtual machine.

  ° It is recommended that the RD Connection Broker and RD Session Host working in redirection mode reside in the same machine.

- **Remote Desktop Web Access**: This role is in charge of providing a graphical interface to users when they want to access the available resources. Having this role available, RD Web Access provides users to retrieve their applications and desktops only by using an Internet browser.

Virtual machines in VDI environments are also accessible via the **RADC** feature (Start Menu) in Windows 7 clients.

For more information about RD Web Access in VDI environments, take a look at this article in the Remote Desktop Services Team Blog: *Publishing in Windows Server 2008 R2* (http://blogs.msdn.com/b/rds/archive/2009/06/05/publishing-in-windows-server-2008-r2.aspx).

- **Remote Desktop Gateway**: This is an optional role in VDI, used mainly in scenarios where we need to extend our implementation outside the network. It is in charge of securing and routing RDP connections over the Internet through a firewall.

- **System Center Virtual Machine Manager**: This is also an optional component, which could help us with the rapid and efficient provisioning of the virtual machines using several features.

# VDI considerations

So far, the explanation and benefits provided by VDI sound very appealing for any of us, but this technology should never be considered a magical solution that can fit into an organization smoothly without resigning any of its benefits. We must first carefully analyze the scenario, requirements, resources, and considerations.

Most VDI implementations that end up in failure are related to the misconceptions generated about the "paybacks", or the considerations that were not analyzed carefully in the cost-benefit equation.

As we mentioned before, each infrastructure, organization, and requirement should be analyzed separately, but as a general guideline, here are some of the considerations when we think about VDI:

- **Do not expect to save money instantly**: Even though we can discuss about the importance of optimizing hardware, VDI by nature, requires a large upfront investment in hardware, plus the time and money we are going to use to run a complete assessment, design, plan, and of course implement and maintain the infrastructure.

  Furthermore, there are several papers and articles we can find, that in general mention VDI as a more expensive solution than using a normal desktop. For more information about this, take a look at the Microsoft paper *Microsoft VDI TCO Whitepaper* (TCO = Total Cost of Ownership) at http://www.microsoft.com/download/en/details.aspx?id=25114.

Here, we can find several interesting analyses about VDI and its costs, including this graphic about annual direct costs using normal desktops and VDI:

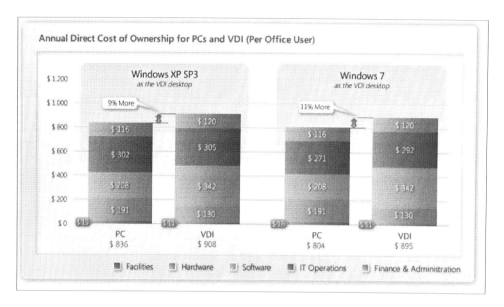

- **VDI incorporates new operations and new complexity**: Disassociating desktops from hardware also includes incorporating other variables in our daily tasks to accomplish a successful VDI implementation.

  The following new challenges appear:

  - Incorporate new processes for a more effective and proactive monitoring of hardware health and performance.

  - Incorporate new processes into desktop support, maintenance, and deployment.

  - A complete analysis about backups: tools necessary, sizing, schedule, and so on.

  - Define new processes in **Disaster Recovery Plans (DRP)**.

  - A possible new approach on patching operating systems and applications to maintain them without major disruptions.

  - A possible new approach on security matters, such as the use of antivirus and other connectivity.

○ Infrastructure maintenance and upgradation. These two tasks that appear normally in our datacenter should be carefully analyzed, since we could be directly affecting users' productivity when we perform any of these two.

- **Set expectations properly**: The idea of VDI is to maintain user experience similar to that of a normal desktop, but most likely, there are going to be some features and processes that will not be the same. Our job is to set these expectations properly in order to complete the implementation without affecting perception or the users' productivity.

- **Take a good review about the current use of desktop resources**: Not only is understanding the right size of each desktop important, we must also review current memory, processor, network, and disk throughput, in order to complete a correct sizing.

  Since all desktops will be stored in the datacenter, we have to make sure that these virtual machines will receive necessary resources when they are needed. Hyper-V R2 supports **Second Level Address Translation (SLAT)** in CPUs, which introduces several improvements in performance.

SLAT uses special CPU functions available in newer processors that add a second level of paging below the architectural x86/x64 paging tables in x86/x64 processors, providing an indirection layer from virtual machine memory access to physical memory access.

By doing this, the Hypervisor CPU time is significantly reduced, and more memory is saved for each virtual machine. RemoteFX technology requires SLAT present in processors in order to function.

For more information about RemoteFX and VDI take a look at *Microsoft RemoteFX for Virtual Desktop Infrastructure: Architectural Overview* (http://www.microsoft.com/download/en/details.aspx?id=13864).

Microsoft has a great document about resources and host capacity planning in VDI environments; take a look at *RD Virtualization Host Capacity Planning in Windows Server 2008 R2* (http://www.microsoft.com/download/en/details.aspx?displaylang=en&id=17387).

- **Evaluate VDI carefully before implementing it**: If this is going to be your first VDI and App-V implementation, before jumping into those two at once, evaluate VDI very carefully. As we discussed in App-V design, VDI needs a proper analysis regarding its architecture, components, and the differences we can find in non-virtualized environments.

  Moreover, if we don't have any experience in VDI or App-V, implementing these two, integrated, could be extremely harmful with any approach. And most likely, users' perceptions about their new desktop will not be any good.

- **Whether using App-V or not, review all the applications included with desktops**: Even though we are not using App-V as our application platform, understanding each application in the work environment is crucial, not only for user experience, per se, but also to define the right "golden image" of VDI, and of course, to handle a correct sizing.

- **Review VDI licensing options**: As we mentioned earlier, VDI requires several components to work using the Microsoft platform, and if want to combine other vendors (such as Citrix XenDesktop, VMware View, and so on), there are also licenses applied in those scenarios.

  Microsoft provides a very useful FAQ section about licenses in VDI; take a look at the *Licensing Windows for VDI environments* document, at http://download.microsoft.com/download/5/0/5/5059CBF7-F736-4D1E-BF90-C28DADA181C5/Microsoft%20VDI%20and%20Windows%20VDA%20FAQ%20v2%200.pdf.

Other useful documents about VDI and Microsoft:

*Achieving Business Value through Microsoft VDI Together with Session Virtualization*: http://www.microsoft.com/download/en/details.aspx?id=21112

*Microsoft Desktop Virtualization Data Sheets*: http://www.microsoft.com/download/en/details.aspx?id=10617

# Integrating App-V with VDI

As we've seen already, VDI is not a simple server we can just install in our organization to evaluate; this technology requires deep analysis before jumping into a decision to try it. Careful analysis is to be done when we decide to implement it, in order to smoothly complement our existing infrastructure.

If we have already implemented App-V 4.6 successfully in our organization, and we are evaluating VDI and its integration, the most important benefit we can take is the **shared cache** feature.

# Shared cache and its benefits

As we already know, even when we are working with streaming servers (App-V Management Server, Streaming Server, or SCCM), the App-V client does not stream the application every time a user tries to access it; the actual streaming occurs with the App-V cache located in the client machine.

If we are using RTSP as a native protocol, the App-V client looks for an updated version of the application, and if there isn't any, the client works with the cached version of the application. So far, this looks good, but if we are thinking about VDI environments and the App-V cache of each Windows 7 computer (App-V client cache can store up to 1TB), this is going to be really expensive in terms of storage.

Using the App-V 4.6 shared cache feature will let us determine a common place (or file; in this case, `SFTFS.FSD`) for this App-V client cache from which all clients can retrieve the already streamed application, letting us save a lot of money in storage costs.

Because of this cost-saving aspect, the shared cache feature appears as a crucial aspect when we are determining whether "to VDI or not VDI" our environment.

Let's consider a VDI scenario with 1,000 users. The complete package of applications takes 50GB; that translates into around 50TB of storage, just for the applications. But using a shared cache, we can transform it into just 50GB (or maybe a bit more, if we don't want to use just one file); the math is really simple, I guess.

This is a great graphic from which we can identify how a shared cache fits into our VDI scenario:

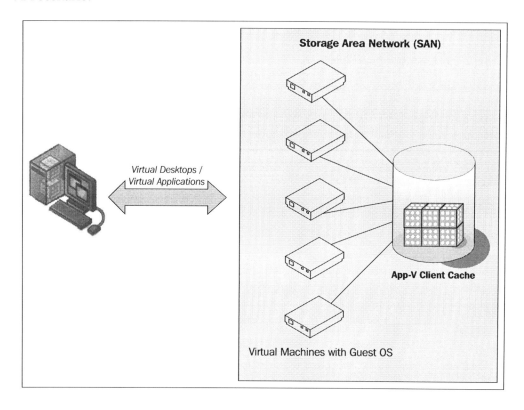

Using all applications from a shared cache also includes other benefits besides saving disk space:

- **Network usage**: Since the applications will not be streaming down from a server, there is a large impact on the network usage

 We are considering, in this case, that the shared cache location is set in the VHD mounted in the image. If we are using a network location for the cache file, this benefit will disappear, and most likely, the network usage will be a disadvantage.

- **Faster application access**: Applications accessed from the App-V cache open up faster than those that must be streamed down first

- **Less processor usage**: The App-V client takes a few CPU cycles when the application is streamed down and even more usage if the SFT file is compressed; using the applications in the cache avoids having this CPU load

# Using the App-V shared cache

The technical specifications will be covered in this chapter, but let's take a look at the general process as a quick review about how we complement VDI clients with shared cache:

1. VDI platform in place with all its basic components and functioning properly.

> An App-V Full Infrastructure platform in place and functioning properly.
> The App-V shared cache is only supported in the Full Infrastructure model (using the App-V management server). There are some workarounds we can use to actually get it to work, but there's no guarantee, so please avoid using it without an App-V management server handling client requests.

2. Using a client Windows image from the VDI platform, we configure the App-V client and log in with a user with access to all the applications we would like to store in the shared cache.

   We must also guarantee that the applications are fully loaded into the cache and not only the Primary Feature Block (FB1). We can use the SFTMIME command line to accomplish this.

3. Extract the App-V client cache and place it in a location where other images in VDI can access it (such as a shared folder in a separate LUN in the storage).

4. Configure App-V clients to use the shared cache instead of a local cache. Accessing this cache will also configure the cache as "read-only" to avoid any inconsistencies with other clients.

In order to review the technical process described here, we are going to take the scenario from scratch, by creating a simple VDI environment with basic resources.

# Creating your own VDI environment

We can set up a VDI environment using just a few resources; in this example, these are the assets we will be using:

- 1 x Hyper-V as the Remote Desktop Services Virtualization Host
- 1 x Windows Server 2008 R2 (virtual machine in the same Hyper-V) as the RDS Session Host, Web Access, and Connection Broker
- 1 x Windows 7 (virtual machine in the same Hyper-V) as the virtual desktop
- 1 x Windows Server 2008 (virtual machine in the same Hyper-V) as Domain Controller with Windows Server 2008 functional level

For more information about using Hyper-V with VDI technology and the benefits associated, take a look at this Microsoft document: *Why Hyper-V for VDI whitepaper* (http://www.microsoft.com/download/en/details.aspx?id=3045).

> We are only using the basic components to set this "minimalistic" scenario for VDI; as mentioned earlier, there are several roles and services that could be required for other functionalities: System Center Virtual Machine Manager, RDS gateway, RDS licensing, and so on.

Using this scenario, let's review the step-by-step process:

1. .Install and configure the Remote Desktop Services roles.
2. Assign and configure virtual desktops to RDS.
3. Test the environment.

# Installing and configuring RDS roles

The first step in this procedure starts with the configuration of the Remote Desktop Services roles in all hosts, to get this scenario functional:

1. Access the Hyper-V machine and open Server Manager to add the role.
2. The role we must select is **Remote Desktop Services | Remote Desktop Virtualization Host**; complete the wizard.

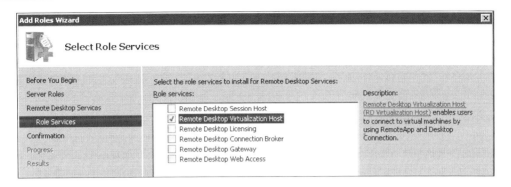

After completing the wizard, there's no reboot needed.

3. Access the Windows Server 2008 R2 virtual machine to configure the RDS roles using Server Manager.

4. The roles we should select in RDS are **Remote Desktop Session Host**, **Remote Desktop Connection Broker**, and **Remote Desktop Web Access**:

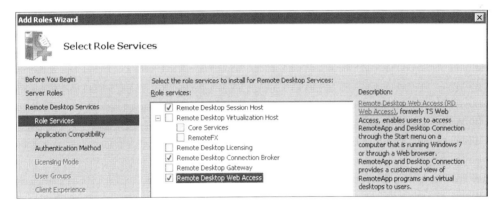

Since we are adding the web access role in RDS, we will require to install IIS with several features.

5. Complete the wizard, configuring **Authentication Method, Licensing Mode,** and **User Groups**.

6. In **Client Experience**, there's no need to configure anything in particular. The RDS Session Host will act as a redirector to the Windows 7 virtual machine; it will not provide any of the client experience to the user.

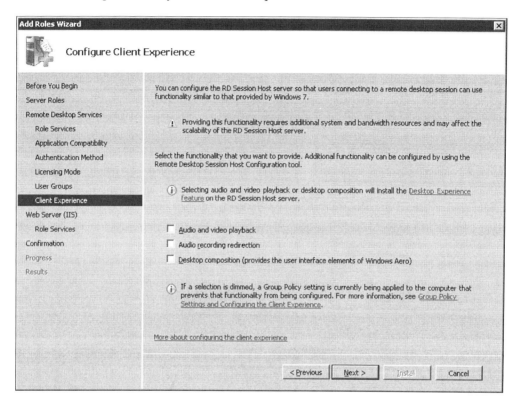

7. Finish the wizard and reboot the machine.

# Configuring and assigning virtual desktops to RDS

Once we've completed the **Add Roles Wizard** for RDS, we must configure the RDS
Connection Broker to include the recently configured Hyper-V virtualization host.
Next, we need to add and configure the virtual desktop to be included in the
RDS scenario.

1.  In the RDS server installed, access the **Remote Desktop Connection
    Manager** console.

2.  Click on **Configure Virtual Desktops**.

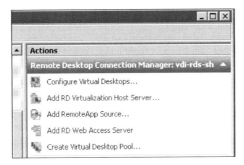

3.  In the new wizard, insert the name of the Hyper-V server and click on **Next**.

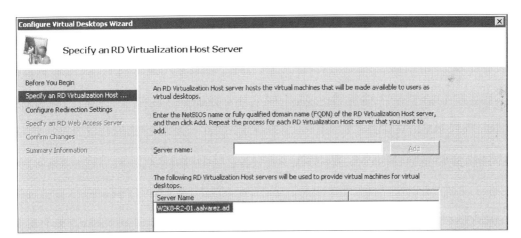

4.  In the next window, we need to configure the RDS Session Host that will act as the "redirector" to client requests. In this scenario, the server NetBIOS name is **vdi-rds-sh**.

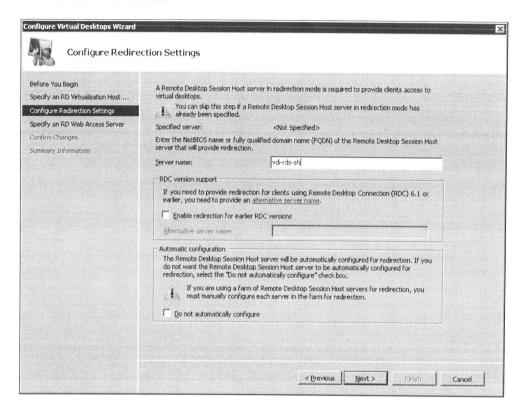

5.  In the following window, we must enter the RDS server that is in charge of providing web access to users. In this scenario, the same server provides that service.

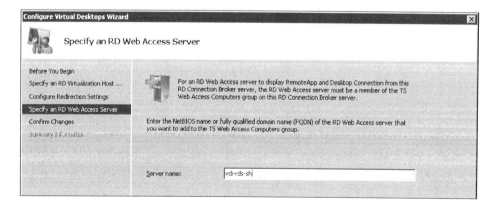

6. Confirm changes and click on **Apply**.

7. In the **Summary** window, we will get the result of the process. and by clicking **Finish** we also have the ability to start assigning virtual desktops.

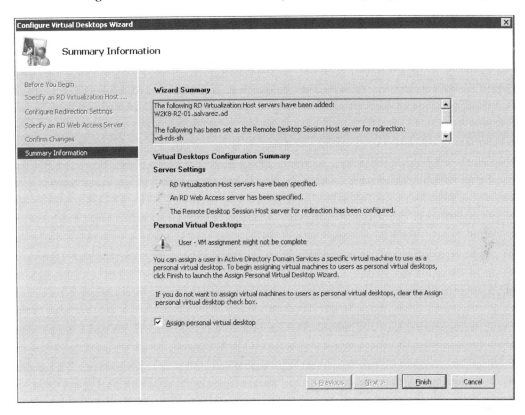

Prior to assigning desktops, the Windows 7 virtual machine must already be added to the Hyper-V server, and the name used in the Hyper-V console must be the same as the current FQDN.

In this scenario, the name used is **vdi-w7-01.aalvarez.ad**. If you use a different name, you cannot complete the assignment wizard.

8. Once we've clicked **Finish**, a new wizard will appear. Select the user that will have access to the virtual machine.

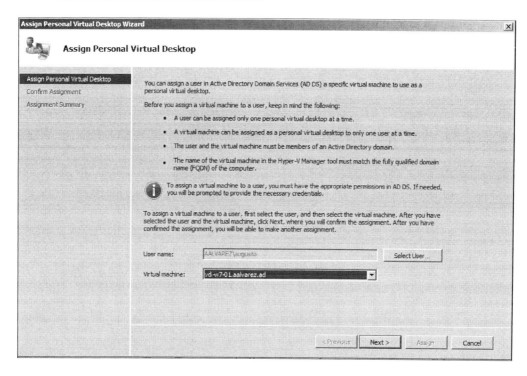

9. Confirm the assignment and complete the wizard.

   Before continuing with the process, there are a few customizations we have to execute in the client machine in order to get it ready to act as a virtual desktop.

   These tasks are: enabling RDP in the client machine, adding the RDP exception in the firewall, adding some RPC management interfaces for RDS to work smoothly with the Virtualization Host (Hyper-V).

   Fortunately, Microsoft provides a simple script to run in the virtual machine golden image to complete all these tasks with minor effort.

The script is available as VBS or as a PowerShell script. It can be accessed in Microsoft's Script Center http://technet.microsoft.com/en-US/scriptcenter/.

*Configure Guest OS for Microsoft VDI (VB Script)*: http://gallery.technet.microsoft.com/scriptcenter/68462b23-0890-4dbd-95b6-8de5763e4f68

*Configure Guest OS for Microsoft VDI (Windows PowerShell Script)*: http://gallery.technet.microsoft.com/ScriptCenter/bd2e02d0-efe7-4f89-84e5-7ad70f9a7bf0/

Group Policy Central additionally developed an interesting article about some considerations and recommendations in Group Policies to be applied to VDI clients. Look at the article *Best Practice: Group Policy for Virtual Desktops Infrastructure (VDI)* at http://www.grouppolicy.biz/2011/11/best-practice-group-policy-for-virtual-desktops-vdi/.

10. Copy any one of these two scripts and save it on the client machine.

11. Open an elevated command prompt and run the script. In this example, the VBS file is used:

If the script was executed successfully, then you should not see any output, as shown in the image.

One final configuration is necessary; RDS Web Access must be set to use RD Connection Broker as the provider to users for connections to virtual desktops..

12. Use a browser to access the RD website provided by our server with the RDS Web Access. In this scenario, the server is the same used for the other roles.

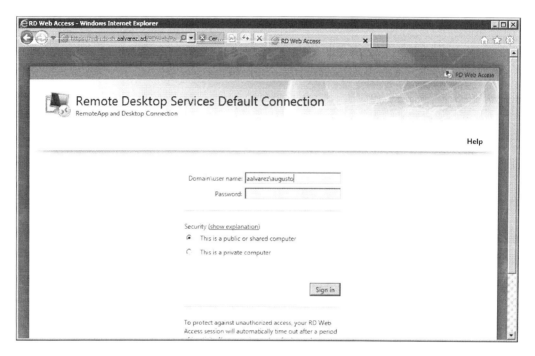

13. Log on to this site using an account that has privileges to manage the RDS configurations.

14. Click **Configuration**, and as source, select **An RD Connection Broker server** and insert the FQDN.

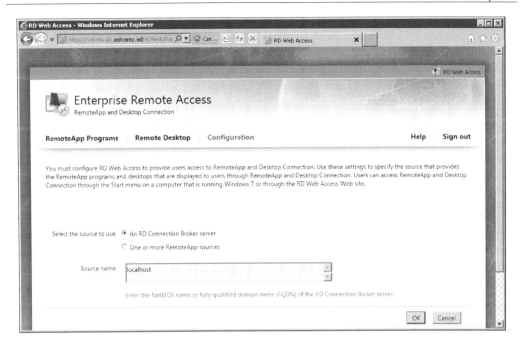

With that, we have our environment ready for virtual desktops.

In Microsoft's Script Center, we can find almost all possible tasks in a Microsoft platform to be executed as a script, including several tasks for VDI environments, such as automating virtual machine creation (a recurrent task in this scenario): *Create virtual machines for VDI* http://gallery.technet.microsoft.com/ScriptCenter/904bd2c8-099d-4f27-83da-95f5536233bc/.

# Testing the environment

With all the configurations in place, we only need to test the virtual desktop connections:

1. From any browser on the network, access the RD website.
2. Log on using an account with access to the RDS environment.

3. We should see now a **My Desktop** icon; click on it.

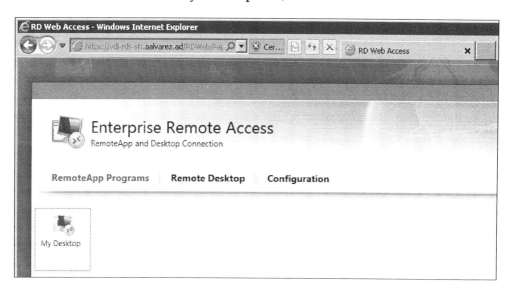

4. The virtual desktop is now available for us.

In this Windows 7 image, we have already installed the App-V client, and any user with the proper permissions will be able to download and execute the virtual applications presented by the App-V management server.

However, as we stated before, each virtual machine, working as a virtual desktop, will download and store in its App-V cache file the applications used for all the users that access this VDI environment; converting it in a very expensive scenario, considering the storage we need

If we want to optimize these resources, using the App-V shared cache feature is the best approach.

# Preparing and extracting the App-V client cache

As we mentioned earlier, the App-V cache is stored in one file: `sftfs.fsd`. Even though we can access this file as any other normal file in the App-V client, there are some considerations that we should be taking care of if we want to extract it properly.

The file is available by default at the following location: `C:\ProgramData\ Microsoft\Application Virtualization Client\SoftGrid Client`.

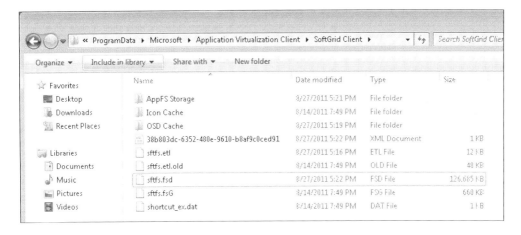

 The `ProgramData` folder is hidden by default, in Windows 7.

Since this file is permanently accessed by the App-V client agent right from the boot time, using and locking it in the virtual drive (our `Q:\`), we cannot just stop the App-V service and copy this file.

Here's a simple procedure to accomplish this:

1. Using a reference App-V client, verify that you've loaded all the applications that you would like to store in this cache file.

   If you are installing the App-V client for the first time, you can use the auto-load triggers to set it to automatically load all applications on login and/or to "Automatically load all applications", but it is recommended that this option be disabled when we are finishing our "golden image".

   Remember that we can use SFTMIME to load/unload applications into App-V cache:

   ```
   SFTMIME LOAD APP:application [/LOG log-pathname | /GUI]


   SFTMIME UNLOAD APP:application [/LOG log-pathname | /CONSOLE | /
   GUI]
   ```

2. Access the **Services** console in this App-V client and set **Application Virtualization Client** and **Application Virtualization Service Agent** to **Disabled**.

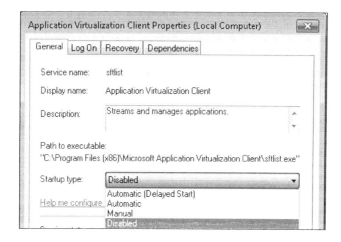

3. Reboot the client machine and verify both services are disabled and not started.

4. Locate the FSD cache file in the `ProgramData` folder and copy and paste it to the location where virtual desktop clients will be accessing it.

Now that we have the cache file available, we need to configure our Windows 7 with the golden image for VDI, to use this shared cache file.

# Configuring App-V clients for a shared cache

A shared cache is not configured by default, in App-V, for obvious reasons; and also, is not an easy-to-access option in App-V when we install the client. There are a few registry entries that we need to create in order to make this feature functional.

Regarding the location for the FSD file, the shared cache can be used in two different types of locations:

- **Network share**: We can place the FSD file in a UNC file that should be accessible to all clients. Using this option significantly affects the network usage between clients and the file server hosting the file, but it can be a viable option if clients have a separate network connected to the shared folder.

   Also, it is important to note that the clients' access to this shared file must be similar to accessing a hard drive, otherwise the usability and performance of the application will be impacted.

- **Mounted VHD drive**: The FSD file can be placed in a separate VHD that can be mounted onto the virtual machines hosting the VDI golden image. Using this ability, we avoid any impact on network usage.

   But again, we must carefully analyze the performance regarding read access to this mounted drive.

Here's the process we need to execute in our Windows 7 golden image for VDI:

1. From **Run,** type `regedit` and locate the following path: `HKEY_LOCAL_MACHINE\SOFTWARE\[Wow6432Node\]Microsoft\SoftGrid\4.5\Client\AppFS`.

   The values available must be something like this:

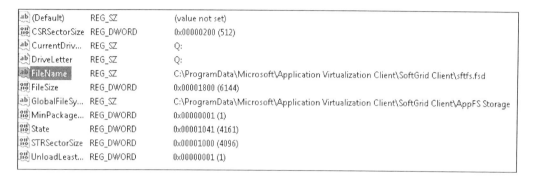

2. In the registry **FileName**, change the **Value data** to the location where the FSD file is located.

   A common best practice is to maintain this FSD file version to keep track of the updated versions of the App-V cache. In this example, a DFS location is used.

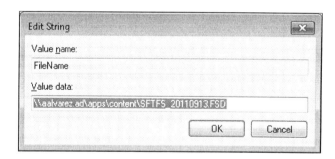

   In this case, we will be using the scenario we've reviewed earlier in the previous chapter with **Distributed File System (DFS)**.

3. In the same registry location, right-click and create a new **DWORD (32-bit) Value** App-V client:

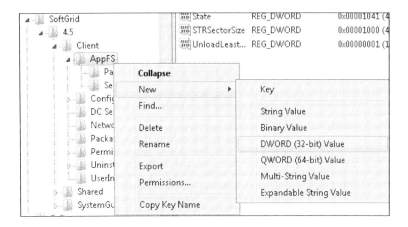

4. Insert the name **ReadOnlyFSD**, and in **Value data** use **1**.

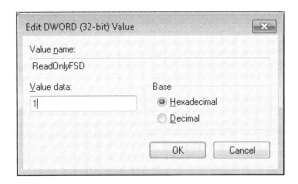

This value is created to configure the App-V client to use the cache file as read-only, guaranteeing consistency for all clients using this same file.

5. Create a new registry in the same path, this time as **String Value**.

6. Insert **ErrorLogLocation** as **Value name**, with a preferred local path to store the error log file. In this example, the folder **C:\Temp** is used, but it can be located in any desired location.

This last step is optional.

7. Now, with these changes applied, we should be looking at something like this:

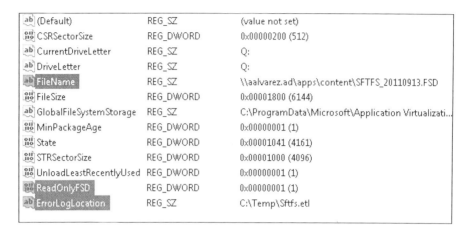

| (Default) | REG_SZ | (value not set) |
| CSRSectorSize | REG_DWORD | 0x00000200 (512) |
| CurrentDriveLetter | REG_SZ | Q: |
| DriveLetter | REG_SZ | Q: |
| FileName | REG_SZ | \\aalvarez.ad\apps\content\SFTFS_20110913.FSD |
| FileSize | REG_DWORD | 0x00001800 (6144) |
| GlobalFileSystemStorage | REG_SZ | C:\ProgramData\Microsoft\Application Virtualizati... |
| MinPackageAge | REG_DWORD | 0x00000001 (1) |
| State | REG_DWORD | 0x00001041 (4161) |
| STRSectorSize | REG_DWORD | 0x00001000 (4096) |
| UnloadLeastRecentlyUsed | REG_DWORD | 0x00000001 (1) |
| ReadOnlyFSD | REG_DWORD | 0x00000001 (1) |
| ErrorLogLocation | REG_SZ | C:\Temp\Sftfs.etl |

8. Since there are not going to be any "load" processes in the cache, it is highly recommended that you disable the **AutoLoadTriggers** and **AutoLoadTarget** options in all clients with a shared cache.

The registry keys can be found in HKEY_LOCAL_MACHINE\SOFTWARE\ [Wow6432Node\]Microsoft\SoftGrid\4.5\Client\Configuration:

- AutoLoadTriggers = 0
- AutoLoadTarget = 0

The App-V team blog in Microsoft TechNet also recommends to copy the OSD and icon files locally in the client operating systems used in VDI to increase the applications response at login, and some considerations about IPv6 and DFS.

Take a look at the *A VDI solution deployed using the Application Virtualization 4.6 SP1 client appears slow to login* article at http://blogs.technet.com/b/ appv/archive/2011/10/12/a-vdi-solution-deployed-using-the-application-virtualization-4-6-sp1-client-appears-slow-to-login.aspx.

With that, our Windows 7 golden image contains all the necessary changes to use the App-V client cache in our customized location with all the pre-loaded applications and is accessible as read-only.

To use this option consistently in all virtual desktops, we should re-use this Windows 7 golden image in our environment or reproduce these changes in all Windows 7 virtual machines available.

# Handling application and cache updates

As we've seen, we can configure the shared cache option to use it consistently in all our Windows 7 images in VDI, but since this feature obligates us to access this file as read-only, applying any changes could be a very painful task with most likely a significant downtime for all the applications.

There are some supported workarounds we can use in this scenario to maintain the consistency of the shared cache without affecting the general availability of the applications. This can be used using Microsoft's symbolic links.

Symbolic links are available in Windows Vista, Windows Server 2008, Windows 7, and Windows Server 2008 R2; basically, by creating a symbolic link we are creating a filesystem object that points to other filesystem objects.

For more information about symbolic links, take a look at this link in Microsoft MSDN: *Symbolic Links* (http://msdn.microsoft.com/en-us/library/aa365680(VS.85).aspx).

Using this option, we can create a symbolic link using a single name in our server; this will be stored as the read-only cache pointing to our current shared cache version. Let's take a look at the steps necessary:

1. In the server containing the FSD cache file, open an elevated command prompt.
2. Locate the path where the App-V cache is stored.

3. Type the following command:

```
mklink symboliclinkname symboliclinktarget
```

In this example, the command appears as follows:

```
mklink SFTFS.FSD SFTFS_20010913.FSD
```

4. Once the command line is executed, we should see our symbolic link created successfully as a simple file.

5. Change the **FileName** registry key we'd modified earlier to use the symbolic link instead of the versioned FSD file.

6. In the Windows 7 image, we must also enable the use of symbolic links. For that, open an elevated command prompt and type the following:

```
fsutil behavior set SymlinkEvaluation R2R:1
```

With these changes applied, every time we need to perform an update to the App-V client cache, we can execute it normally in a reference machine; store it as a versioned FSD file, and update the symbolic link to point to the new file.

In order to perform an update to the symbolic link, we need to first delete the existing file and re-create one using the same procedure shown previously.

> Windows XP does not support file symbolic links. But there's also the possibility of using NTFS junction points as a different workaround. For more information, check the Microsoft Knowledge Base article *How to create and manipulate NTFS junction points* at http://support.microsoft.com/?kbid=205524 and also Sysinternal's tool *Junction v1.06* at http://technet.microsoft.com/en-us/sysinternals/bb896768.aspx.

# Reviewing alternatives in App-V plus RDS integration

In my previous book *Getting Started with Microsoft Application Virtualization 4.6*, we had the chance to take a good look at the different types of integration between App-V and Remote Desktop Services (RDS), formerly known as **Terminal Services**.

RDS, as we have seen in this chapter, has a significant role in VDI environments, but Remote Desktop Services offers several features natively without requiring the use of VDI, and of course, using a shared cache is not the only way of integrating App-V into this kind of platform.

RDS platforms, which are largely implemented in several organizations, include the use of RemoteApp type of applications that have several similarities with App-V. In this section, we are going to examine and understand a little bit more about this.

# App-V versus RemoteApp

RemoteApp programs are applications installed in a RD Session Host server; from there, we can publish them to clients, and users can access these applications from their computers, seemingly as locally installed applications. RemoteApp is integrated directly into a user's desktop, running in a local window and with its own entry in the taskbar.

As for App-V, RemoteApp applications can run with other applications in the client's machine avoiding any conflicts or incompatibilities. We can access RemoteApp applications from a Start Menu (already published by an administrator), from an MSI file, or by using .rdp (Remote Desktop Protocol) files, also created and distributed by an administrator.

## Understanding App-V and RemoteApp differences

After reading this quick overview about RemoteApp, it sounds like it has all the common characteristics that we can find in virtualized applications with App-V. So, what are the differences?

| RemoteApp | App-V |
| --- | --- |
| Installed on RDS servers; published to clients | Sequenced on a similar desktop machine; delivered to clients |
| Uses remote resources (memory, processor, and so on.) | Uses local resources |
| Requires a server hosting the application | Does not require any server, just the package we need to deliver |
| No possibility of using offline applications, since we need an active connection to a server | Can be used for offline deployments |
| We need two servers if we want to publish incompatible applications using RDS (for example, Office 2007 and Office 2010) | We don't need any servers, just the sequenced applications |
| Published applications do not need compatibility with the client operating system | Applications are recommended to be captured and deployed in the same type of operating system |

Without question both technologies, RemoteApp and App-V, can save a lot of time and money. But before deciding on any of these two, we should evaluate, plan, and design the best approach in our deployment, considering also that we can combine App-V with RDS and RemoteApp.

# Combining App-V with Remote Desktop Services

Here are some of the reasons to use App-V along with RDS:

- **Delivering applications to the RDS servers using App-V simplifies the time and effort required to maintain these servers**: Users can directly use the App-V RDS client installed on the RDS server that will be in charge of receiving App-V packages.

- **App-V removes the need to install applications on servers**: RDS requires an existing and installed application on a server for publishing it, making this a risk we have to accept; using App-V, we just need to deliver these applications to the servers without installing any of them.

- **We can optimize resource utilization on our RDS platform**: In complex scenarios, we may need to publish incompatible applications using RDS, for example, HR members need Microsoft Office 2007 and management is using Microsoft Office 2010; for this, we need at least two separate RDS servers to install each of them.

  App-V RDS client can be installed on one RDS server, from where we can deploy both incompatible applications, and clients will still be using one server.

- **Simplified applications deployment:** Installing applications in RDS is a disruptive process. Users must log off and possibly do a server reboot. Using RDS with App-V, the process can be transparent for users, including updating an application.

- **Improving profile experience:** We can avoid the use of roaming profiles for users; App-V supports the redirection for application settings. We can force mandatory profiles (user environment not possible to be modified by users) for RDS clients, while redirecting App-V application data and settings to keep these changes consistent.

You can find the complete reference in the *App-V Remote Desktop Services* document available at the Microsoft Download Center: http://www.microsoft.com/downloads/en/default.aspx.

# Installing and configuring App-V Remote Desktop Services

Using App-V and Remote Desktop Services does not differ much from what we've seen so far in a normal App-V deployment.

The only component for which we need special installation is the App-V client, which uses different installation binaries available in , *Microsoft Application Virtualization Client for Remote Desktop Services*. The rest of the roles — App-V management server (including the management system and data store), Streaming Server, and App-V Sequencer — are exactly the same as we've seen earlier.

To achieve proper co-existence for these two platforms, there are some important matters we should consider and take note of before the implementation; here's a short overview.

## App-V RDS Client considerations

Using RDS, we still have the same deployment process for the App-V applications, but the environment where we will be working is not the same as we've seen earlier. For this reason, here are some of the points we should consider:

- Consider using a network location for the **User-specific Data Location** option. This is where App-V stores the changes made in the applications' packages for each user.

  The default option is the AppData folder of the user's local profile. But, if the scenario is using mandatory profiles, all of these changes will be lost and App-V redirection will be the best approach.

 Keep in mind that, for this redirection, it is highly recommended to use a network location near the clients, to optimize the use of bandwidth and maintain acceptable user experience.

- **Cache pre-load is usually a good approach in an RDS environment.**
- It is highly recommended to standardize the RD Session Host settings across our server farm, maintaining the same configurations on all the servers that we possibly can.

Starting with App-V 4.6 SP1, the shared cache feature is a supported configuration in RD Session host farms. Prior to SP1, this option was not supported. For more information about this, review the f *How to Configure a Read-only Cache on the App-V Client (RDS)* article at `http://technet.microsoft.com/ en-us/library/gg507632.aspx`.

# Deployment considerations

Microsoft provides a very complete and interesting table about some considerations we should evaluate when we are analyzing the applications' delivery methods to the Remote Desktop Servers.

You can find the complete reference in the *App-V Remote Desktop Services* document available in the Microsoft Download Center, at http://www.microsoft.com/ downloads/en/default.aspx.

| Deployment method | Supports user publishing | Supports computer publishing | Upgrade process | Preload App-V cache capability |
|---|---|---|---|---|
| Full Infrastructure with RTSP(s) | Yes | No | 1. Version updated on App-V Management Server<br>2. RD Session Host server placed in maintenance mode<br>3. First client opening the package will upgrade | No |
| Full Infrastructure with HTTP(s) or File Streaming | Yes | No | 1. Version updated on App-V Management Server<br>2. RD Session Host server placed in maintenance mode<br>3. Publishing refresh<br>4. First open of package will upgrade | No |
| Stand Alone Client (MSI) | No | Yes | 1. RD Session Host server placed in maintenance mode<br>2. New version of package MSI executed | Yes |

| Deployment method | Supports user publishing | Supports computer publishing | Upgrade process | Preload App-V cache capability |
|---|---|---|---|---|
| SCCM 2007 R2 | No | Yes | 1. RD Session Host server placed in maintenance mode | No |
| | | | 2. Configuration Manager 2007 R2 Advertisement executes | |
| SFTMIME | Yes | Yes | 1. RD Session Host server placed in maintenance mode | Yes |
| | | | 2. Updated package published with SFTMIME | |

An interesting thing to remember about application publishing is that, when we are working with RDS, if we are using computer publishing, the applications will be available for all users that are connected to the RD Server. User publishing will provide the granular permissions, permissions that are commonly necessary for most environments, only giving access to applications to the right RD clients.

# Publishing App-V applications with RemoteApp

As we've seen, RemoteApp publishes to clients normal installed program. App-V applications do not fit in the "normal" environment for RDS, that's why, if we are seeking application deployment of App-V packages using RemoteApp, it will require some extra configuration.

In this example, the DefaultApp application provided by App-V is used. Let's take a look:

1. Publish the App-V application to the RD Server.

2. Make sure you have copied the EXE or DLL file where the application stores the icons used (available in the Icons folder for the virtual package). This will be necessary to use each virtual application with the appropriate icon.

3. Access the properties from one of the shortcuts shown by the virtual application and copy the application name. The complete name plus version used appears right after the /launch parameter.

   In this case, that would be **DefaultApp MFC Application 1.0.0.1**.

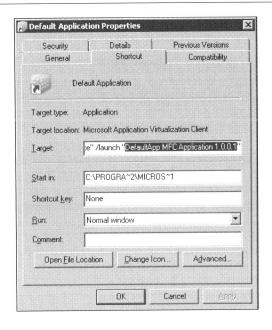

4. Open the **RemoteApp Manager** console and click on **Add RemoteApp programs**.

5. Search for the **Application Virtualization Client** folder located in **Program Files**.

6. Select the **sfttray.exe** file.

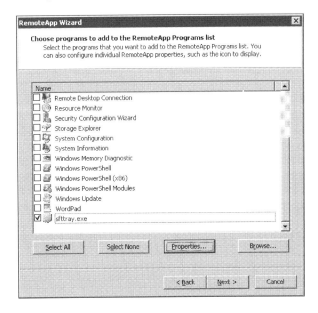

7. Click on **Properties**. Complete the name and alias for the application.

8. Select the **Always use the following command-line arguments** option and insert **/launch** *"Application Name"* (paste the value copied in step 3).

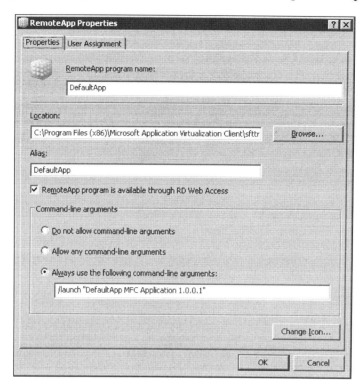

Use the **Change Icon** option to select the proper icon for the application. For that, you will need the EXE or DLL file copied earlier.

Click **OK**.

9. In the **RemoteApp** wizard, click **Next**.

With that, all we need to do is deploy the application using a .rdp or MSI file, or by just accessing it from a web browser. I'll be using the last option.

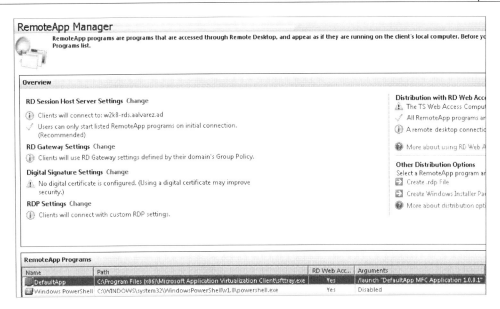

10. From an RD Client, access the web portal for Remote Desktop Services; we
should see **DefaultApp** available.

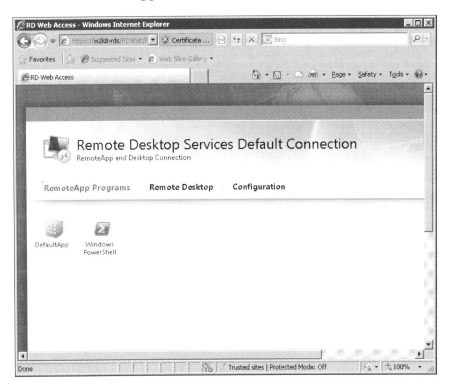

11. By clicking it, we will gain access to the application as if it were deployed locally.

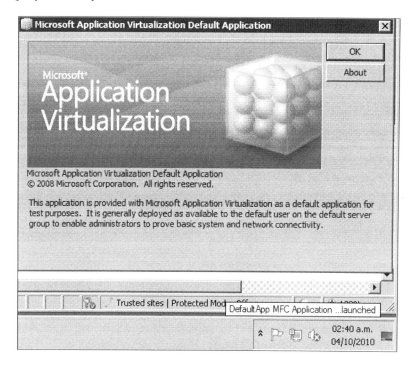

Furthermore, we can verify that the App-V client is also being used from the RD Server (in my case, the server name is w2k8-rds.aalvarez.ad) just by verifying the existing connection in the tray bar.

Using RemoteApp to publish App-V streamed-applications does not involve complex configurations, but it always needs some manual execution, making this not the more scalable solution available.

But, if we deployed App-V packages using SCCM 2007 R2 or an MSI file, these particular steps are not necessary, since the application should be available for selection in the RemoteApp wizard.

# Summary

In this chapter, we've gone through all we need to know about Virtual Desktop Infrastructure and the integrations with App-V. We also had the chance to take a look at the App-V integration with Remote Desktop Services and with RemoteApp programs.

In order to decide whether to integrate VDI and App-V or not, we must first understand all the components and architecture included with each of these platforms. VDI is not a simple technology; there are several variables attached and the cost involved is one of the most important reasons we should carefully analyze the scenario before making any decision.

Fortunately, App-V appears to be one of the main reasons organizations decide to use VDI. The integration, including the option of "shared cache", is vital to avoiding large costs for storage. Using a shared cache, we can reduce many TB of applications to a few GB, while gaining optimization of other resources, such as bandwidth and processor usage, all of which are essential in VDI.

In this chapter, we've also taken a good look at the technical processes included, to configure VDI using just a few resources, extract the App-V cache, and configure the shared cache feature in App-V clients. We've also revised the possibilities when we need to update efficiently this read-only cache file. Finally, in this chapter, we saw that shared cache is not the only way we can integrate App-V with Remote Desktop Services technologies. RDS also includes RemoteApp as a similar approach to App-V, and these two can be combined for a more efficient way to handle the infrastructure of our applications.

In the next chapter, we are going to review a new kind of App-V integration, using System Center Configuration Manager 2012.

# 8
# Integrating App-V with System Center Configuration Manager 2012

Optimizing our infrastructure and operations is a concept that we have revisited several times within this book. **System Center Configuration Manager (SCCM)** is a platform vastly used in several organizations with the purpose of this optimization, and with its new version, we now have several improvements in management and operations.

**App-V** integration is also an important topic that we must consider, analyze, design, and implement, if we already have the Configuration Manager platform in place. If we choose App-V as the desired solution for handling the application's lifecycle, we must consider SCCM as an important part in this solution.

Even though these two platforms were designed not only for integration but also to be deployed as highly scalable platforms, there are some considerations that we should carefully review in the process. And since SCCM appears in the application's deployment process, we must understand some of its capabilities and how they differ from an App-V implementation without any coexistence.

With the analysis completed, we can easily evaluate it, as this integration is quite a powerful solution. SCCM 2012 and its new enhancements tremendously facilitate application management and enhance user experience, not only for the IT administrator but also the final end user.

In this chapter, we are going to cover the following:

- Understanding SCCM 2012 and its new functionalities

- Reviewing the benefits of, and considerations regarding, the SCCM+ App-V integration

- Naming the components involved in this integration and the application delivery methods present

- Implementing the SCCM + App-V integration (starting with the SCCM 2012 installation and how to distribute the App-V Client to clients)

- Creating and deploying virtual applications using SCCM 2012

# SCCM 2012

**System Center Configuration Manager 2012** is the new version of this robust and scalable solution from Microsoft.

SCCM is in charge of defining your organization structure in order to improve most of our operational tasks in the IT platform, such as software deployment, compliance settings management, and comprehensive asset management of servers, desktops, laptops, and mobile devices.

The basic functionality of SCCM is to work with client agents (discovered initially and commonly using Active Directory), which are deployed to users' devices. These components are then put in an inventory for both hardware and installed software. This data is stored in a central database, and that data is then used to target application deployments to collections of client computers or users.

Some of the common tasks we can perform and integrate with SCCM are software lifecycle management, operating systems deployment, patch management, guaranteeing clients security compliance by integrating it with the **Network Access Protection (NAP)** platform, and so on.

## SCCM 2012 improvements

System Center Configuration Manager 2012 introduces significant changes to its predecessor, SCCM 2007 R3. To summarize, the main focus of the new features is *the user*, not only the administrator in charge of managing the platform. SCCM 2012 now contains a far simpler UI, and the final user has an improved interaction with the SCCM resources available.

Let's review the main improvements in SCCM 2012:

- **Improved Management Console**: This feature is likely to surprise you the most, at first, since it has a fresh, new, and considerably different design, as compared to what we've seen in earlier versions.

  The Management Console is divided into four sections: **Administration**, **Software Library**, **Monitoring**, and **Assets** and **Compliance**. The new console also adds a nice-looking ribbon at the top with all the basic operations, and most of the basic tasks have been regrouped in order to facilitate usage.

  We can assure you that the new SCCM 2012 console will give administrators an incredibly improved experience.

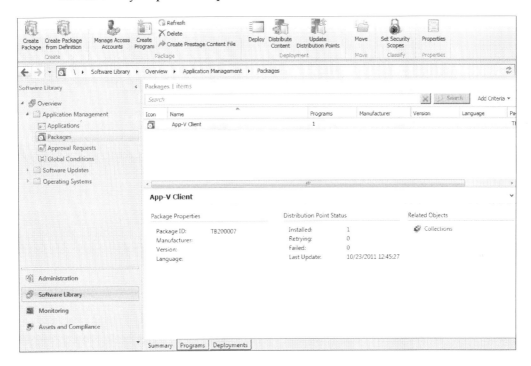

- **Improved setup options**: The installation steps are configured to run with simplified options, but the main improvement here is the option **Site Recovery** included in **Setup Wizard**.

- **Including Software Center as the main end-user interaction interface**: SCCM 2012 includes the SCCM client in a portal where users can handle their resources, provided by Configuration Manager. Using **Software Center** users now have more control of the software they have available in all of its devices (laptops, desktop or smartphone). Within Software Center, users can also request new applications.

- **New and enhanced options for applications management**: There are several new features included in all the lifecycles of applications, for example, multiple deployment instances of the same application—one application can include different ways to deploy it—handling a virtual package for one device but full binaries in another device.

- **Retirement**: SCCM 2012 uses application retirement for all applications. This "retirement" option was only available for virtual applications in SCCM 2007 R2/R3.

- **Requirements and dependencies**: We can set different types of requirements to deploy an application, for example, number of processors available, memory, free disk space, existing registry key, and so on. We can now also use other applications as dependencies.

- **Supporting smartphones natively**: SCCM includes the possibility of managing smartphones in our organization, not only for the Windows Phone series but also Symbian and Nokia devices. This new feature (essential for several organizations) appeared basically because Microsoft offered, without much success, a previous version for smartphone management—System Center Mobile Device Manager. This platform is included in SCCM 2012, natively.

- **Infrastructure and roles improvements**: There are several changes in the infrastructure itself in SCCM 2012. It is now simpler than the previous version. Some of the changes are as follows:

  - Central Administration sites can't have any users assigned. This role is only used to manage replication and for management hierarchy tasks between sites.

  - Sites are no longer configured for mixed or native mode, instead you secure client communication endpoints by configuring individual site system roles to support client connections over HTTPS or HTTP.

  - Client agent settings are now defined at the collection level, instead of at the site level.

  - Content distribution is now the responsibility of SQL Server replication.

- **SCCM 2012 is a 64-bit only platform**: It can only run in Windows Server 2008 64-bit version or Windows Server 2008 R2. For the database instance, SQL Server 2008 or SQL Server 2008 R2 in 64-bit are supported (to be discussed later—the SP and update level of each).

The System Center Configuration Manager distribution points role can still run in 32-bit.

As we can see, there are tons of improvements in this new platform and several others that we don't have the chance to review just yet. For more information about these changes, please read *What's New in Configuration Manager* at `http://technet.microsoft.com/en-us/library/gg699359.aspx`.

# Reviewing SCCM and App-V integration

Integrating the System Center Configuration Manager with App-V is much simpler with the new versions of these two platforms. Let's review some of the benefits, considerations, delivery methods, and components required.

# Benefits of integrating SCCM and App-V

There are several benefits of using SCCM and App-V as an integrated platform instead of separate technologies. Let's review some of the most important ones:

- **Optimizing your infrastructure**: If we have already implemented SCCM in our environment, not integrating with App-V could translate into larger costs for management, troubleshooting, complexity, and hardware. Since we will need to implement the Streaming Server functionality separately from distribution points, this role in Configuration Manager can fulfill the streaming process without acquiring big changes in our implementation.

- **Improving client targeting**: System Center Configuration Manager brings you the possibility of deploying normal and virtual applications with an enhanced level of targeting, depending on collections and capabilities of the systems involved.

  There are several possibilities of "client targeting" we can include while deploying virtual applications. For example, dependencies on other applications and client requirements, such as memory available, processor type, and so on.

- **Complementing App-V with SCCM assessments**: App-V includes user targeting for their packages. By integrating with Configuration Manager, we can combine these possibilities with software metering, asset intelligence, and **Wake-on-LAN** features for the deployment of the virtual applications.

- **Virtual applications delivery as a complement in Operating System Deployment**: One of the most important features in SCCM is **Operating System Deployment (OSD)**, which can be combined and scaled up with other features, such as Software Updates, software and hardware inventory, targeting for implementing operating system drivers, and so on. Using App-V, we can deliver applications as soon as the operating system is deployed, saving considerable time to deliver a ready-to-go operating system.

- **Background delivery of App-V applications**: In unstable or slow networks, BITS protocol can be leveraged, allowing application delivery as network connections permit. The SCCM client performs the download of the App-V application into the SCCM cache from where it is then imported into the App-V cache. This offers much more flexible application delivery but comes with a storage penalty on the client. The application will exist in both the SCCM and App-V client cache and cannot be purged from the SCCM client cache. This means in this delivery model that there is at least a doubling of the storage required on the client for this delivery model.

# Some considerations about the integration

SCCM does not provide the exact functionalities we can find in the native App-V components implemented. The idea of SCCM integration is to complement the App-V platform. But, because of the Configuration Manager architecture, there are some considerations we should review.

Most of the integration features remain undocumented by Microsoft at the moment, but analyzing the infrastructure using the Beta and Release Candidate version of SCCM 2012 appears to maintain basic architecture definitions better than the previous version—SCCM 2007 R2/R3. Here are some of the considerations we can find so far:

- **We must re-advertise an application when there's an Active upgrade**: As we've mentioned before, **Active upgrade** is the process that we run in an App-V package to update the application using a **service pack** or any other type of modification. The App-V Full Infrastructure model automatically delivers the new version to clients. SCCM does not handle updates in the same package as a delta that must be delivered to clients, so we will need to make a new advertisement every time there's a virtual application update.

- **Reduced reporting**: App-V Full Infrastructure provides a very important set of reports about our virtual application that we can execute and retrieve; Configuration Manager does not provide the same level of reporting. Using Local Delivery (as used earlier) as the preferred method for delivering applications, it is not possible to report on how many times an application has been used.

- **Targeting applications for Remote Desktop Services requires users to log off and log on in their sessions**: This is not only a limitation for virtual applications; it applies to all Configuration Manager Clients' user targeted and/or user interaction with the SCCM client. The SCCM client only allows software distribution to the console session of a terminal server system (`mstsc.exe /console`). Therefore, if application delivery targets users that are using a remote session on the terminal services system, they will not be able to execute the advertisement.

- **Asset Intelligence** (for reporting and inventory features): This feature in SCCM requires `Feature Block 1` present in the virtual application to be streamed to clients. Asset Intelligence cannot inventory virtual applications that co-exist with the same version of an application installed locally. As we mentioned, virtual applications live within their own environment, making it possible for the same application to work as locally installed and virtually deployed. If that's the scenario, Asset Intelligence won't inventory this App-V application.

- In order to use **Dynamic Suite Composition** (**DSC**) in virtual applications, both interconnected packages must be advertised and registered with the App-V Client. That's why using the delivery method **Local Delivery** (downloading and execution), to be discussed later, is the recommended option when we are using DSC.

  We can also use dependencies in SCCM to guarantee that both packages can be delivered normally.

# Components involved

In this integration, we must understand which components are interacting in these two platforms:

- **App-V Sequencer**: The process of capturing it is the same, and we don't need to introduce any changes in that phase

- **SCCM Site Server**: In charge of managing and handling the actions performed by the SCCM Distribution Points

- **SCCM Distribution Point**: Storing and distributing the App-V applications

- **SCCM client**: This client agent communicates with System Center Configuration Manager and receives virtual applications

- **App-V Client**: SCCM Client and App-V Client work together — the SCCM Client delivers the virtual application to the App-V Client, which has the responsibility of executing it

# Understanding delivery methods

Using SCCM to deploy virtual applications includes two types of delivery methods that we can use to fit any specific scenario. These two delivery methods are the same that appeared in the App-V + SCCM 2007 integration (covered in my previous book *Getting Started with Microsoft Application Virtualization 4.6*).

The delivery methods remain the same, but SCCM 2012 adds some twists to the configurations that we can achieve, using some options that we are going to review later, such as *Persist content in the client cache* and *Enable peer-to-peer content distribution*.

Applying the different delivery methods will basically depend on the type of connectivity the client machine has with the SCCM distribution point, converting this integration into a highly scalable one since we can discriminate the type of user with a specific type of streaming delivery.

Let's go through each type; they are **Streaming Delivery** and **Local Delivery** (downloading and execution).

## Streaming Delivery

This delivery method represents the one similar to that which we discussed in *Chapter 1, Taking a Deep Dive into App-V* about **Electronic Software Distribution (ESD)**. As we discussed, this is a role we can install on a server that will execute nothing more than delivering applications; this server can be a System Center Configuration Manager Server configured for Streaming Delivery.

When using this delivery method, the App-V Client will be configured to receive applications using HTTP/HTTPS (**Standard Distribution Point**) or **SMB (Branch Distribution Point)** streaming.

Delivery in the streaming mode occurs as shown in the following screenshot:

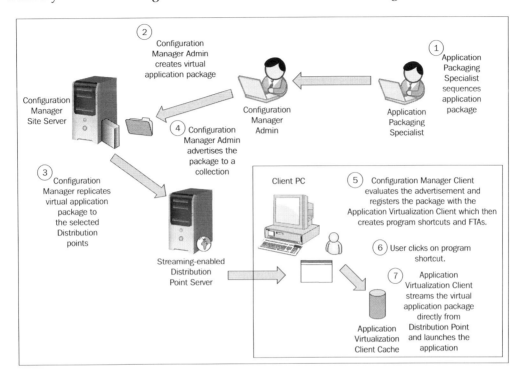

In this process, we can evaluate the entire workflow in the Streaming Delivery, from the moment the application is sequenced. These set of steps should be familiar to us if we already know and understand how a Streaming Server works with virtual applications, but note the following:

- The App-V Client does not stream an application until one of the shortcuts of this application is double-clicked

- Once the streaming process has started, the same behavior occurs at first— `Feature Block 1` is delivered from the SCCM Distribution Point to the App-V client cache

- Once the application is running, the rest of the package is streamed down by the App-V Client

The Streaming Delivery method must be considered when the clients and servers live on the same LAN; remember that the streaming process requires high-bandwidth connections. Another good example of using this method is when we have applications that are constantly updated, and the updates occur in the Distribution Point that delivers the new package to clients. Avoid using this method when we have several offline users.

# Local Delivery (downloading and execution)

The Local Delivery (downloading and execution) method is self-explanatory. The initial task is executed by the client who downloads the application and complete package, and then executes it.

In this downloading process, the application is delivered to the SCCM client cache, and then the SFT file is streamed from the SCCM clients' cache into the App-V clients' cache. Basically, the SCCM client works as a local Streaming Server for the App-V Client.

Delivery in this mode occurs as shown in the following screenshot:

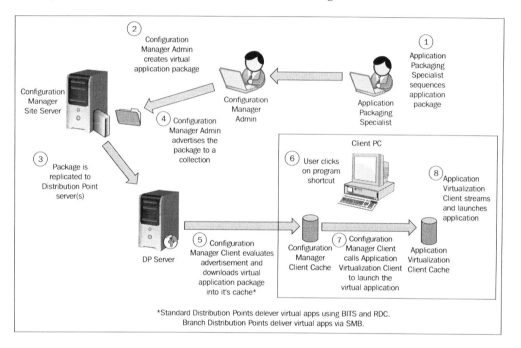

*Standard Distribution Points delever virtual apps using BITS and RDC.*
*Branch Distribution Points deliver virtual apps via SMB.*

In this process workflow, we can clearly see how the SCCM Client is in charge of downloading the entire content of the package as soon as it's advertised. The App-V Client streams the application to the cache from the SCCM Client cache, and then it completes the launch process only when the user clicks on any of the shortcuts from the application.

The application stays in the App-V cache, ready to be launched, as long as the advertisements in Configuration Manager are maintained.

Local Delivery is the best approach when we are using slow networks between servers and clients, and of course for offline users, who can work normally with the application, even when they are not connected to the network.

Local Delivery also needs a considerable amount of storage, three times the size of the application package: one for the SCCM Client, another for the App-V Client, and the third one is stored for calculating differentials when the application receives an update.

# App-V Client and the OverrideURL setting

As we reviewed, in both delivery methods the SCCM client streams down the published applications to the App-V client cache; to accomplish this, the App-V Client includes a new registry value `OverrideURL`.

This value can be changed to use an alternate server in charge of delivering the virtual applications. All of this process is transparent to the user; the value is changed by the SCCM client and the streaming process is redirected to the Configuration Manager Distribution Point in charge of the delivery.

This is a simple diagram where we can see the interaction between the SCCM Client and the App-V Client:

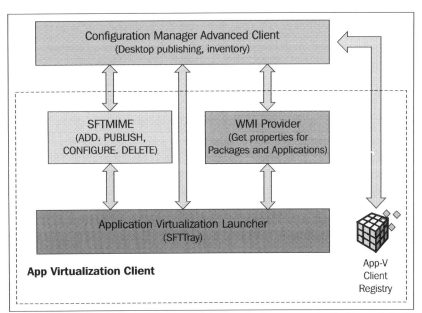

Image used from Microsoft official guide "Virtual Application Management with Microsoft Application Virtualization 4.5/4.6 and System Center Configuration Manager 2007 R2".

Even though this concept appeared in the integration of App-V and SCCM 2007 R2, the basic functionality remains in this new version SCCM. By reviewing the deployment of App-V applications using SCCM, we can confirm that the OverrideURL behavior is maintained. There's an example of the **Winamp** virtual application (deployment reviewed later in this chapter) and the registry settings in the App-V Client.

The **OriginalURL** setting displays the configuration used in the OSD, and the **OverrideURL** uses the SFT location in the SCCM Client cache:

| Name | REG_SZ | Winamp |
|---|---|---|
| OriginalURL | REG_SZ | RTSP://appv-server:554/Winamp.sft |
| OverrideURL | REG_SZ | FILE://c:\windows\ccmcache\content_5dc317e8-23f1-44cf-adc5-ea2abf7cf679.1.system |
| PkgURL | REG_SZ | FILE://c:\windows\ccmcache\content_5dc317e8-23f1-44cf-adc5-ea2abf7cf679.1.system |

# Requirements for the SCCM + App-V integration

In order to accomplish this smooth integration without adding significant load to our operations, we must understand each of the requirements involved.

The requirements do not differ much from what we've seen earlier in SCCM 2007 R2, which is an important advantage if we already have this platform implemented and are considering migrating to SCCM 2012.

The two important requirements we are going to analyze are: platform requirements in SCCM 2012 and storage requirements for sizing the SCCM client cache.

## Platform requirements in SCCM 2012

Even though it could sound pretty obvious at this point, always remember that having a healthy environment in SCCM is an important requirement before starting with changes in the environment.

Regarding System Center Configuration Manager 2012 components, the basic platform requirements are as follows:

- **Primary site**
- **Site Server**: A Site Server with the following roles installed:
    - Site System
    - Site Server
    - Component Server

- ° Distribution Point
- ° Fallback Status Point
- ° Management Point
- ° Reporting Point

- **Distribution Points**: At least one available and working Distribution Point, with IIS and streaming enabled for BITS application delivery, is required. This server will be in charge, of course, of the package distribution.

- **Clients**: SCCM clients must be installed and work properly. We'll review how to push clients' agents in SCCM 2012, later in this chapter.

For more information about **Site System Servers** and **Site System Roles**, refer to the following article in Microsoft TechNet: *Fundamentals of Configuration Manager* (`http://technet.microsoft.com/en-us/library/gg682106.aspx`).

# Storage requirements

The storage requirements for SCCM 2012 + App-V remain the same as the SCCM 2007 integration.

These considerations depend primarily on the type of the delivery method chosen in the environment. As for the App-V environment, we must size the storage considering clients, App-V cache, and server distribution points in SCCM. A general guideline for the storage requirements is as follows:

- SCCM Client cache must be configured considering the full size of the App-V packages to be distributed.

- It is recommended to size the App-V client cache considering the SCCM client cache defined. The App-V client cache should be configured with a free disk space threshold option, adding 1 GB more to the SCCM client cache value.

  When using an SCCM Client cache with 4 GB, the App-V Client cache should be configured with a free disk space threshold of 9 GB.

- SCCM Distribution Points should allocate space considering the size of the package multiplied by three. The triple-sizing consideration, as said, depends on the delivery method, current version of the package, upgrade version, App-V client cache version, or differential files while constructing an upgraded version of the package.

In the official guide provided by Microsoft, *Virtual Application Management with Microsoft Application Virtualization 4.5/4.6 and System Center Configuration Manager 2007 R2*, we can find a complete reference about all the necessary requirements, including the storage considerations. We can download this guide from the Microsoft Download Center, at `http://www.microsoft.com/downloads/en/default.aspx`.

> To configure the SCCM Client cache, we can check the following official article by Microsoft: *How to Manage Clients in Configuration Manager* (`http://technet.microsoft.com/en-us/library/gg712288.aspx`). See the section titled *Configure the Client Cache for Configuration Manager Clients*.

# Implementing SCCM and App-V integration

Finally, after reviewing all the benefits, requirements, and considerations about the integration, it is time to get our hands into the SCCM 2012 and App-V integration.

As mentioned earlier, the scope of this chapter will not focus on understanding how to use the System Center Configuration Manager platform, but we'll take a closer look at the basic operations tasks, such as handling SCCM client installations.

In this section, we are going to review the following topics and step-by-step procedures:

- Installing System Center Configuration Manager 2012
- Distributing the App-V Client with SCCM 2012
- Using virtual applications in SCCM
- Creating virtual applications
- Deploying virtual applications

# Installing SCCM 2012

This section will consist of an overview of SCCM 2012 installation using the **Release Candidate** bits of SCCM.

## SCCM 2012 requirements

Configuration Manager is a robust platform and must be analyzed and sized carefully in every environment. In this example, we will be using a minimalist scenario.

For the primary site, the following configuration is required:

- Active Directory and DNS platform in place and working properly
- Installing SCCM requires an Active Directory schema extension (the same extension used in SCCM 2007)
- If the current AD platform was already extended for SCCM 2007, there's no need to extend it again

 For more information about this matter, please see the article *Determine Whether to Extend the Active Directory Schema for Configuration Manager*, at http://technet.microsoft.com/en-us/library/gg712272.aspx.

- Windows 7 client machines
- For the SCCM 2012 Primary Site, general requirements for installation are the following:
  - Memory: 2 GB minimum; 4 GB or more recommended
  - Windows Server 2008 R2
  - IIS role installed with the following features:
    - Common HTTP features: Static Content, default document, directory browsing, HTTP errors, and HTTP redirection
    - Application Development: ASP.NET, .NET Extensibility, ISAPI Extensions, and ISAPI Filters
    - Health and Diagnosis: HTTP logging, logging tools, and **Request Monitor Tracing**
    - Security: Windows Authentication and Request Filtering
    - Performance: **Static Content Compression**
    - Management Tools: IIS Management Console, IIS Management Scripts and Tools, IIS 6 Metabase Compatibility, and IIS 6 WMI Compatibility

- The following features also have to be added:
    - ° .NET Framework 3.5.1
    - ° **Background Intelligent Transfer Service (BITS)**
    - ° Remote Differential Compression
    - ° SQL instance available with one the following characteristics:
        - ° **SQL Server 2008 SP2 with Cumulative Update 6**
        - ° **SQL Server 2008 R2 SP1 and Cumulative Update 3**

**IMPORTANT:**

These requirements are based on a simple and minimalistic SCCM 2012 implementation; depending on the installation type and SCCM roles involved, the requirements at this stage will vary.

There are other optional components available, which are not present because of the scope of this book. For example, **Windows Server Updates Services (WSUS)**.

For more information about requirements in SCCM 2012, please visit the following Microsoft TechNet link: *Supported Configurations for Configuration Manager* (http://technet.microsoft.com/en-us/library/gg682077.aspx).

# Installing SCCM 2012

Let's review the step-by-step process for installing **System Center Configuration Manager 2012 Beta 2**:

1. Launch the **Install** option in the SCCM 2012 setup window.
2. The option we are going to use is **Install Configuration Manager Primary Site server**.

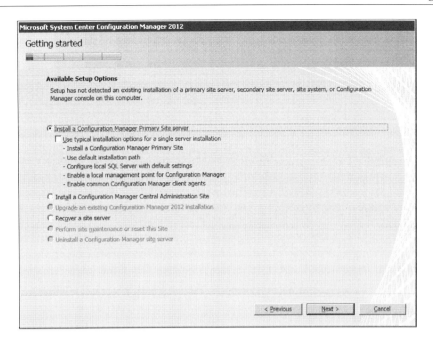

3.  In the setup process, SCCM 2012 (as well as its predecessor) requires a folder where the platform will download the latest updates for Configuration Manager.

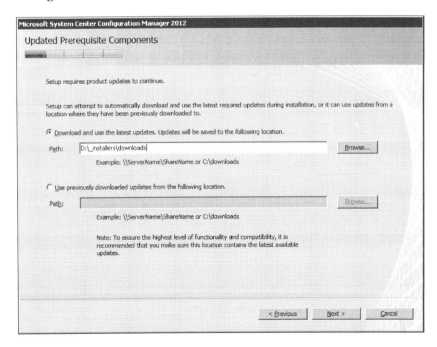

4.  Configure the site information necessary for the Primary Site configurations—**Site Code** and **Site Name**. Also, leave the option for **Install Admin Console** selected.

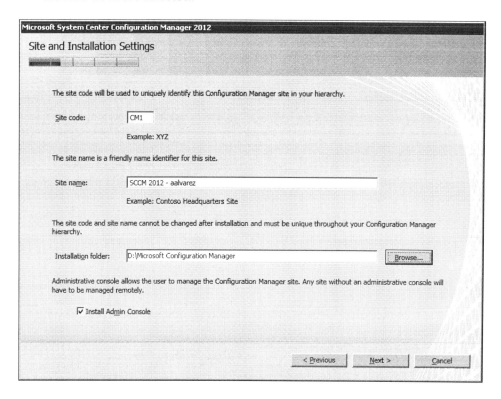

5.  Since this is the first SCCM Server and there's no existing Central Site, select the option, **Primary site will be installed as a standalone site**.

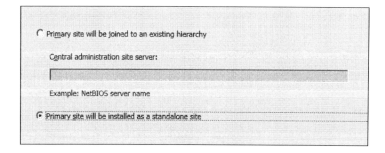

**Central Sites** do not process any client data, do not accept client assignments, and only have some certain functionality related to coordinate sites replications.

For more information about site differences in SCCM 2012, please refer to *What's New in Configuration Manager*, at `http://technet.microsoft.com/en-us/library/gg699359.aspx`.

6. Configure the database server. Remember that the only SQL instances supported in this version are SQL Server 2008 SP2 with Cumulative Update 6 and SQL Server 2008 R2 with SP1 and Cumulative Update 3.

There have been some changes between the SQL supportability in the SCCM 2012 Beta versions and the Release Candidate. There could be some changes for the RTM version also, but there is no official word from Microsoft about it.

7. Enter the NetBIOS name for the server where the SMS provider will be installed; in this case, it is the same server.

8. In **Client Computer Communication Settings,** choose for client machines to be able to use HTTP and HTTPS for communication. Remember that HTTPS communications require a healthy PKI infrastructure in all servers and clients. However, that topic goes beyond the scope of this book.

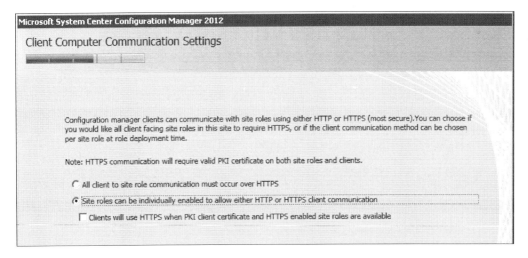

9.  Make sure also that **Management Point** and **Distribution Point** are using **HTTP** for communication.

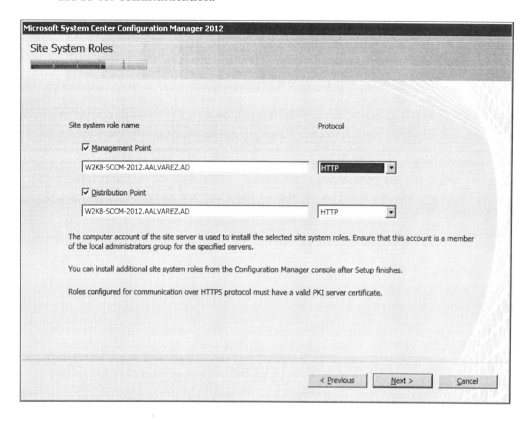

10. Complete the wizard to start installation. The process will take a while, so be patient.

Once the installation is complete, we will be able to appreciate a refreshed SCCM console with some great UI improvements and also standardize the entire System Center suite to fit with the same configuration.

SCCM 2012 includes four panes from which we can handle the entire suite: **Administration**, **Software Library**, **Monitoring**, and **Assets and Compliance.**

Within **Administration**, we can find all the options for managing the SCCM infrastructure (sites, client options, security, distribution points, and so on). Some of the initial tasks we can perform are about the discovery options from which clients will be presented.

For example, using **Active Directory System Discovery**, SCCM will find client machines by searching for computer objects in AD Domain Services.

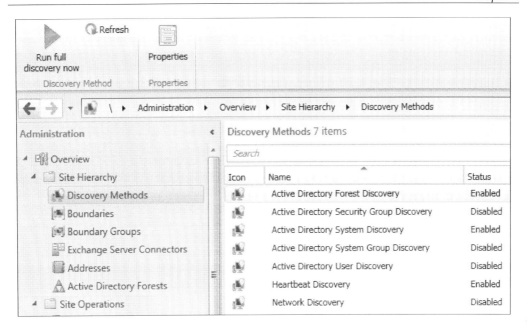

Under **Site Operations**, we can review all the sites we have configured in our platform, accessing each site's properties we can configure general parameters involved in that scope, including for example, the ports used by Configuration Manager to communicate with clients.

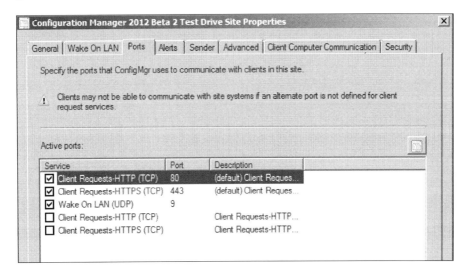

Within **Site Operations**, there are several client configurations available; one important one is **Client Installation Settings**, from which we can define how the **Configuration Manager Client** agent (necessary in SCCM) will be installed.

If you wish to install the client agent as soon as the computers are discovered, check **Enable automatic site-wide client push installation**. Take note that, if we have several machines deployed in our **Active Directory** domain, this action can be network-intensive.

For manual deployments of the Configuration Manager, we can use the **Assets and Compliance** pane. In **Devices**, we have all the default collections created, and in **All Systems**, we can find the discovered computers.

In this example, we will be using a created collection, **Windows 7**, which contains one computer: **W7-CLIENT**.

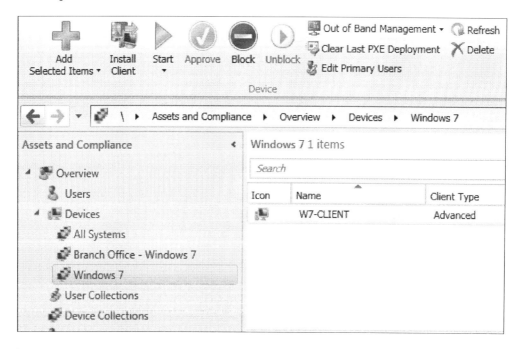

By selecting **Install Client**, we will receive a new wizard to confirm the SCCM Client installation. In this example, we will be using the specific site of **Configuration Manager 2012 Beta 2** (pre-configured VHD available from Microsoft).

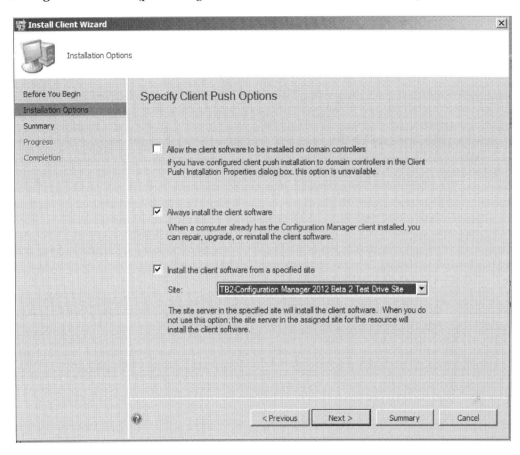

This task can usually take several minutes to complete, depending on several factors. If you've had the chance to work with SCCM previously, you'll know that this kind of task is never completed immediately.

Still, we can review the latest status of each client in the same console. In the **Push Information** section, we will retrieve the latest status of the client installation.

# Distributing the App-V Client with SCCM 2012

Since the SCCM 2012 platform is installed and the client agents are deployed successfully, we are going to learn how to install the App-V Client in a given SCCM Collection, in this section.

SCCM 2012 provides a new experience in UI for handling applications and packages, but basically, the steps for deploying the App-V Client will not differ much if we have already completed them in SCCM 2007.

In this example, we will use the `setup.exe` file, which installs the prerequisites in the same process. The file `setup.msi` can be used separately, but the prerequisites must also be installed separately.

> Distributing the App-V Client using SCCM is not necessary for the integration to take place; this is an optional step and should not be considered if the App-V Client is already installed in all clients.
>
> Once the SCCM client is installed for all the virtual applications distributed with SCCM, the necessary configurations will be completed automatically.

Let's look at the process for adding and installing the App-V Client package:

1. Within the **Software Library** pane, we have several options available, since this "application" contains several files necessary to completing a successful installation. Under **Application Management**, right-click **Packages** and select **Create Package**, as shown in the following screenshot:

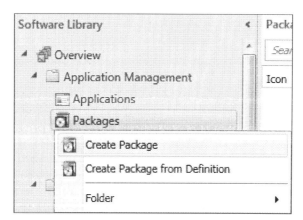

2. Specify the package name, and enable the **This package contains source files** option.

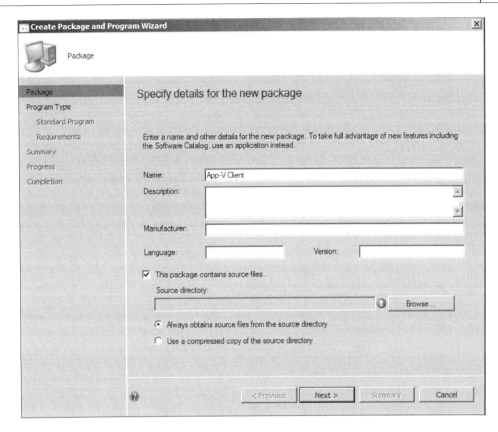

3. In **Set Source Directory**, select the UNC path for the installation files.

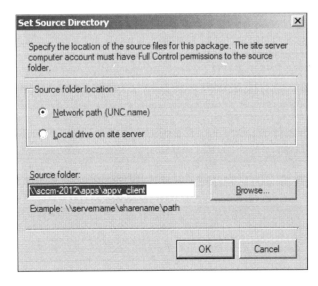

One great improvement in SCCM usability is how we use the **Programs** assets, which are basically the command lines to be used for deploying packages or scripts.

Using SCCM 2012, as soon as we try to add a package, we will be asked to insert a new program (previously, this program had to be created separately).

4. In **Program Type**, select **Standard Program**.

5. Select the program command line and other parameters. Since I'm using the .exe file, the command line used is `setup.exe /s /v"/qb-! SWICACHESIZE=\"6144\"`.

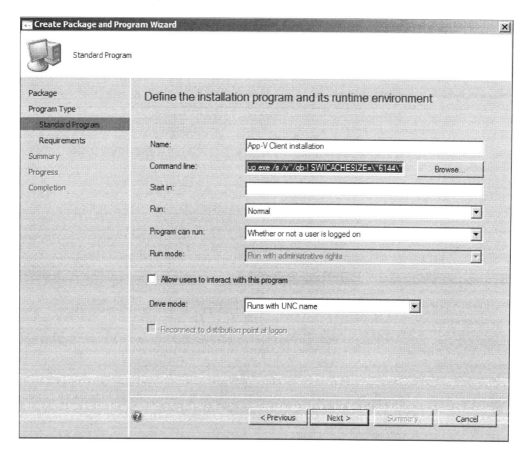

6. In **Requirements**, we can configure several parameters prior to running this program, for example, the client platforms to be installed or the estimated disk space.

7. Complete the wizard.

8. As soon as the package is added, we can select the option **Deploy**, in the SCCM 2012 console for that package.

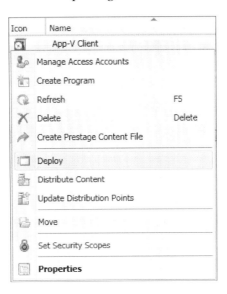

9. In the **Deploy** option, we will receive a new wizard. The first option will let us select the **Collection** to be used for this deployment.

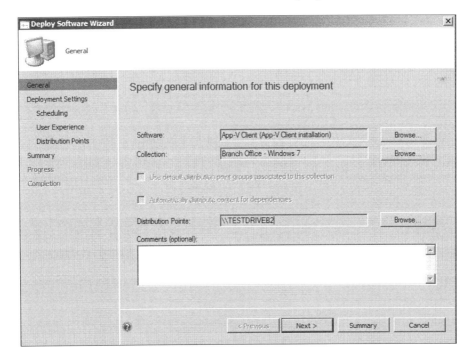

10. In **Deployment Settings**, we can configure how to deploy this package. **Available** is used to let the package be available to the client and let the user decide when to install it, whereas **Required** will automatically install the client.

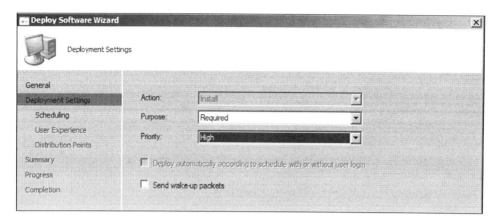

11. In **Scheduling**, we can configure the schedule options for this package to be installed. In my example, I'm using **As soon as possible**.

12. In **UserExperience**, we can configure options about the possibilities each user receives when the installation or assignment is taking place.

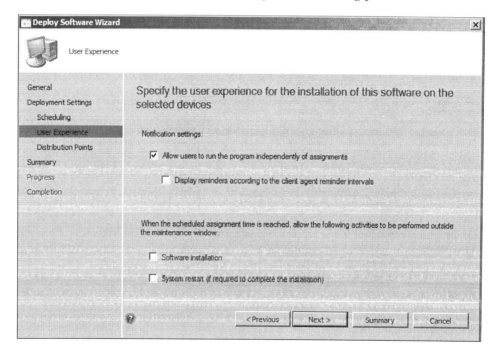

13. In the next window, we will receive the options regarding the type of delivery methods, whether Streaming Delivery or Local Delivery (downloading and execution):

    ○ **Download content from distribution point and run locally** represents the Local Delivery method.

    ○ **Stream content from distribution point** represents Streaming Delivery.

    ○ Note also that we can configure a different type of delivery, depending on whether the client is connecting from the same LAN or using a slow connection.

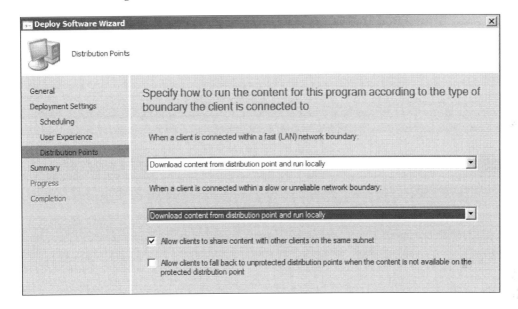

14. In **Summary**, review the deployment settings for the package and finalize the deployment configuration.

Using the **Monitoring** pane, we can review the current status of the deployment, including **Completion Statistics**, which retrieves a simple and easy report overview of the deployment without requiring running any specific report.

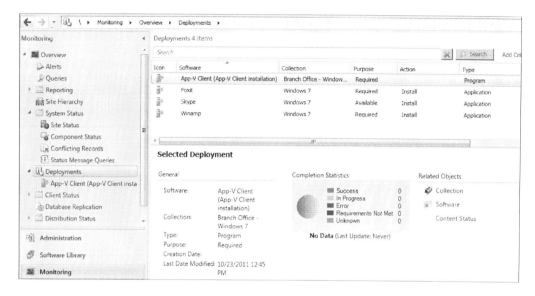

Also, in this section, we can modify the deployment properties configured recently for the same package.

# Using virtual applications in SCCM 2012

Creating, handling, and deploying virtual applications within SCCM 2012, has been simplified compared to what we needed to configure when we were using SCCM 2007 R2. Virtual applications are supported by default without requiring any execution change in the platform.

In this section, we will learn about the following:

- Creating virtual applications in SCCM 2012
- Deploying virtual applications in SCCM 2012
- Reviewing the deployment of virtual applications in clients

# Creating virtual applications

The concept of "importing" virtual applications does not apply any more in SCCM 2012; "creating" is the right word in this case. However, the basic steps remain the same. To create a virtual application, we need the basic component: the manifest (XML file).

Let's look at the process step-by-step, as follows:

1. In **Software Library | Application Management**, right-click on **Applications** and select **Create Application**.

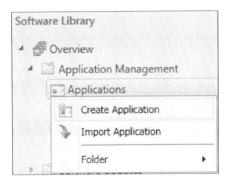

2. Select the path for the application manifest using the UNC. In this example, we will be using the **Winamp** virtual application.

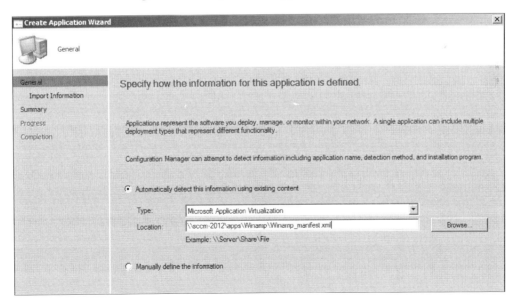

3. Complete the information about the application: name, version, and so on.

4. Once the wizard is completed, the application will be added into SCCM.

As soon as the application is added, we can configure its deployment using the same section in the console.

# Deploying virtual applications

The deployment process of App-V packages is pretty much the same used in SCCM 2007, but some interesting options are added in the process.

Some of these new capabilities are not actually new, but the usability of these features has been simplified in order to optimize our deployments. Some of the interesting capabilities are: handling deployment types or generating alerts depending on success and/or fail rate.

Let's take a look at the deployment process in SCCM 2012 for virtual applications:

1. In the **Software Library** section, using the applications list, we can right-click the application we would like to deploy and select the relevant options.

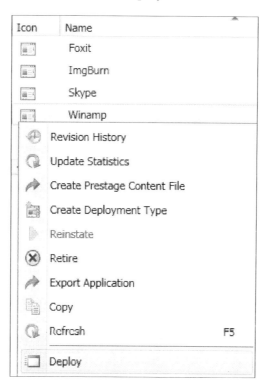

2. Select the **Collection** of devices where we would like to deploy this app, and also use the associated distribution point from which the clients will retrieve this application. In this example, the Distribution Point **TESTDRIVEB2** is used with the **SCCM 2012 Beta 2** installed:

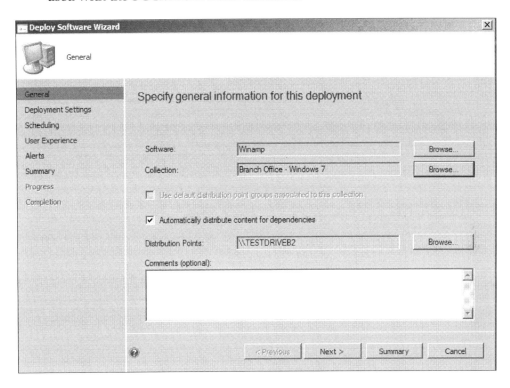

3. In **Deployment Settings**, we have the same options seen earlier — **Available** and **Required**.

4. In **Scheduling**, as seen before, we can define when this application will be available for deployment on client devices.

5. In **User Experience**, we have similar options to the ones we've seen in the App-V Client package. In this section, we can configure it to **Hide all notifications** for the users. This option is not selected as we will be reviewing the installation process in the client later.

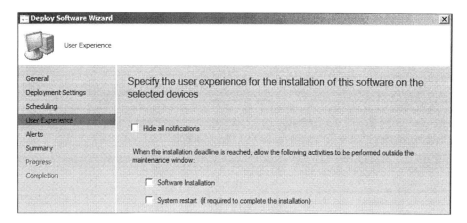

6. Deploying software also includes the possibility of managing the alerts regarding this process. We can configure this deployment to elevate alerts for SCCM and/or **System Center Operations Manager (SCOM)**.

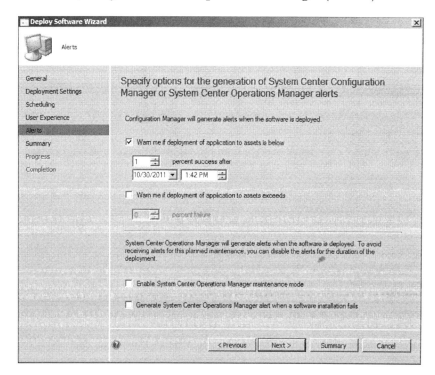

In the SCCM section, we can configure the following options:

- ○ Warning if the deployment success rate is below the selected percentage.

- ○ Warning if the deployment failure rate is below the selected percentage.

- ○ And for SCOM, we must enable the option to generate alerts in Operations Manager. By enabling this option, the SCCM client will communicate with the SCOM agent in the same machine to elevate this warning.

7. Review the **Summary** and complete the wizard.

Once the steps are completed, in the **Software Library** section, we can also review the **Deployment Types** records existing for the applications.

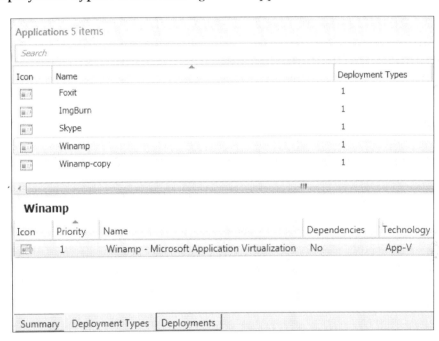

Double-clicking the deployment type, we will get the parameters configured earlier, plus a few more we should consider. Let's take a look:

- In the **Content** tab, some of the options available are as follows:

    - ○ **Persist content in the client cache**: This option is used when we want to store this application in the cache and prevent an automatic deletion (which must be configured manually) for the files used.

- ° **Enable peer-to-peer content distribution**: This option is used for client machines to distribute the content with other client machines that are near. This parameter is not yet documented by Microsoft, so we cannot confirm how it works exactly.

- ° **Load content into App-V cache before launch**: Again, this option is not documented by Microsoft yet, but what we assume is that the package is loaded completely into the App-V cache prior to launch, instead of just `Feature Block 1`.

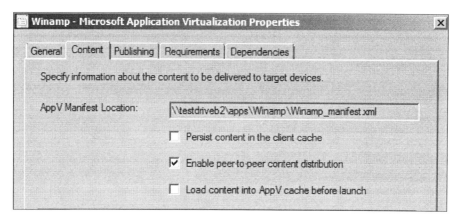

- ° In the following options, as we saw earlier, we can find the behavior of the delivery types—Streaming Delivery or Local Delivery (downloading and executing).

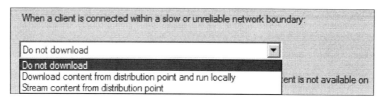

- In the **Requirements** tab, we can configure the dependencies for the deployment. In this case, there's only **Operating System**, but there are several other options, such as client's memory, disk space, processor, existing registry path, and so on.

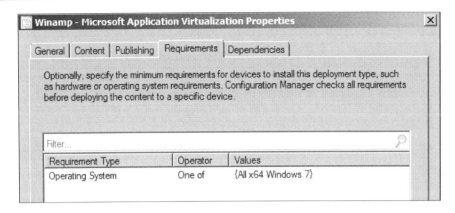

Here's an example of creating a *Global Condition* (selecting a *Custom* require-ment) to be included as a requirement in application deployment—we will be using it to be assessed by the client prior to deployment; if the file exists, the deployment continues:

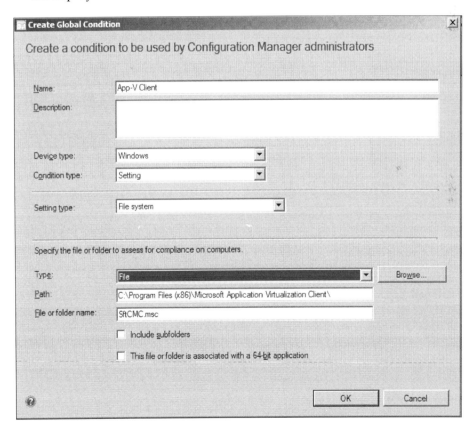

As a reference, we will be using the `Program Files` App-V Client default installation folder and selecting the App-V Client Management Console (`SftCMC.msc`).

- In **Dependencies**, we can configure an existing application as a dependency to deploy the application.

- Each dependency can be configured with a selected **Priority**. This option is used with an `Auto Install` parameter. The application with higher priority will be installed first.

 We cannot configure an existing SCCM package as a dependency. The only possibility is a previously added application.

## Deployment Types

The **Deployment Types** are basically a deployment profile configured for an application. Using this option in SCCM, we can configure different parameters for an application deployment to take place.

Take note that these Deployment Types are used to set parameters in the process of deployment behavior, but not parameters in the application settings.

For every application, we can have different deployment types, which can be configured by just right-clicking the application and selecting **Create Deployment Type**.

Within the wizard, we will get the chance to configure all the necessary parameters for deployment. After completing this option, we will have different Deployment Types. Thus, we can be certain to fit each deployment process in every scenario.

Here are some examples.

- We might need to choose different *Requirements* for 32-bit and 64-bit clients. For example, the App-V Client installs on a different `Program Files` folder, and adds different drivers, in each case.

- For roaming users, we would like to use Local Delivery (downloading and execution) for client machines, guaranteeing that users can run the application by loading locally and not depend on a Streaming Server.

# Deploying applications in clients

Once we have configured the application and the deployment process, we just need to wait till that package is deployed to the SCCM client.

SCCM 2012 includes **Software Center** for every client machine deployed. Using **Software Center**, we can retrieve the latest status of applications available and installed for the client machine, as well as information about each package.

In this example (shown in the following screenshot), the client machine shows the virtual applications that are already installed as well as virtual applications available for installation. For those applications marked as **Available**, we must manually select **Install**, to complete installation.

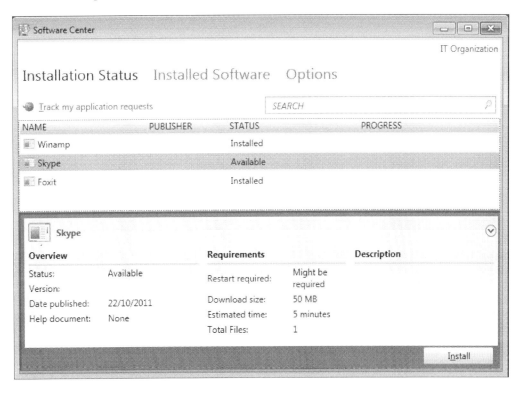

The installation of the package depends on the package size and the deployment parameters we've configured.

Since we had configured the system to not suppress notifications earlier, we should receive all the messages about the deployment processes.

Also, we can review the current applications deployed in the App-V Client console. We can verify that the package URL for each application deployed using SCCM must be directed to the local SCCM cache (the default location is `C:\Windows\ccmcache`).

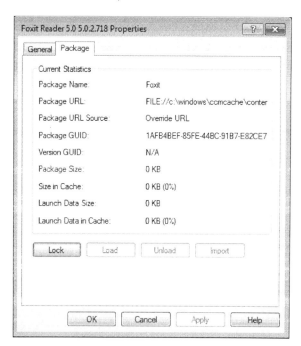

With those verifications, we can confirm that our **SCCM + App-V integration** is working properly for deploying applications.

If we need to troubleshoot virtual application deployment, the SCCM client also includes a log file dedicated to virtual apps. This log file can be found, along with the rest of SCCM logs, in C:\Windows\CCM\Logs\VirtualApp.log.

We've completed the SCCM 2012 and App-V integration successfully. There are other possibilities within this integration, such as understanding **Asset Intelligence** in the SCCM console, that are beyond the scope of this chapter.

# Summary

In this chapter, we've completed a comprehensive analysis of the App-V integration with System Center Configuration Manager 2012, not only analyzing the main benefits, requirements, and considerations, but also putting our hands into the deployment of SCCM 2012.

Integrating App-V application with System Center Configuration Manager 2012 is much simpler than what we've seen with SCCM 2007. There are a few suppressed steps (such as enabling virtual application support in SCCM or adding programs manually to the console, to deploy a package), and the UI improvements facilitate the work of all of IT administrators.

In this chapter, we've looked at the basic concepts in SCCM and App-V integration—components involved and the delivery methods existing for distributing virtual applications. This last topic is an important matter when we are designing our infrastructure, since an incorrect delivery method could result in several infrastructure problems as well as provide bad user perception.

With the considerations completed, we had the chance to complete the necessary steps to implement SCCM 2012 in a minimalistic scenario. And with that, we also reviewed the process involved for deploying the App-V Client component.

As a final step in this chapter, we had a closer look at the management of the virtual applications in SCCM 2012. We had a look at creating and deploying virtual applications to our clients and also understood how the Deployment Types appear with an important role in this integration.

In the next chapter, we are going to review another type of App-V integration—private clouds and **System Center Virtual Machine Manager 2012**. This time, we are not going to consider desktop virtual applications, but server virtual applications.

# Integrating Server App-V with Private Clouds

**9**

Organizations are no longer obligated to think about their infrastructure (hardware, roles, services, and other assets) as static; the current market considers businesses as 24 x 7 x 365. Application virtualization appeared in order to provide companies with a way to solve most of the problematic issues that we usually have on the desktop.

The acceleration of virtualized environments in the last few years has also included the necessity to increase agility in the deployment process and the scaling of our business applications and the platforms they run on. Server App-V, integrated with **System Center Virtual Machine Manager 2012 (SCVMM 2012)**, appears as one of the principal instruments to accomplish that.

Server App-V allows IT administrators to virtualize typical server software and platforms, applying similar benefits gained from Desktop App-V, such as removing installation and configuration procedures in the deployment of applications. But, it also includes new ones, for example, separating the configuration used by each server application in one file, facilitating the deployment of several instances of the same application, or moving server workloads from development to the production environment.

System Center Virtual Machine Manager performs an important role in this agility and dynamics, as it not only provides the concept of *service* in our infrastructure, but also includes the ways to generate, manage, operate, and scale out these services, whenever they are needed.

In this chapter, we will cover the following topics:

- Basic concepts and applications supported by Server App-V, including the differences between Server App-V and Desktop App-V
- Understanding the SCVMM platform and the Service template concept
- Installing and running initial configurations in SCVMM 2012 (Release Candidate (RC))
- Sequencing MySQL server with Server App-V
- Deploying a MySQL server package using PowerShell Cmdlets
- Deploying a MySQL server package using SCVMM Service templates

# Server App-V

Microsoft has been working on this project for a few years now, to deal with some real problems IT administrators usually have, plus adding some important value, agility, and a dynamic experience for the platforms we provide as server applications.

Basically, Server App-V is a technology that enables the virtualization of server applications, removing the dependency of a server application in a specific Windows Server instance (whether that instance is running in a virtual machine environment or directly on hardware).

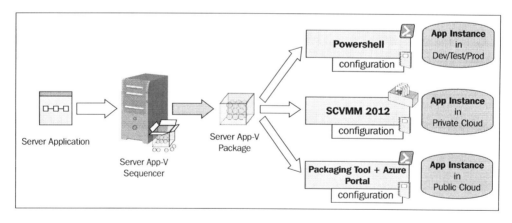

Server App-V represents an evolution of Desktop App-V. This technology includes other aspects in the application virtualization approach, which fit more accurately in server platforms, for example:

- Server App-V works with a Virtual Environment, but this interacts with the operating system and vice-versa, for example, virtual services are visible to the OS.

  This is particularly important as we can use monitoring tools, such as System Center Operations Manager, to monitor the functionality of our virtual server application.

- In the sequencing process of an application, Server App-V also detects and includes in the package, several additional components that Desktop App-V does not. The Local Users and Groups that the application might create, IIS applications, COM+ and DCOM components, WMI providers, performance counters, and all other components Desktop App-V detects and includes within the package.

- Server App-V appears as a *Private Cloud* concept in the way to offer **Software as a Service (SaaS)** and/or **Platform as a Service (PaaS)**. This is the ability to deploy software or a platform without requiring to install it.

  Even though we usually use the concept of "application" in the same way as "software", the term SaaS in Server App-V does not represent the entire scope of the platform. Server App-V includes the ability to provide "as a Service" platforms, such as database engines, or in the near future, Exchange roles or SharePoint.

- One of the main goals of Server App-V is to have a predictable and repeatable way to deploy server applications.

  Some of the common problems we usually find in organizations are that moving platforms from testing or pre-production to production is never an easy ride; often, several inconsistencies might be found.

- Server App-V includes the ability to separate the configuration of the server application, in order to accomplish scalability in the deployment process. This way, we can have the server application package with **Configuration "A"** deployed on one server and the server application package with **Configuration "B"** deployed on another server.

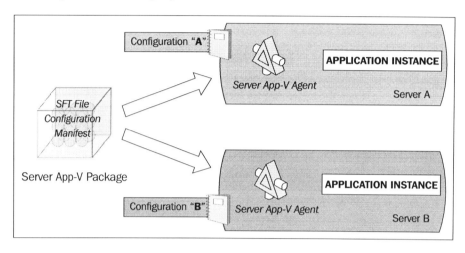

- Server App-V also handles state management operations. This is accomplished by backing up the current state of an application and restoring it in a separate instance of the application.

- There are no more streaming processes in Server App-V. Client agents still exist but the interaction with the Server App-V packages can include using just PowerShell Cmdlets or using System Center Virtual Machine Manager 2012.

Windows Azure represents Microsoft's "Public Cloud", from which we can use a remote platform to handle software (SaaS), services/platforms (PaaS), and infrastructure (IaaS).

At the moment, Windows Azure is available only to selected clients by a closed beta.

Server App-V is not compatible just yet with the worker roles in Windows Azure, but it will be in the near future.

For more information about Server App V, read the article *Microsoft Server Application Virtualization* at this Microsoft TechNet link: `http://technet.microsoft.com/es-ar/library/hh397409(en-us).aspx`.

# Reviewing applications supported by Server App-V

In this current version, with System Center Virtual Machine Manager 2012 in Release Candidate, Server App-V is oriented to business applications (mainly dynamics and web apps), but it is possible to include others.

Some of the features supported by Server App-V are the following:

- **Windows services**: Server App-V includes the possibility of virtualizing Windows services with a different approach than the one we've seen in Desktop App-V. With Server App-V, the service is installed and placed in the OS as a normal installation of the server application. This way, we can monitor it as any local service.

- **Web applications hosted in IIS**: We can virtualize web applications entirely (websites, virtual directories, and application pools) on IIS 6, IIS 7, and IIS 7.5.

- **WMI**: Server App-V Sequencer also captures the WMI providers and/or classes created during an installation.

> There are some scenarios where we can find WMI conflicts when we are trying to deploy applications using a particular provider or class. The Server App-V team blog has a complete approach on how to address this issue, outlined here: *Overcoming WMI Deployment Conflicts in Microsoft Server App-V* (http://blogs.technet.com/b/serverappv/archive/2011/12/01/overcoming-wmi-deployment-conflicts-in-microsoft-server-app-v.aspx).

- **SQL Server Reporting Services**: Even though the SQL server engine is not supported for virtualization, the applications that install **SQL Services Reporting Services** (**SSRS**) are supported.

- **COM/DCOM/COM+ objects**: These components are registered in the deployment process; this way, other applications in the server can access them.

- **Local users and groups**: If the application is creating users and/or groups during installation, Server App-V Sequencer captures and maintains the application, including SID, for next deployments.

To name some of the existing supported applications:

| Applications supported in Server App-V | |
| --- | --- |
| Apache | Petshop |
| BuildTracker Server and client | PHP 5.3.3 |
| Business Objects Xi 3.1 (SAP) | PHPMyAdmin |
| Commerce Server 2007 | PostgreSQL |
| DasBlog | SQL Server Express |
| Dexterity Sample Application (Dynamics GP) | SQL Server Web Data Administrator |
| DotNetNuke | SSRS 2005 |
| Drupal | SSRS 2008 |
| Dynamics AX | StockTrader |
| Dynamics GP | WordPress |
| Dynamics NAV | Real Server G2 |
| Dynamics Point of Sales | App-V Management Server |
| Dynamics Retail Management System | Diskeeper Server Edition |
| eScrum | HP OpenView 8.1 |
| Harmony (Sliq) | IBM Tivoli Workload Scheduler |
| IBM DB2 | Lieberman–Enterprise Randmon Password Manager |
| Malevinch Code Review | Print Queue Manager (PQM) |
| MySQL | Tivoli Storage Manager (IBM) |
| WS_FTP Server | XenApp (Citrix) |

 This list has not yet been officially released by Microsoft; we are assuming that there are going to be some known supported applications, when the final version is released.

Some of the considerations for the applications not supported are as follows:

- **We cannot capture Windows Server Roles**. Deploying these kinds of roles is a task performed by SCVMM 2012.

    ◦ We can virtualize web apps, but we cannot virtualize IIS.

    ◦ In IIS, virtualizing web apps and virtual directories is supported.

    ◦ The **Web Deploy** tool is used in this process of deploying web apps. For more information, take a look at *Web Deploy 2.0*, at `http://www.iis.net/download/webdeploy`.

- **SQL Server is not supported in this version**. SQL Server Express is supported, but there's no official guideline on how to capture it, by Microsoft.

- **Device drivers are still not supported in Server App-V**. For using workaround methods for this, take a look at *Chapter 5, Troubleshooting App-V*.

- **SharePoint and Exchange Server roles**. They are not supported in this release but are priorities for the next version.

An important part of understanding Server App-V is to differentiate it from Desktop App-V. In the following section, we will see the basic differences between these two platforms.

# Differentiating between Server App-V and Desktop App-V

Server App-V and Desktop App-V work similarly. But, there are some important differences between the two, and we must understand them in order to ascertain whether Server App-V fits in our environment.

| Desktop App-V | Server App-V |
| --- | --- |
| Natively provides a streaming process as the method for deployment. | There's no streaming process. Packages are added or deployed as services. |
| OS cannot interact, by default, with virtual applications. | OS can interact with virtual applications. There's no possibility of absolute isolation of the package. |
| Several virtual applications can co-exist in the same OS. | Server App-V is not focused for multi-tenancy support. Multiple applications in the same OS can present problems. |
| Application files are not visible. | Application files are visible. |
| Specific components are registered in the environment. | Several components, besides the basic ones, are registered (WMI providers, local users and groups, performance counters, and so on). |
| We need a different package version to use a different configuration in an original package. | Using an XML file, we can provide, to the same package, different configuration parameters. |
| No native support for PowerShell Cmdlets. | PowerShell is natively supported. |

# PowerShell Cmdlets available

Server App-V depends directly on the PowerShell Cmdlets; the operations are executed using the library for Server App-V. Let's review the Cmdlets available:

- **Get-ServerAppVAgent**: Lists information, such as the Server App-V version of the machine and the logging level of Server App-V.

- **Get-ServerAppVPackage**: Gives you information about Server App-V packages added to the system: package name, version, and size of the package.

- **Add-ServerAppVPackage**: Adds a Server App-V package into the environment. We will review the detailed utilization of this Cmdlet, later.

- **Set-ServerAppVPackage**: Applies a deployment configuration document (the XML file) to the specified package.

- **Start-ServerAppVPackage**: "Start" means that all Windows Services, IIS sites, and other applicable processes of your package that would normally start at system startup will be started by the Server App-V agent.

- **Stop-ServerAppVPackage**: Represents the reverse of Start-ServerAppVPackage. It will stop all the processes that belong to your package.

- **Remove-ServerAppVPackage**: Removes the package and all of the registration associated with the package from your machine.

- **Backup-ServerAppVPackageState**: Backs up package current state. You can do a backup state operation on the machine and restore the state on your new machine, so that you don't lose any data.

- **Restore-ServerAppVPackageState**: Uses the output from Backup-ServerAppVPackageState and restores the generated state.

- **Remove-ServerAppVPackageState**: Removes the associated state from the package. This is equivalent to running Remove-ServerAppVPackage and Add-ServerAppVPackage Cmdlets.

# Understanding the SCVMM and the Private Cloud concept

System Center Virtual Machine Manager (SCVMM) is the platform provided by Microsoft to manage our virtual environment—virtualization hosts (such as VMware ESX, Hyper-V, and XenServer), virtual machines, and the resources associated with them (Windows Clusters, network connectivity, storage, and so on).

SCVMM 2012 represents the fourth stable version for this platform (2007, 2008, and 2008 R2 were the previous), and it not only provides a centralized management for all of these assets, but also includes several important features, such as the following:

- **Manage third-party virtualization platforms**: Add and manage Citrix XenServer and VMware ESX Hosts and Clusters.

- **Physical to virtual conversions**: Using simple procedures, we can convert physical machines into virtual machines.

- **Virtual to virtual conversions**: VM located in hosts can be converted to Hyper-V-compatible virtual machines.

- **Self-service portal**: Users can provision VMs (within self-service policy settings) without administrator actions.

- **Intelligent placement**: This is the capacity planning technology that ensures the maximum optimization in your hardware resources. Using an algorithm and settings, we define the intelligent placement of VMs to ensure optimization.

- **Library management**: This is for common resources such as ISO files, VM templates, applications, and so on.

- **Hyper-V and Cluster lifecycle management**: Deploys Hyper-V to bare metal server, creates Hyper-V clusters, and orchestrates patching of a Hyper-V Cluster.

- **Cloud Management**: This is to abstract server, network, and storage resources into "Private Clouds". It also delegates access to Private Clouds with control of capacity, capabilities, and user quotas.

This is just a summary of most of the features of, and possibilities with, SCVMM. To understand a bit more about the technology, go through the following links:

- SCVMM Key Features: `http://www.microsoft.com/en-us/server-cloud/system-center/virtual-machine-manager-features.aspx`

- *Virtual Machine Manager (VMM) for System Center 2012 Release Candidate Documentation* available at the Microsoft Download Center (`http://www.microsoft.com/download/en/default.aspx`)

- *Virtual Machine Manager for System Center 2012* at Microsoft TechNet (`http://technet.microsoft.com/es-ar/library/gg610610(en-us).aspx`)

# Integrating SCVMM and Server App-V

Server App-V is included in the release of System Center Virtual Machine Manager 2012, currently in Release Candidate version.

Even though it could sound strange at first, it makes sense when we think that Server App-V does not include a management or Streaming Server, like Desktop App-V does. The basic components in Server App-V are the client, Sequencer, and their PowerShell Cmdlets.

So, why include Server App-V as part of SCVMM 2012? Server App-V appears as the Private Cloud solution to implement Software as a Service (SaaS) or Platform as a Service (PaaS). These two are important aspects in the service provisioning of SCVMM, including Infrastructure as a Service (IaaS), which of course is not the focus of Server App-V.

As we can see, the *service* concept appears a lot. The *Cloud* concept in SCVMM is based on these services, also including the ability to provide 'Service templates' from the VMM console.

# What is a Service template?

SCVMM 2012 includes the use of Service templates as the ability to group a set of virtual machines that are configured with several components, including applications, and that can be treated as one. The same concept appears for System Center Operations Manager and their *distributed applications.*

Services in VMM can include one or several virtual machines. When the service includes one virtual machine and a particular application/configuration, we call this a *single-tier service*. A service with several VMs (for example, two web servers and one database server) is called a *multi-tier service*.

The use of services can have several scenarios where we can gain efficiency, if we integrate it with SCVMM:

- View common services in our organization as one entity, managing and configuring those is simpler.

- Separate the operating system configuration from the application installation, which allows operating common tasks—such as OS or application patching—easier, and without major disruption of the service.

- Scale up our services dynamically whenever needed. We can add/remove virtual machines to support the load necessary for our business application without requiring to redefine the architecture or causing downtime.

In this chapter, we are going to take a detailed look at the process of creating and handling Services templates in Virtual Machine Manager, oriented of course to Server App-V applications.

# Installing and configuring SCVMM 2012

In this section, we are going to take a quick look at the process of installing System Center Virtual Machine Manager 2012 RC and running the initial configurations in the platform.

These steps will be necessary for the following topics in this chapter:

- Deployment of virtual applications available using SCVMM depends on having virtualization
- Library Servers in place
- Using virtual machine templates

## Installing SCVMM 2012

If we've had prior experience with the System Center Virtual Machine Manager installation process, then we won't have any problem installing it. And, if we haven't had any experience, the steps are simple to follow.

### SCVMM 2012 requirements

Considering one server that is using the roles of VMM Management Server and VMM console, the requirements for the platform are the following:

- Hardware (recommended configuration, less than 150 hosts):
  - Processor: Dual-Core, 2.8 GHz (x64) or greater
  - RAM: 4 GB
  - Hard drive: 40 GB

- Operating system:
  - Windows Server 2008 R2
  - Core installation not supported
  - The VMM console can be installed in Windows 7

- Microsoft .NET framework 3.5 SP1.
- **Windows Automated Installation Kit (AIK)** for Windows 7.

- SQL server instance available (supported versions):
    - ° SQL Server 2008 SP2 or higher
    - ° SQL Server 2008 R2 SP1 or earlier

- A machine joined to an Active Directory domain.

- For the VMM self-service portal, the web server (IIS) role needs to be installed.

- Optional components that can be used with SCVMM 2012:
    - ° **Windows Deployment Services (WDS)**: Service used to deploy new operating systems
    - ° **Windows Software Update Services (WSUS)** 3.0 SP2 64-bit: Service used for handling the patches in the operating systems

- Ports and connectivity: Depending on the type of connection established to/from the SCVMM server, there are several ports required. We will be covering those in the installation steps.

For a detailed description of the requirements, please refer to the article *System Requirements: VMM for System Center 2012,* at `http://technet.microsoft.com/en-us/library/gg610592.aspx`.

SCVMM can be installed on a virtual machine, but we must keep in mind some considerations and recommendations in a scenario where SCVMM is managing itself as a virtual machine:

- We cannot migrate the SCVMM virtual machine to a different host, using the VMM Administrator console. As the VMM service will be in charge of the migration, the virtual machine will become unavailable and will disrupt the process.

- If we implemented **Performance and Resource Optimization (PRO)** in SCVMM, in order to avoid any migration, we should also exclude the virtual machine hosting SCVMM from the PRO feature. Otherwise, if any resource in the host is compromised, the migration process will start.

- For more information about Performance and Resource Optimization (PRO), take a look at *Performance and Resource Optimization (PRO)* at the following link in Microsoft TechNet: `http://technet.microsoft.com/en-us/library/cc764283.aspx`.

# Reviewing installation steps

The installation steps only require following an installation wizard. As mentioned previously, even if we don't have any experience installing SCVMM, the steps are easy to follow.

For the detailed installation steps, visit *Installing VMM for System Center 2012*, at `http://technet.microsoft.com/en-us/library/gg610617.aspx`.

Let's take a quick look:

1. Start the installation wizard and select the components you would like to install.

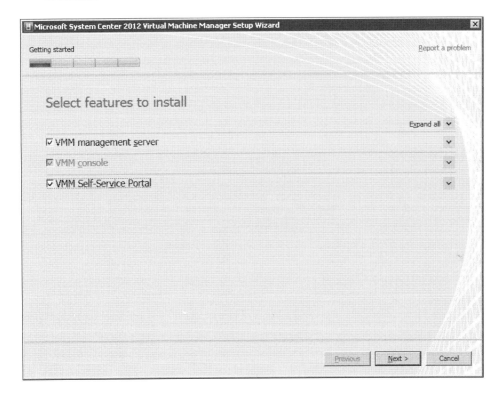

2. Select the installation path for SCVMM.
3. Verify the prerequisites of SCVMM. There are several warnings that can be ignored, for instance, **Insufficient computer memory**, in case the OS does not have the 4 GB available.
4. Complete the information for the database and the SQL server hosting this database.

5. Confirm the **Service Account** for the SCVMM.

6. Verify the ports used for connections, and confirm that these are going to be available for the client-server connections.

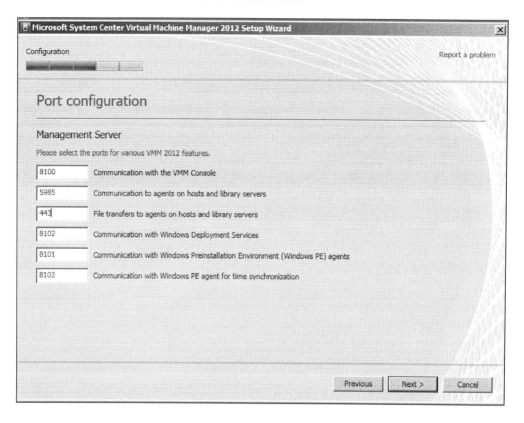

7. If we've selected the self-service portal, confirm the VMM server and connection port.

8. In the **Library Share** section, we can create a library share on the same host we are installing it on or use an existing library.

> SCVMM installs the VMM agent to the computer holding the Library Share, so don't try to set a common file share if this agent was not installed first.

9. Complete the installation steps and start the VMM console.

# SCVMM initial configuration and features

We are also going to take a glance at some of the basic configurations in SCVMM. These configurations are also necessary to understand, in order to get virtual applications working properly.

## Adding virtualization hosts

To start working with our virtualization servers that will be hosting the virtual machines and services we will be providing, we need to run a simple wizard:

1. Open the VMM console and, in the **VM and Services** section, select **Create Host Group**. This is an optional step, as we don't need to use groups to manage servers, but of course, it is highly recommended.

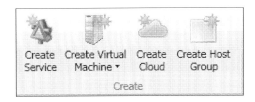

2. Once the group is added, we'll get the option to add the kind of server we want, by right-clicking on it.

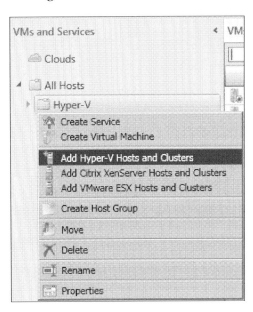

3. Adding a Hyper-V host in this case requires running a simple wizard. There are several scenarios available; select the appropriate one.

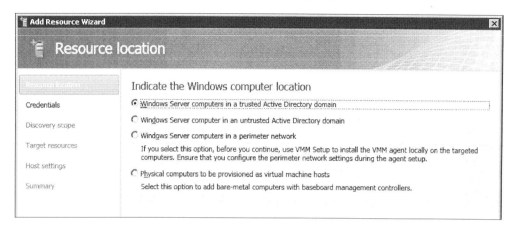

4. Insert the credentials used to discover computers. This account will also be in charge of installing the VMM agent, so it will need administrative permissions on the host.

5. Specify the host name and confirm it in the next step.

6. In the following step, we can also add the **virtual machine placement paths**; the directory inserted here will be used to deploy VM.

7. Complete the wizard and verify whether the host was added correctly.

For more information about adding Hyper-V hosts, refer to the guide *Adding Hyper-V Hosts and Host Clusters to VMM*, at `http://technet.microsoft.com/en-us/library/gg610605.aspx`.

Also, for adding VMware ESX and Citrix XenServer hosts, take a look at *Managing VMware ESX and Citrix XenServer in VMM*, at `http://technet.microsoft.com/en-us/library/gg610687.aspx`.

# Adding Library servers

Adding Library servers is usually a common task in the SCVMM administration, because most likely, all of our virtual machines, installation media, and applications will not be stored in Virtual Machine Manager.

The process of adding a library is also quite simple and just requires selecting the server. It will retrieve the **Shared Folders** available, and we just need to select the folders that we want to use.

Make sure you have organized the virtual machine templates, applications, and other resources available.

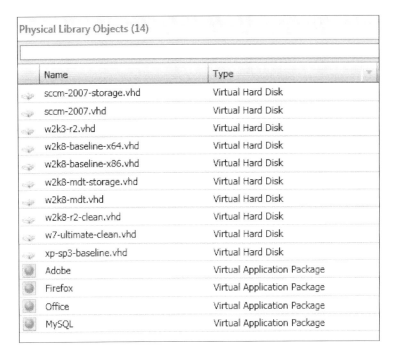

# Handling and creating VM templates

Creating virtual machine templates is a crucial step, if we want to integrate SCVMM with Server App-V applications. These templates are going to be used to deploy services by Virtual Machine Manager, which can include these virtual applications.

Here are some quick facts about virtual machine templates in SCVMM:

- We can create a template using a virtual hard disk located in a library or from an existing virtual machine in a host managed by VMM.

- Operating systems inside the virtual machines must be generalized in order to be compatible with other deployments.

  This process is achieved by the **sysprep** utility contained in all Windows operating systems.

  For more information about the **sysprep** utility, take a look at *What Is Sysprep?*, at http://technet.microsoft.com/en-us/library/dd799240(WS.10).aspx.

As a quick reference, here's the command line used to generalize an OS and shut it down after the process:

```
sysprep /oobe /generalize /shutdown
```

- System Center Virtual Machine Manager 2012 includes several customizations we can achieve in these VM templates; these customizations can save us tons of hours in the deployment process:

    ○ Basic information, such as computer name, product key, domain/workgroup, time zone, and so on.

    ○ Operating system configurations such as roles and features included in the deployment process.

    ○ Configure the VM template to include applications and specific configurations for each of them. We can configure the SQL data tier, virtual application, web application, application script, or just a script that can be executed pre- or post-installation or even pre- or post-uninstallation.

The process of creating our VM template requires going through the steps of a simple wizard, as follows:

1. In the **Library** section of the VMM console, select **Create VM Template**.

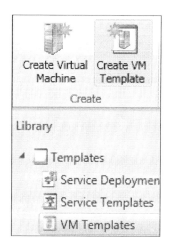

2. Select the source—an existing VHD or an existing VM deployed in a host. Remember the requirement for generalized operating systems mentioned earlier.

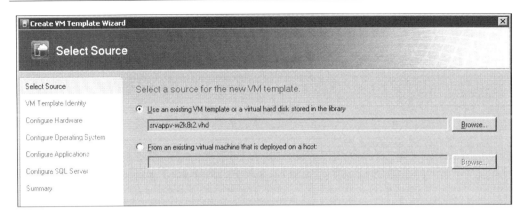

3. Complete the VM template name.

4. In the **Configure Hardware** section, pay special attention to **Cloud Compatibility Profiles**, which will set the platforms supported to deploy this template.

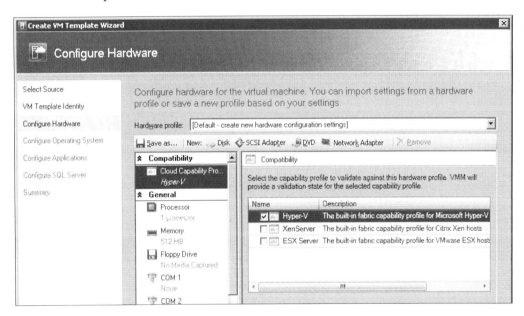

5.  Also, validate the **Classification** field for the VHD, as to whether this virtual hard drive will be placed in **Local Storage** or **Remote Storage**.

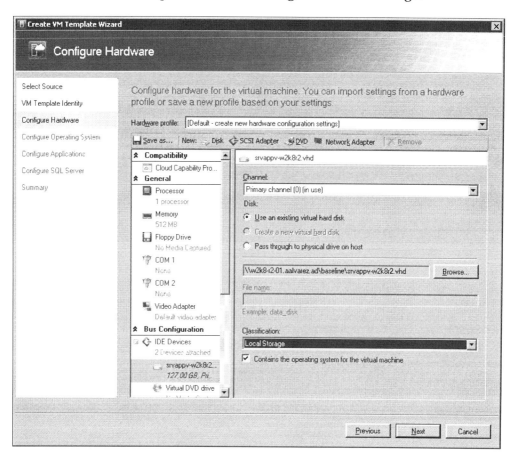

6.  Use the **Roles and Features** section to add any necessary components to this template.

    Take note that the options selected here will be added in the deployment process of the template.

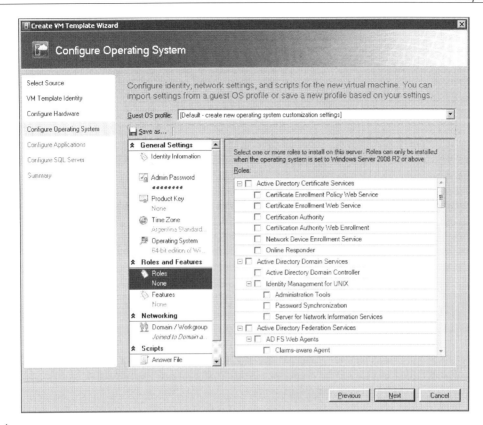

7.  Since we are going to add our virtual application later, complete **Configure Applications**, with no applications configured by default.

8.  As we are not interested in creating a SQL server template, we can skip the last step.

**IMPORTANT:**

When we sequence a Server App-V application, by default, there are going to be some requirements associated with this application regarding the **Roles and Features** existing in Server App-V Sequencer.

For example, if our Server App-V Sequencer includes the .NET Framework 3.5 SP1 feature added (using Windows Server 2008 R2 features), every application sequenced in this server will include the requirement every time the application is deployed. That feature must be enabled in the client, otherwise the deployment process fails.

For that, it is highly recommended that if we already captured a Server App-V application with a Server Role or Feature, we include those natively in the template VHD (prior to the sysprep process).

# Sequencing applications with Server App-V

The sequencing process in Server App-V is quite similar to the process we already know in Desktop App-V. Prior to working with Server App-V Sequencer, we must remember the basic differences we've talked about in the Desktop App-V experience such as isolation—Server App-V packages are not meant to co-exist in the same OS.

Bearing these differences in mind, let's take a quick look at an example of sequencing Server App-V applications.

## Preparing Server App-V Sequencer

Preparing Server App-V Sequencer does not require anything but creating a baseline OS with Server App-V Sequencer in place.

We must keep in mind that, since the sequencing process is the same used in Desktop App-V, most of the common operations and best practices are included, such as:

- **Using the same base OS in Server App-V Sequencer and client machines**. This particular best practice appears as a default requirement in Server App-V.

  When a Server App-V application is sequenced, it includes, by default, the roles and features enabled in the sequencer and sets those as requirements for the Server App-V clients.

  If we think about it, it makes sense, as we are using server applications that interact with several OS components. Server App-V applications will malfunction, if there is any inconsistency in the OS.

- **Sequencing the application to Q drive, if possible**.

- **Using virtual machines and snapshot capabilities with Server App-V Sequencer, and of course, always sequencing a new application with a clean OS image**.

If we have the base operating system in place, we just need to install Server App-V Sequencer, which only requires running the installation wizard:

1. Locate the installation binaries for the Server App-V platform in the SCVMM 2012 installation folder.

   By default, we can find it in `C:\Program Files\Microsoft System Center 2012\Virtual Machine Manager\SAV`.

2. Run the `SeqSetup` installer and complete the wizard.

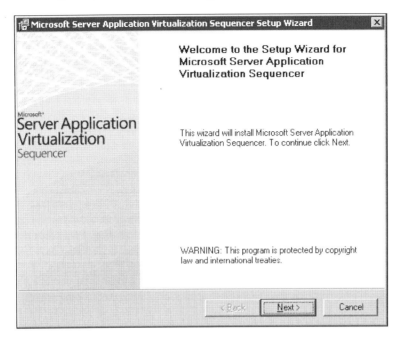

3. Also, install Server App-V Sequencer Cmdlets included in the binaries: `SequencerCmdletsSetup`.

   These are PowerShell Cmdlets included to use PowerShell to generate a Server App-V application without using the GUI.

4. Once the installation is completed, generate your VM snapshot.

# Sequencing MySQL with Server App-V Sequencer

Once our Server App-V Sequencer is prepared, it is time to get our hands into the sequencing process, which as we said before, is similar to the process we already know in Desktop App-V.

In this example, we are going to take a server application such as MySQL and capture and customize it with Server App-V Sequencer.

Let's take a look at the capturing process:

1. Run the Server App-V Sequencer application. The GUI is presented in the same way as for the Desktop App-V Sequencer.

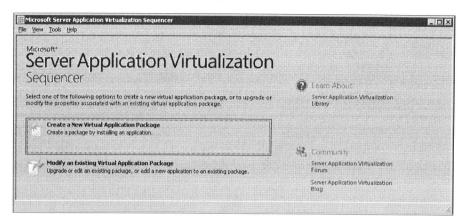

2. Select **Create a New Virtual Application Package**.

3. The wizard will also verify that we are following the best practices in Server App-V Sequencer — clean image ready, other applications running, and so on.

4. Select the installer for the application we are trying to install, or choose to **Perform a custom installation**.

5. Enter a **Package Name**.

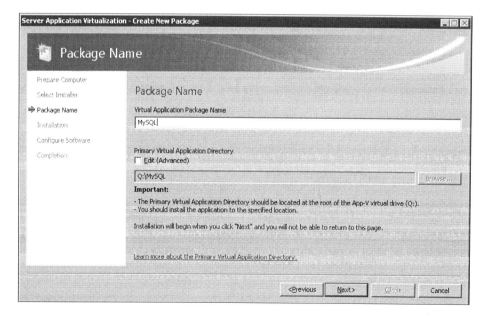

6. Once the environment is prepared, run the MySQL installation. In this example, we are using **MySQL Server 5.5**:

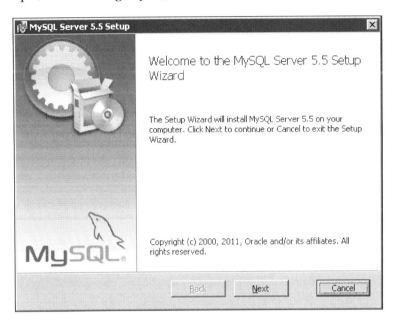

7. As we are going to use a personalized installation, select the **Custom** setup type.

8. Select the component we would like to install in MySQL, and also select the *Q* drive as the default path for the platform.

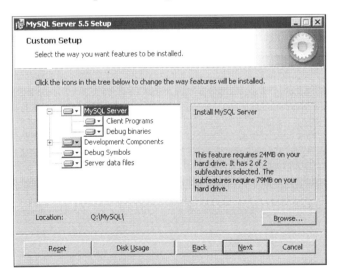

9. Complete the installation steps. The last step will require running the **MySQL Server Instance Configuration Wizard**.

> We are going to use some basic configurations in MySQL, but for more information about the instance configuration in this platform, take a look at the MySQL official article *MySQL Server Instance Configuration Wizard*, at `http://dev.mysql.com/doc/refman/5.0/en/mysql-config-wizard.html`.

10. As we would like to redirect some of the MySQL paths, select **Detailed Configuration**.

11. The following screen is used to set some basic performance parameters in MySQL, depending on the type of machine we are configuring. In this example, we will use **Dedicated MySQL Server Machine**.

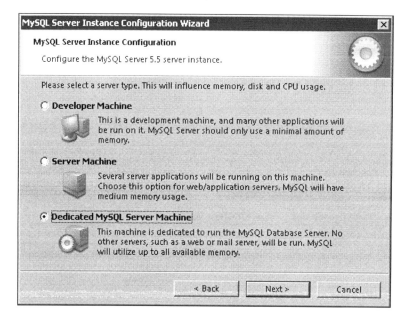

The configuration we set here is placed in the `my.ini` file of MySQL that can be altered later; this file is also included in the Server App-V deployment options that we are going to use later.

12. Select the type of the databases that this MySQL instance will contain.

13. Select the location for the **InnoDB** file (in this example too, **Q:\** is used).

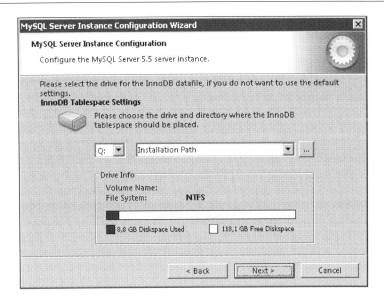

InnoDB represents the storage engine used by MySQL and uses this file to store some critical data.

14. Select the TCP/IP options in MySQL, including the port used by the engine.

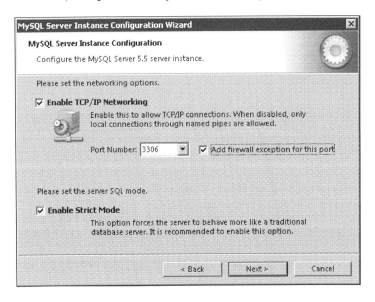

The port used here can also be modified later, in the **Deployment Configuration** option available in Server App-V.

15. Since Server App-V can use Windows Services as normal services in client machines, we can also choose to create the Windows Service.

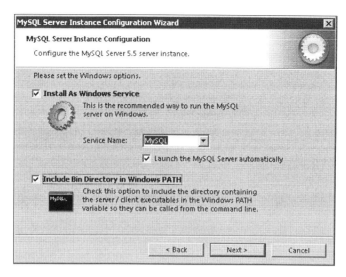

16. Complete the security options and password used by the root user.

17. The installation should be completed with no warnings. Click on **Finish**.

18. In the Start Menu, we should have **MySQL 5.5 Command Line Client** available.

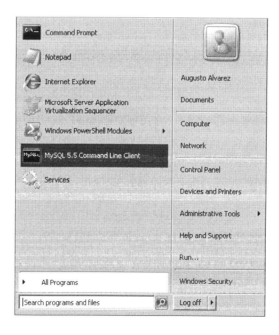

Also, the **MySQL** service should appear in the **Services (Local)** console.

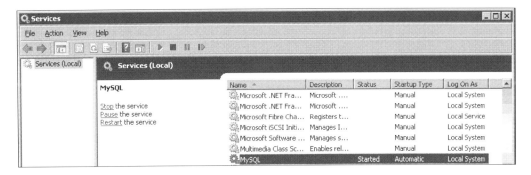

19. To verify the usability for the engine, access the command-line client. In this example, the user created is `augusto` and the database used is `test`:

```
CREATE USER 'augusto' IDENTIFIED BY 'Passw0rd';

CREATE DATABASE IF NOT EXIST test;
```

20. Back to the sequencer wizard; complete the capturing process of the installation.

21. We should have **MySQL 5.5 Command Line Client** and the Windows command prompt as the detected applications.

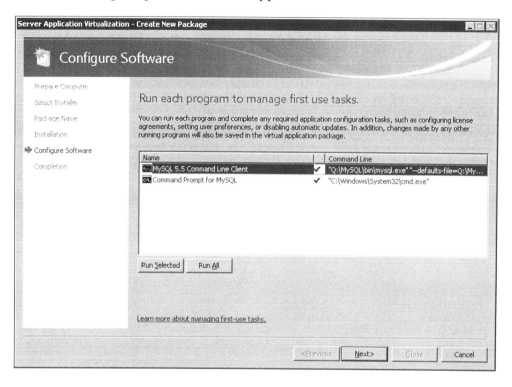

22. Complete **Configuration Software**, in case there are other parameters needed to be set in the platform.

23. Once we have completed configurations, Server App-V Sequencer sets up a quite similar configuration window to finish our application.

Prior to saving the package, we are going to take a look at the options available in Server App-V Sequencer, once the capturing process is completed.

# Understanding the available Server App-V Sequencer panes

At first glance, once we complete the Server App-V Sequencer capturing process of the application, the window shows a similar GUI to the one we see in Desktop App-V, except for a few differences.

The main difference resides in **Deployment Configuration Item**. This is the main difference we find in Server App-V when compared with the Desktop App-V options available.

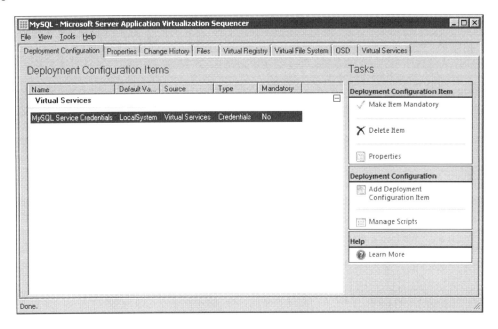

These are the tasks we can complete in this window:

- **Review and modify Windows Services detected**: The services included in the application should appear here and we have the ability to change some of their configurations, such as user credentials used for starting/stopping the service.

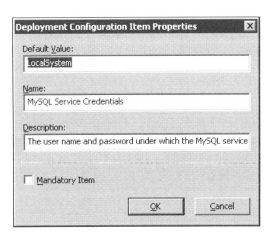

- **Manage Scripts**: We can select scripts to be used when the application is deployed on Server App-V clients. The scripts can be executed inside the virtual environment of the application or outside, in the operating system.

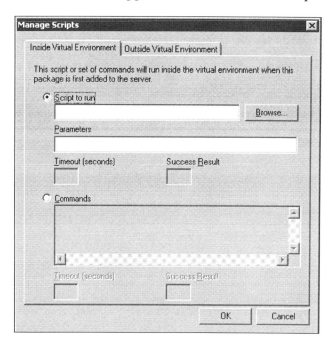

- **Add Deployment Configuration Item**: This option is crucial in the Server App-V applications deployment; we can add more options available in the application.

  The options that can be added will depend on the configuration files used by the application. We can add/modify the options that usually appear in the installation process of the application, without re-sequencing the application into a different package.

  In this example, I've searched for the keyword **port** and it retrieves the options available in the configuration files that can be added or modified in the Server App-V package:

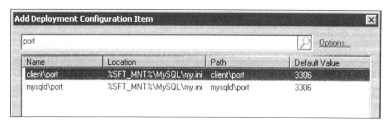

---

Also, by selecting each item as **Mandatory**, we will be forcing to re-define this item every time it is deployed.

Having this option can let us re-deploy the application as many times as we want to, and in every deployment, change the port used.

The rest of the options available apply in the same way as we've seen previously in Desktop App-V.

 In the case of web applications, we should also see an *IIS* pane added in Server App-V Sequencer, from which we can modify IIS settings that apply in the package we are creating.

The result of the package saved also seems the same as we have seen in other App-V packages: OSD, SPRJ, SFT, and XML files are created.

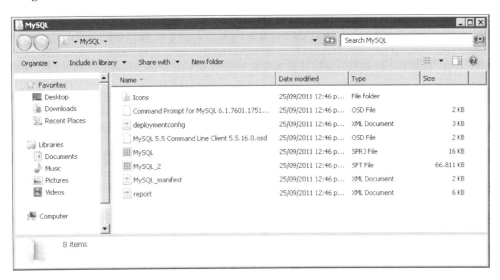

Take note that the options we've seen in **Deployment Configuration Item** are generated into one file: deploymentconfig.xml. This file contains all the items and their configurations included in the package we've just sequenced.

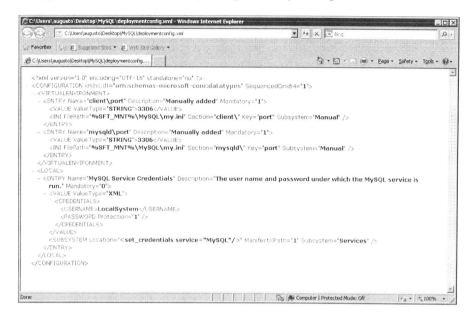

This deploymentconfig.xml file is attached on each deployment. This way, items we've considered as "mandatory" can be re-defined with particular values every time the application is deployed.

# Deploying Server App-V applications

Deploying Server App-V applications has some big differences from the process we already know, basically for one specific reason—there's no streaming. The deployment of the Server App-V applications depends directly on the PowerShell Cmdlets.

There are two deployment possibilities in Server App-V:

1. **Using PowerShell**: The process is quite similar to the one in the standalone mode. With the Server App-V client installed, we use Cmdlets to add the package in the same way we use SFTMIME.

2. **Using SCVMM 2012**: Using this platform, we can deploy our Server App-V applications using Service templates. When we deploy a virtual machine, we can include the Server App-V application with the necessary parameters.

Let's review both of these scenarios.

# Deploying Server App-V applications using PowerShell

If we are used to handling SFTMIME commands to add/remove packages, using PowerShell Cmdlets won't be much different.

Let's review the process of deploying Server App-V applications using PowerShell Cmdlets:

 Remember to use the same base OS, with the same roles and features installed when the application was sequenced.

1. Install the Server App-V agent and the Cmdlets onto the client machine.

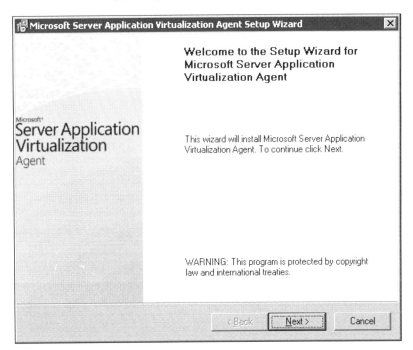

The installers can also be found in the SCVMM installation folder—C:\ Program Files\Microsoft System Center 2012\Virtual Machine Manager\SAV. The installation binaries are represented by AgentSetup and AgentCmdletsSetup.

2. Since there is no configuration needed in the installation, we can complete the installation wizard normally.

   Microsoft Visual C++ 2005 and 2008 SP1 Redistributable Package (x86) are installed in the process.

3. Once the installation is completed, we can find the Server App-V client management console, which is the same used for Desktop App-V.

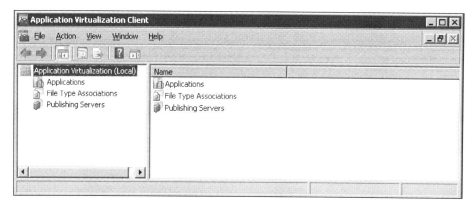

 We are assuming that this GUI could change in the following versions, not only because there's no reference to Server App-V, but also because it includes **Publishing Servers** in the pane. Publishing servers cannot be used for Server App-V applications.

4. Access **Windows PowerShell** in the client machine. We need to add the Server App-V library into the environment, but first, we must enable ExecutionPolicy, to allow this kind of library:

```
Set-ExecutionPolicy Remotesigned -Scope Process -Force

Import-Module ServerAppVAgent
```

For more information about ExecutionPolicy in PowerShell, visit the article *Set-ExecutionPolicy* on the Microsoft TechNet website, at http://technet.microsoft.com/en-us/library/ dd347628.aspx.

5. Once the library is imported, we can add the package using the following command:

```
Add-ServerAppvPackage –Name packageName -Manifest packageName_
manifest.xml -SFT packageName.sft -Configuration deploymentconfig.
xml
```

Using the MySQL example, I've placed the package on the user's desktop C:\ Users\augusto\desktop\MySQL. The execution looks as follows:

```
Add-ServerAppvPackage –Name MySQL -Manifest C:\Users\augusto\
desktop\MySQL\MySQL_manifest.xml -SFT C:\Users\augusto\desktop\
MySQLMySQL_2.sft -Configuration C:\Users\augusto\desktop\MySQL\
deploymentconfig.xml
```

```
Administrator: Windows PowerShell                                          _ □ ×
PS C:\Users\augusto> Add-ServerAppvPackage –Name MySQL -Manifest C:\Users\augusto\Desktop\MySQL\MySQL_manifest.xml –SFT
C:\Users\augusto\Desktop\MySQL\MySQL_2.sft -Configuration C:\Users\augusto\Desktop\MySQL\deploymentconfig.xml

Please wait while the package(s) are added or upgraded.  This operation may take a long time...


Name          : MySQL
Version       : 2
PackageGuid   : 3f400825-0268-49c3-963a-bf3da261c717
MountPoint    : Q:\MySQL
ComputerName  : SRUAPPU-CL
CachedLength  : 664042095
TotalLength   : 664042095


PS C:\Users\augusto> _
```

Depending on the package size and configurations, the process of importing a Server App-V application could take several minutes.

The output should include the package name, version, GUID, mount point, client computer name, and package length.

Take note that the package is fully cached and there's no compression of the package.

6.  Once the package is added, we should notice the shortcuts added for the application.

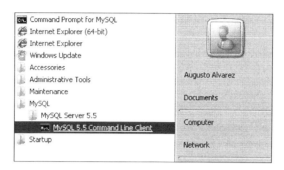

Also, the services must be installed and must be visible to the operating system:

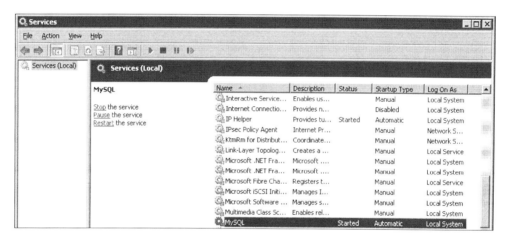

7.  As a final verification to check the consistency of this application, in this example also, I'm verifying that the root password maintains `augusto` as user and `test` as database.

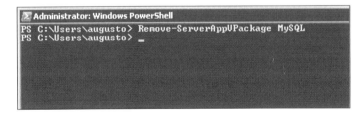

Within these steps only, we were able to import a package into our client OS. The scalability we can gain using PowerShell is very valuable. Automation processes can be achieved and can also be integrated with other common operations in our platform.

As Server App-V offers us the portability experience for our server applications, we could easily remove an existing package from an operating system and quickly deploy it into another OS.

To remove an existing package, we just need to execute the following command:

```
Remove-ServerAppVPackage MySQL
```

PowerShell Cmdlets also interact in the SCVMM 2012 deployment process, but this is transparent to the user. Virtual Machine Manager uses VM and Service templates to deploy Server App-V applications.

# Deploying Server App-V applications using SCVMM 2012

This is not a complex process, if we have the correct environment in place:

- A VM template compatible with the Server App-V package to be deployed
- At least one virtualization host available with necessary resources to deploy the package
- A library available to VMM, with the Server App-V package included:
  - [Optional] An existing application profile to be included

## Configuring an application profile

Before getting our hands into configuring and deploying a service template, let's take a look at the **application profile** included in SCVMM 2012.

Application profiles are SCVMM assets that provide necessary parameters and information for installing Server App-V packages, Microsoft Web Deploy applications, and Microsoft SQL Server data-tier applications (DACs). Application profiles also include the possibility of running scripts when we are deploying applications.

Application profiles are not necessary for deploying Server App-V packages using SCVMM, but the application profiles generate some default configurations that could accelerate the deployment process.

Let's take a quick look at how to create application profiles in SCVMM:

1. In the VMM console, open **Library | Profiles**. Right-click on **Application Profiles** and select **Create Application Profile**.

2. A window will open. In the **General** tab, include the application profile name and description, in the appropriate fields.

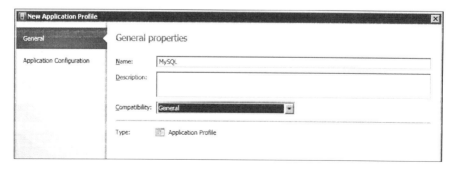

If you are planning to use this application profile to deploy SQL Server
DAC packages or SQL server scripts to an existing SQL server in your
environment, then in the **Compatibility** list, select **SQL Server
Application Host**.

3. In **Application Configuration**, select the **OS Compatibility** option with all
   the compatible operating systems for this application.

4. Click on **Add** and select **Virtual Application**.

5. Select the virtual application package existing in your library.

6. In the virtual application settings, note that we can configure the parameters
   we've added earlier in the sequencing process such as: MySQL service
   credentials and ports used, which are selected as **Mandatory**.

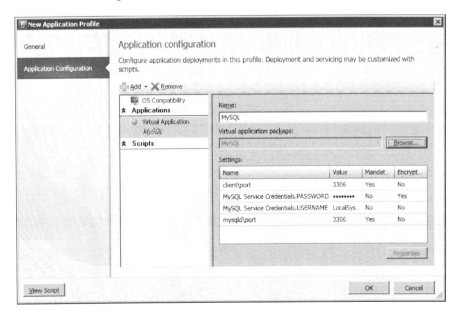

7. Click **OK** and the application profile will be added to the **Profiles** section in VMM.

We can create as many application profiles as we require to, setting the particular configurations we need in each case; this can be very helpful when we start creating our Services templates.

# Configuring and deploying a Service template

As we've seen earlier, the Service template concept in SCVMM 2012 is a logical grouping of resources, such as a virtual machine with applications, which are treated as one.

Virtual Machine Manager includes an easy-to-use Service template designer, from which we can drag-and-drop these resources, in order to create ourselves a personalized service to be deployed.

> For more information about how to deploy Services in SCVMM 2012, take a look at *Creating and Deploying Services in VMM*, at http://technet.microsoft.com/en-us/library/gg675074.aspx.

Let's review the process of creating and deploying a service within VMM:

1. In the VMM console, open **Library | Templates**. Right-click on **Service Templates** and select **Create Service Template**.

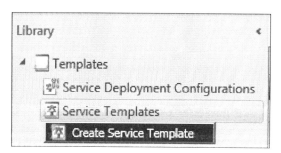

2. The Service template designer will show up, and the initial tiers selection will appear. In this case, as it is a service with one virtual machine, the option must be **Single Machine**.

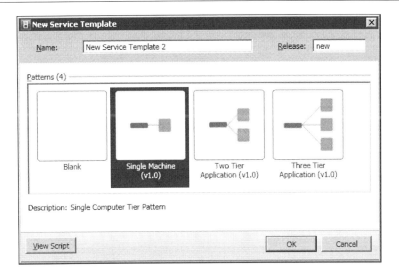

3.  As soon as we select it, we will see a default service diagrammed in the console. Using the options provided, we can start modifying this service as we like.

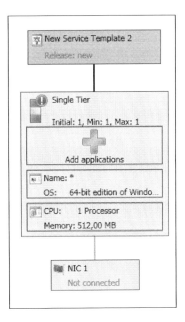

4. We should add the VM template we've created earlier, which is the base OS to deploy our Server App-V application.

Take note that we can drag-and-drop the components into the designer.

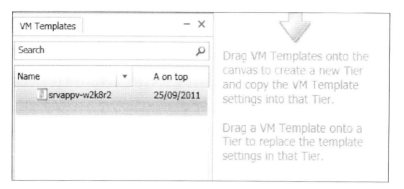

5. Accessing the properties of the Service template will show us more information and configuration options we need to set. In the **General** tab, we can configure the behavior of this machine using the scale-out options.

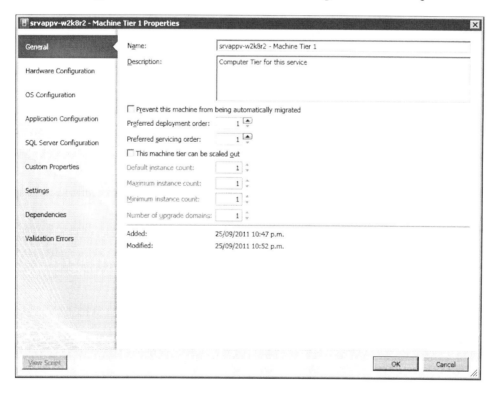

Scaling out a service is a pretty interesting option to use. It applies to scenarios where you have your service deployed but may need to improve the capabilities.

For example, you are using a web application and the number of hits in your site is increasing. Scaling out your service can include more machines into the service to support the increasing traffic.

6. In **Hardware Configuration**, we retrieve the settings included in the VM template when we created it. Verify that all options are in place.

7. In **OS Configuration**, we will also receive the options available for the operating system that we configured earlier in the VM template.

8. In **Application Configuration**, we can use the **Application profile** created earlier, or we can add the application in this instance by just clicking **Add | Virtual Application**.

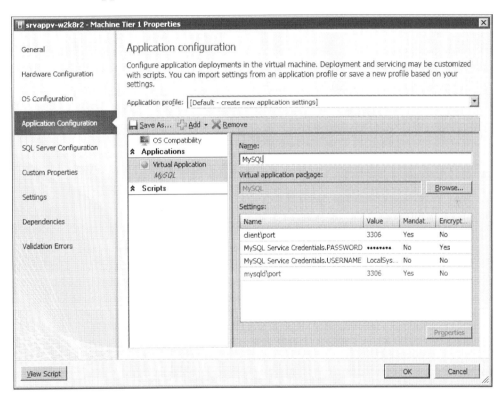

9.  We can complete the remaining configuration options without any particular value added or modified.

    - **SQL Server Configuration**: Only applies when we have a SQL Server Profile configured, which of course can only be applied to SQL server machines.

    - **Custom Properties**: This is a feature that appeared in SCVMM 2008 R2 and enabled scripts to be very generic and not require updating when your infrastructure changes.

    - We can use *Custom1* to equal the hardware vendor (for example, Dell or HP). So, when a script runs it can query *Custom1* and only run against HP hardware, for example.

    - **Settings**: Applies to scenarios where we can use this virtual machine in a self-service portal, establishing a deployment quota.

    - **Dependencies**: Lists the number of library elements included in the service.

10. When we have the service ready, we are ready to start deploying it.

    In the lower section of the designer, we can review any warnings and errors that may appear in the configuration.

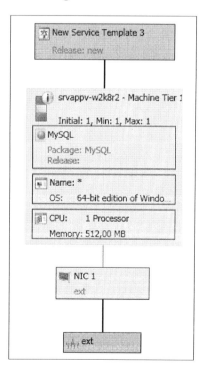

11. In the **Home** pane, click on **Configure Deployment**. We can start configuring our deployment. Enter the service **Name** and **Destination**.

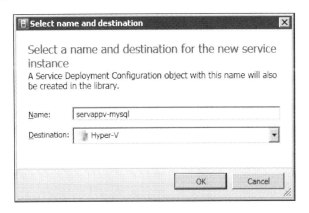

12. Review the deployment options in the **Deploy Service** window — virtual machine name, location, and resources used.

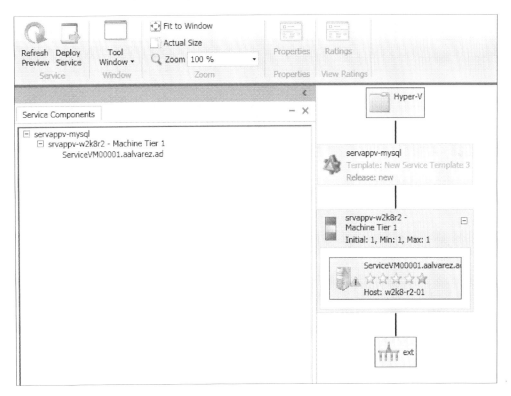

13. Click on **Deploy Service** and the process will start.

14. We can monitor the process in the **Jobs** section in SCVMM 2012.

15. In the process, Virtual Machine Manager deploys the Server App-V agents, in order to get the virtual package running.

16. Once it is completed, we can review the details of the deployment.

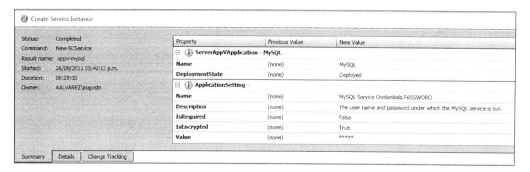

With that, we've completed the service deployment, including a Server App-V application. As we've seen, there are some incredible possibilities for Server App-V applications within the Service templates in SCVMM.

We should consider this technology and these processes in our environment, even if we don't have virtual applications; we can simplify and optimize our infrastructure deployments using just a few steps.

> In case we need to troubleshoot the deployment of the Server App-V applications there are some similarities to the troubleshooting we need in Desktop App-V. The Server App-V Team Blog has an interesting article *Accessing Virtual Application Resources* about the approach we should take, at http://blogs.technet.com/b/serverappv/archive/2011/11/11/accessing-virtual-application-resources.aspx.

# Summary

In this chapter, we've reviewed the basic concepts of Server App-V and the differences with Desktop App-V. Even though the technology works in a similar way, the design goals of each are different.

We've also reviewed the important features of SCVMM 2012, which is highly integrated with Server App-V, providing a way to deploy our server applications as services, facilitating the management of our infrastructure. SCVMM also includes several important features in virtualization management.

Sequencing applications was, of course, covered in detail in this chapter, taking MySQL Server as the selected server application. We've seen that the sequencing process is quite similar to the Desktop App-V experience, but with Server App-V, we gain several other components we should also analyze, for example, including the configuration of our application in one file (`deploymentconfig.xml`) that can be personalized each time the application is deployed.

In the deployment process, we've also covered the two ways we can deploy Server App-V applications—PowerShell and using Service templates in SCVMM 2012. When we have our platform and resources in place, both the processes are simple with no major complexities.

We will review the tools we can find from Microsoft and other vendors, to optimize our App-V infrastructure, in *Appendix, Reviewing App-V Microsoft and Third-party Tools*.

# Reviewing App-V Microsoft and Third-party Tools

One of the most important aspects in any given platform is represented by the acceptance it has among users, administrators, and decision-makers in every organization. App-V is definitely one of them, since it represents the application virtualization technology with the highest number of clients deployed worldwide.

Contributions and knowledge-based communities are other aspects of the platform. These contributions include blog articles, technology forums, and additional tools and add-ons that we can implement to optimize our platform management, usability, and processes.

Microsoft has developed several tools and add-ons that we can use to get more functionality out of the platform. One quick example is the **DSC** (**Dynamic Suite Composition**) configuration tool (covered in *Chapter 2*, *Sequencing in Complex Environments*), from which we can automate the dependency configuration between packages.

Microsoft also offers some key tools we need to use to scale up our platform, for example, the App-V administrative template, from which we can deploy consistent configurations among clients in our Active Directory domain. Those are two of the only few offered by Microsoft.

We will also look at community contributions to App-V tools and add-ons. There are several applications, free as well as paid, that offer administrators important features for managing the App-V platform but also increasing functionalities, troubleshooting, and so on.

In this appendix, we'll be focusing on:

- Microsoft tools for App-V: General characteristics, requirements, and download links

- Third-party tools for App-V: General characteristics, requirements, and download links

# Microsoft tools for App-V

Microsoft includes an important set of tools completely free and available for use by App-V administrators and sequencing professionals. There are several of these tools that we can use even if we are App-V beginners, but there are a few oriented towards the more experienced administrator or sequencer.

 In this appendix, we include the official links offered by Microsoft to download these tools, but, in case those become unavailable, they can still be found at the *Microsoft Download Center* home page, http://www.microsoft.com/download/en/default.aspx.

# Application Virtualization Dashboard

The Application Virtualization Dashboard is a key component for those App-V administrators looking to retrieve statistics and usage reports from the platform. Some of the features included in this application are as follows:

- Built-in reports available—top five applications used, top five users, applications never used, application usage for a specific user, system utilization, and so on

- Administrators can create their own dashboards with a simple process

- The graphical dashboard lets customers view any App-V dataset in near-real time

The Application Virtualization Dashboard, supported by App-V 4.5 and 4.6, interacts with SharePoint services to generate these kinds of reports.

Additional details:

- License: Free
- Download link: `http://www.microsoft.com/download/en/details.aspx?displaylang=en&id=16183`
- Requirements:
  - Same OS supported by App-V 4.5/4.6 servers
  - Microsoft Application Virtualization 4.5 or 4.6
  - Windows SharePoint Services 3.0 SP2
  - Microsoft .NET Framework 3.5
  - Internet Explorer 7.0 or higher

# Application Virtualization Dynamic Suite Composition tool

The Dynamic Suite Composition tool offered by Microsoft simplifies the task of editing OSD files to add or remove dependencies between packages. This task can be executed without the tool, although even with the right guidelines, is not a complex process; making any mistake could lead to serious problems in the application.

Additional details:

- License: Free
- Download link: http://www.microsoft.com/download/en/details.aspx?displaylang=en&id=6655
- Requirements:
  - Windows 7, Windows Server 2003, Windows Server 2008, Windows Server 2008 R2, Windows Vista, or Windows XP
  - Microsoft .NET Framework 2.0 or higher
  - Microsoft Application Virtualization 4.5 or higher

In *Chapter 2, Sequencing in Complex Environments*, we had a good look at using this tool.

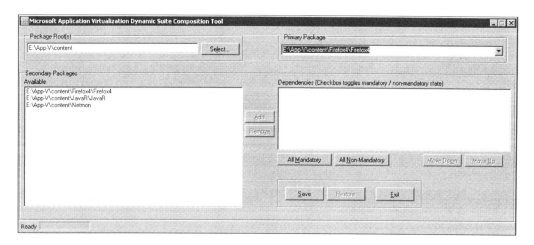

# Application Virtualization Administrative template (ADM template)

The ADM template represents an important component in the administration process of the App-V environment. Using the ADM template, we can easily configure App-V Desktop and Remote Desktop Services Client settings, including communication and client interface, using only Group Policy settings.

In *Chapter 4, Handling Scripting and App-V Command Lines*, we've learned how to configure our App-V clients using the manual procedure (registry) and the Group Policy procedure (using the ADM template).

Additional details:

- License: Free
- Download link: http://www.microsoft.com/download/en/details.aspx?displaylang=en&id=25070
- Requirements:
    - Windows Server 2003, Windows Server 2008, Windows Vista, or Windows XP
    - Application Virtualization 4.5/4.6 Client for Windows Desktops or Remote Desktop Services

# Application Virtualization Best Practices Analyzer

The App-V **BPA (Best Practices Analyzer)** is a simple tool that we can run to evaluate common best practices for App-V Management or Streaming Servers 4.5. Best Practices Analyzer generates an HTML report with all the information about warnings and guidance for configuration settings that should be adjusted.

Additional details:
- License: Free
- Download link: `http://www.microsoft.com/download/en/details.aspx?displaylang=en&id=4022`
- Requirements:
  - Windows XP or Windows Vista
  - Microsoft .NET Framework 2.0 or greater
  - Microsoft Baseline Configuration Analyzer v1.0
  - App-V Streaming Server version 4.5 or App-V Management Server version 4.5

# Application Virtualization 4.5 Security Configuration Roles

The Security Configuration Roles tool will help administrators to harden their App-V platform, disabling unnecessary ports in the server. The components involved are: Management Server, Streaming Server, and Management Service.

A guide on how to use it can be found in Aaron Parker's blog at `http://blog.stealthpuppy.com/virtualisation/microsoft-application-virtualization-45-security-configuration-roles/`.

Additional details:
- License: Free
- Download link: `http://www.microsoft.com/download/en/details.aspx?displaylang=en&id=21863`
- Requirements:
  - Windows Server 2003 or Windows Server 2008
  - Microsoft Application Virtualization 4.5

# Application Virtualization Sequencing SuperFlow

The Application Virtualization Sequencing SuperFlow is not actually a tool per se but could be very helpful for those just starting out with sequencing. SuperFlow provides an interactive interface to view and understand the App-V Sequencing process, step by step, best practices, sample log entries, troubleshooting guidance, and so on.

Additional details:

- License: Free
- Download link: `http://www.microsoft.com/download/en/details.aspx?displaylang=en&id=5262`
- Requirements:
  - Windows 7, Windows Server 2003, Windows Server 2008, or Windows Vista
  - Microsoft .NET Framework 3.5 Service Pack 1

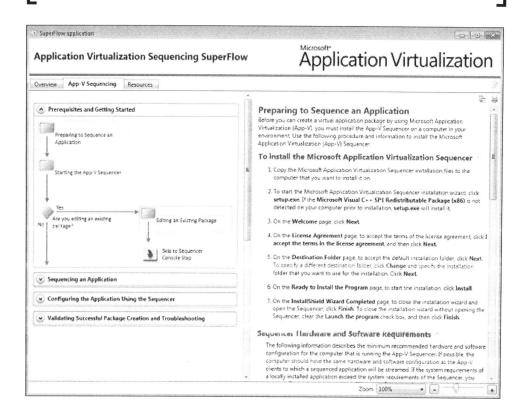

# Application Virtualization Listing tool

The Application Virtualization Listing tool detects and lists all the virtual processes running in the system; this way, we can easily detect the virtual applications running. Also, it retrieves the priority and owner of the process, virtual memory, and so on.

Additional details:

- License: Free
- Download link: `http://www.microsoft.com/download/en/details.aspx?displaylang=en&id=8901`
- Requirements:
    - Windows 7, Windows Server 2003, Windows Server 2008, Windows Server 2008 R2, Windows Vista, or Windows XP
    - Microsoft Application Virtualization 4.5 or higher
    - Microsoft .NET Framework 2.0 or higher

# Application Virtualization Client Log Parser utility

This tool helps administrators to simplify the use and understanding of App-V client log files. The Client Log Parser filters the information in log files and generates an output file with the following fields: `System`, `OS`, `Build`, `Date`, `Time`, `Module`, `Log Level`, `hApp`, `App`, `User`, `Thread`, and `Message`.

This information can also be imported into Excel using a CSV file. More information about log files can be found in *Chapter 5, Troubleshooting App-V*.

The Client Log Parser is not supported by Microsoft Support channels. Additional details:

- License: Free
- Download link: `http://www.microsoft.com/download/en/details.aspx?displaylang=en&id=24492`
- Requirements:
    - Windows 7, Windows Server 2003, Windows Server 2008, Windows Server 2008 R2, Windows Vista, or Windows XP
    - Microsoft Application Virtualization 4.5 or higher

# Application Virtualization SFT View

SFT View is a simple tool that allows "mounting" (creating a view as `.dir` folders) the SFT file with all its files and folders into a directory for read-only access. Within these browsing capabilities, we can permit antivirus software to scan these files and folders for any malware.

This tool includes two important disclaimers:

- This application is not supported through the official Microsoft Support channels. That means if we detect any problem within our packages using this tool, the Support team will not support any analysis or information using this software.
- SFT View should NOT be installed on App-V Streaming Servers.

Additional details:

- License: Free
- Download link: `http://www.microsoft.com/download/en/details.aspx?displaylang=en&id=8897`
- Requirements:
    - Windows 7, Windows Server 2003, Windows Server 2008, Windows Server 2008 R2, Windows Vista, or Windows XP
    - Microsoft Application Virtualization 4.5 or higher

# Application Virtualization SFT Parser tool

The SFT Parser tool is a tool for advanced App-V Sequencer professionals and displays detailed information for SFT files. Some of the tasks we can perform are:

- Process corrupted SFT files and recover information from corrupted SFT files
- List files in the SFT file
- Provide statistics about properties of the SFT metadata
- Display size, timestamps, attributes, and version information associated with the package

Additional details:

- License: Free
- Download link: `http://www.microsoft.com/download/en/details.aspx?displaylang=en&id=12350`
- Requirements:
  - Windows 7, Windows Server 2003, Windows Server 2008, Windows Server 2008 R2, Windows Vista, or Windows XP
  - Microsoft Application Virtualization 4.5 or higher

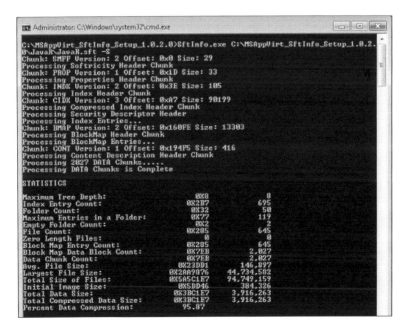

# Application Virtualization Cache Configuration tool

The Cache Configuration tool allows administrators to reconfigure the cache size set in any given App-V client. Remember that the cache size is only configured in the installation process of the App-V client; it cannot be redefined using the Management Console. This tool uses a scriptable command line interface to set the desired parameters.

This application is also not supported by Microsoft Support channels. Additional details:

- License: Free
- Download link: `http://www.microsoft.com/download/en/details.aspx?displaylang=en&id=5927`
- Requirements:
  - Windows 7, Windows Server 2003, Windows Server 2008, Windows Server 2008 R2, Windows Vista, or Windows XP
  - Microsoft Application Virtualization 4.5 or higher

# Application Virtualization MSI Compat Transform

The MSI Compat Transform is quite a helpful tool, if we are migrating App-V 4.5 to 4.6 client machines. It basically transforms the MSI created, using an App-V Sequencer 4.5, to be compatible with an App-V Client 4.6.

This application is also not supported by Microsoft Support channels. Additional details:

- License: Free
- Download link: `http://www.microsoft.com/download/en/details.aspx?displaylang=en&id=5927`
- Requirements:
  - Windows 7, Windows Server 2003, Windows Server 2008, Windows Server 2008 R2, Windows Vista, or Windows XP
  - Microsoft Application Virtualization 4.5 or higher

# Microsoft Application Virtualization DemoMate demo

**DemoMate** is a platform where we can easily create any particular demo and package it to use it later as guidance in a presentation. In this case, Microsoft offers a download to use preloaded demos of App-V regarding:

- Handling package upgrades and permissions
- Handling Dynamic Suite Composition
- App-V metering
- App-V Sequencer usage

Additional details:

- License: Free (only preloaded demos)
- Download link: `http://www.microsoft.com/download/en/details.aspx?displaylang=en&id=11523`
- Requirements:
  - Windows Vista or Windows 7

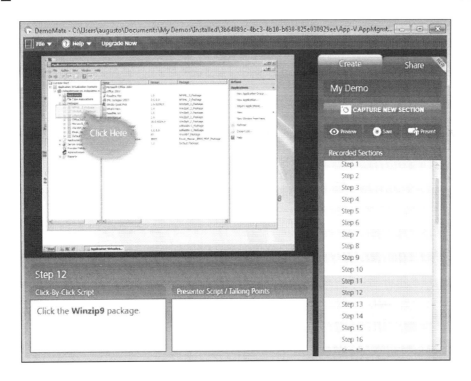

# Third-party tools for App-V

The App-V community also offers a lot of features and add-ons we can implement in our App-V platform in order to optimize our processes.

As we said earlier, we need to evaluate which tools are actually going to add a significant value in our scenarios, considering also that several of these tools are not free.

## App-V Ping tool

The App-V Ping tool, from Immidio Resource Kit, is a simple tool from which we can quickly verify whether the connection to our App-V management/Streaming Server is working properly. This is a basic task we must perform in order to understand whether our clients can receive applications.

The tool verifies the 554 connections with a little more detail than the **telnet** client, but it will not verify whether the "content" folder is shared or whether the user has permissions in any application.

Additional details:

- License: Free
- Download link: `http://immidio.com/resourcekit/`
- Requirements:
    - Any Windows version (apparently there's no OS restriction)
    - App-V Management or Streaming Server

## App-V Client Diagnostic and Configuration (ACDC) tool

The ACDC tool, created by Log In Consultants, is one of the most powerful available tools to monitor, configure, and diagnose in App-V client. Some of the tasks we can perform are as follows:

- Launch predefined and custom commands within the virtual environment of each application
- See the impact of the App-V client and the available virtual applications on your system by calculating package size, cache size, user delta file size, log file size, and so on

- Diagnose problems with App-V applications by parsing the App-V client log file (in real time) and search any message online
- Configure settings that are not visible in the App-V client GUI, such as **Predictive Streaming**, **Allow Stream from File**, **Max Package Age**, and many more
- Give an overview of application and package information by merging important WMI, registry, and OSD information in one single window

Additional details:
- License: Free (registration required)
- Download link: `http://www.loginconsultants.com/index.php?option=com_docman&task=doc_details&gid=69&Itemid=149`
- Requirements:
  - ○ Windows Server 2003, Windows Server 2008, Windows Server 2008 R2, Windows 7, Windows Vista, or Windows XP
  - ○ Microsoft .NET Framework 2.0
  - ○ App-V Desktop/Remote Desktop Services Client 4.5 or later

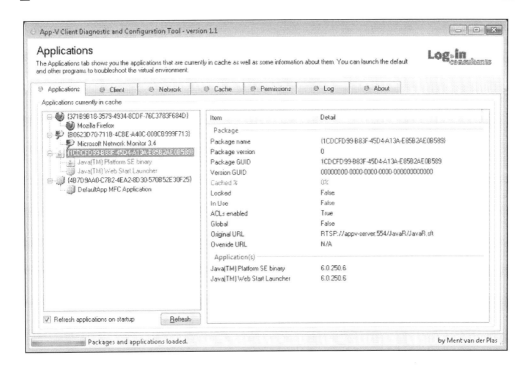

# App-V USB tool

The App-V USB tool, created by Log In Consultants, works with App-V client to automatically add and import App-V packages located in a USB drive.

We can manually add selected applications or just select to detect and import all applications with one click.

Additional details:

- License: Free (registration required)
- Download link: http://www.loginconsultants.com/index.php?option=com_docman&task=doc_details&gid=40&Itemid=149
- Requirements:
    - Windows XP, Windows Vista, or Windows 7
    - App-V Client 4.5 or higher

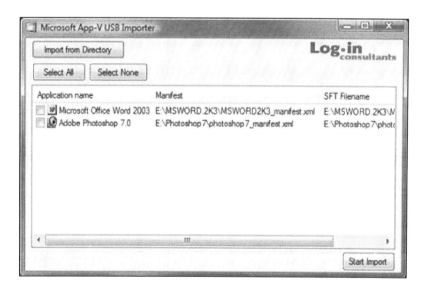

# App-V add-on ADM 2.0

This add-on, created by Log In Consultants, extends the App-V Administrator template offered by Microsoft with a new ADM that includes several very interesting options, such as:

- Global cache file location
- Read-only cache file configuration (used in VDI environments)
- Enhanced logging settings
- User cache location
- Publishing server configuration: server host and server type
- Tray icon settings
- Communication settings
- `SFT_SOFTGRIDSERVER` system variable

Additional details:
- License: Free (registration required)
- Download link: `http://www.loginconsultants.com/index.php?option=com_docman&task=doc_details&gid=70&Itemid=149`
- Requirements:
  - Windows Server 2003, Windows Server 2008, Windows Vista, or Windows XP
  - App-V 4.5 or later

# Application Virtualization Explorer

This tool, created by Gridmetric, simplifies several common tasks performed by advanced sequencer professionals. Some of the tasks we can perform using the attractive GUI are: configure application dependencies and file type associations, view and edit OSD scripts, and so on.

It also includes the option for browsing PKG files of any given package.

Additional details:

- License: Paid (trial version available)
- Download link: `http://www.gridmetric.com/products/ave.html`
- Requirements:
  - Windows XP SP3, Windows 2003 Server SP2, Windows Vista SP1, Windows 7, Windows Server 2008 SP1, or Windows 2008 R2
  - Microsoft .NET Framework 2.0 SP2

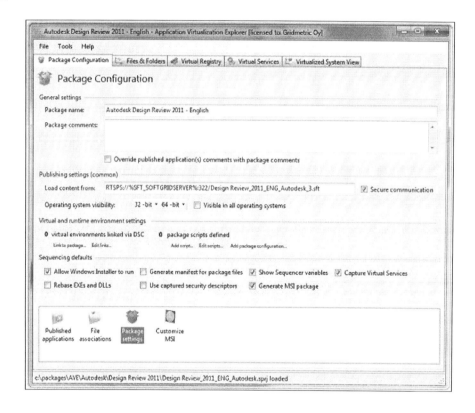

# App-V Client Setup Kit

The App-V Client Setup Kit, by Log In Consultants, is a tool that helps App-V administrators to generate a universal Visual Basic script to deploy the App-V client. This script can later be used manually or with any deployment tool.

Additional details:

- License: Free (registration required)
- Download link: `http://www.loginconsultants.com/index.php?option=com_docman&task=doc_details&gid=20&Itemid=149`
- Requirements:
  - Any Windows OS

# Application Virtualization Analyzer

The Application Virtualization Analyzer, developed by Log In Consultants, is a suite from which we can obtain basic and important information from all of our App-V packages. The tool is oriented to quickly detect any conflicts present.

Using an Excel file, all of the information is parsed and organized to list your App-V packages. In the same Excel file, all of the conflicts are detected and listed separately.

Additional details:

- License: Free (registration required)
- Download link: `http://www.loginconsultants.com/index.php?option=com_docman&task=doc_details&gid=118&Itemid=149`
- Requirements:
  - Windows Server 2003 or higher
  - PowerShell V2

# AppV_DeployApp and AppV_PublishApp

This set of tools, developed by TMUrgent (Tim Mangan), was created to simplify the App-V implementations without requiring any Management/Streaming Servers. It improves the standalone implementations by automatically loading applications in a file share and using Active Directory User Groups to define permissions.

Additional details:

- License: Free
- Download link: `http://www.tmurgent.com/AppVirt/DeployNPublish.aspx`
- Requirements:
  - Windows XP, Windows Vista, or Windows 7
  - Microsoft .NET Framework 4.0 (setup includes automatic installation, if it's not present)

# LaunchIt

LaunchIt, developed by TMUrgent (Tim Mangan), is a tool that can be included in App-V packages in order to add a warning message to the user when it shuts down the application with all the processes that are going to be terminated with that action. This only applies when we configure, in the package, the `TERMINATECHILDREN=TRUE` value.

Additional details:

- License: Free
- Download link: `http://www.tmurgent.com/AppVirt/DownloadLaunchIt.aspx`
- Requirements:
  - Any Windows OS

# App-V OSD editor

The App-V OSD editor, by Log In Consultants, represents a GUI for reviewing and editing OSD files. This is an "old" application, so it does not support the Windows 7 OS tag in OSD editing.

Additional details:

- License: Free (registration required)
- Download link: `http://www.loginconsultants.com/index.php?option=com_docman&task=doc_details&gid=27&Itemid=149`
- Requirements:
    - Windows XP, Windows Vista, or Windows 7

# OSD Illustrated

OSD Illustrated, developed by TMUrgent (Tim Mangan), is a simple interactive web application available, from which we get a complete reference about the OSD tags available.

Additional details:

- License: Free
- Download link: `http://tmurgent.com/OSD_Illustrated.aspx` (no need to download actually)
- Requirements:
    - Internet Explorer 7 or higher

# Batch+

Batch+ is a tool, created by AppPlus, that allows administrators to quickly edit several OSD files at once with the parameters we decide, for example, adding the Windows 7 tag to all packages.

Additional details:

- License: Free (registration required)
- Download link: http://www.intercept-it.com/AppPlus/ Community/CommunityTools/BatchFreeEdition/ BatchHighlights.aspx
- Requirements:
  - ° Any Windows OS

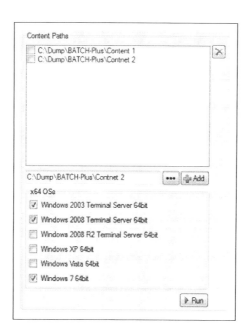

# Add OS to OSD

This tool, created by Fabian Meister, simply adds an OS tag to a selected OSD file. It does not check the OS tag we are using; it just adds the tag.

Additional details:

- License: Free
- Download link: `http://local.micro.biol.ethz.ch/appv/Add_OS_to_OSD.zip`
- Requirements:
    - Any Windows OS

# OSD+

This tool, developed by AppPlus, includes several functionalities to handle, edit, and launch App-V packages, without requiring an App-V platform. Some of the features included are the following:

- File streaming capabilities into App-V client
- Launch application from inside the GUI
- Launch troubleshooting tools inside the application's virtual environment
- Create manifest files for SCCM and third-party delivery software integration
- Create "dynamic suite compositions" with the click of a button
- Import registry files into the OSD file
- Restore OSD files to previous save points

Additional details:

- License: Paid
- Download link: `http://www.intercept-it.com/AppPlus/Products/OSD/Highlights.aspx`
- Requirements:
    - Undocumented

# App-V Helper

The App-V Helper tool developed by *mayankjohri* and available on Source Forge, is another tool to facilitate package deployment. We can select any given package and the computer where we would like to deploy and execute the process.

Additional details:

- License: Free
- Download link: `http://sourceforge.net/projects/softgridhelper/`
- Requirements:
  - Any Windows OS

# Softricity File (SFT) Checking utility

The Softricity File Checking utility, created by Kalle Saunamäki, permits administrators using a command line to retrieve detailed information about SFT files. Some of the information that can be retrieved is about block size, GUIDs, and FB1 size.

Additional details:

- License: Free
- Download link: `http://www.virtualapp.net/sft-check.html`
- Requirements:
  - Any Windows OS
  - Microsoft .NET Framework 2.0

# LogTools for SoftGrid client

This suite, created by Kalle Saunamäki, includes several command-line utilities to handle App-V client log files efficiently. The tools included are:

- `logloader` - tool to convert log files to XML format for further processing (application launch/shutdown events)
- `logxml2csv` - tool to convert XML-formatted files to CSV files for easy viewing and processing in, say, Microsoft Excel

Additional details:

- License: Free
- Download link: `http://www.virtualapp.net/client-logtools.html`
- Requirements:
  - Any Windows OS
  - Microsoft .NET Framework 2.0
  - Minimum log-level for App-V Client(s) set to 4 - Information

For more information about App-V client logs and their log level, see *Chapter 5, Troubleshooting App-V*.

# SFT Encoder Express

The SFT Encoder Express, created by Kalle Saunamäki, represents the free version of the Virtualization Encoder. This tool permits us to package, into a standard App-V package, any directory we choose; the SFT Encoder creates the necessary files (SFT, OSD, and SPRJ).

The files are created using the SoftGrid 4.1 and 4.2 standards.

Additional details:

- License: Free
- Download link: `http://www.virtualapp.net/sft-encoder.html`
- Requirements:
  - Any Windows OS
  - Microsoft .NET Framework 2.0

# Virtualization Encoder

Virtualization Encoder represents the paid and professional version of SFT Encoder Express. Besides permitting administrators to package any given directory, it includes several other options, such as upgrade or downgrade package versions (App-V 4.6 SP1 is supported) or editing a package without the need to create a new version of this package.

Additional details:

- License: Paid (trial version available)
- Download link: `http://www.gridmetric.com/products/sftencoder.html`
- Requirements:
    - Windows XP SP3, Windows 2003 Server, Windows Vista SP1, Windows 7, Windows Server 2008, or Windows 2008 R2 operating system.
    - Microsoft .NET Framework 2.0 with SP2

# App-V Migration tool

The App-V Migration tool was created in 2008 (last version) by Log In Consultants; it allows administrators to automatically create App-V packages using the installer MSI for the application.

The process basically executes an "unattended" installation for the application, with the parameters we define; the tool completes the installation and generates the App-V package.

Additional details:

- License: Free (registration required)
- Download link: `http://www.loginconsultants.com/index.php?option=com_docman&task=doc_details&gid=28&Itemid=149`
- Requirements:
    - Windows XP, Windows Vista, or Windows 7
    - Microsoft .NET Framework 2.0
    - App-V Sequencer 4.5

# Lib-V

This suite, also offered by Gridmetric, is oriented for specific companies' business applications; basically, it is a .NET 2.0 library that allows applications to handle and edit App-V components on their own.

This way, if the application was created to be virtualized, we can customize it in order to understand, handle, and edit any of the App-V components (such as SFT, OSD, SPRJ, XML, and MSI files) without requiring manual editing by a sequencer professional.

Additional details:

- License: Paid (no trial version available)
- Download link: `http://www.gridmetric.com/products/libv.html`
- Requirements:
  - Microsoft .NET Framework 2.0
  - The rest is undocumented

# AppScriber

AppScriber, created by Immidio, represents a platform from which we can provide end users with an application portal. Users can now subscribe/unsubscribe from applications just by using this portal.

AppScriber is not App-V-exclusive. It also supports Microsoft System Center Configuration Manager, Citrix XenApp, and Symantec Altiris Deployment Solution.

This application works in a way similar to Software Center, offered by SCCM 2012, which we had the chance to review in *Chapter 8, Integrating App-V with System Center Configuration Manager 2012.*

This suite is not free, but Immidio also offers the AppScriber 3 Express edition at no charge.

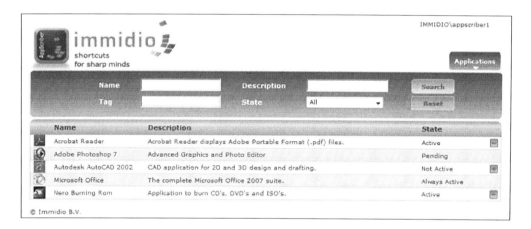

Additional details:
- License: Paid
- Download link: http://immidio.com/appscriber/
- Requirements (for back-end servers):
  ○ Windows Server 2003 or later
  ○ Microsoft .NET Framework 2.0 SP2
  ○ IIS 6 or later
  ○ SQL Server/SQL Server Express 2005 or later
  ○ Internet Explorer 7 or higher (client machines)

# AdminStudio

AdminStudio, created by Flexera Software, is a robust suite for application management and optimization using MSI files. It permits application packaging with all the necessary parameters and customizations, plus adding features, such as testing and validations, generate reports, centrally manage permissions, and so on.

AdminStudio also includes a virtualization package that supports App-V packages for quickly converting MSI files into App-V packages, validating and testing for conflicts, editing packages without the App-V Sequencer, and so on.

Additional details:

- License: Paid
- Download link: `http://www.flexerasoftware.com/products/adminstudio/editions.htm`
- Requirements:
    - Windows Server 2003 or later
    - SQL Server 2005/SQL Server 2005 Express or later
    - IIS 6 or later
    - Microsoft .NET Framework 3.5 SP1

# App-V Tool suite

The App-V Tool suite represents a set of applications composed by **Duplicate Root Detector**, **Permission Copy**, and **App-V Search**.

Duplicate Root Detector will scan a folder for `.sft` files and report whether any of those files use the same root (`asset`) directory. `.sft` files that are part of the same package are not reported as using the same root directory. It also scans for duplicated package IDs among SFT files.

Permission Copy allows the user to copy the Access Permissions from one App-V application or application group to another.

App-V Search is a simple search tool that allows you to search the names of applications, application groups, and packages for a given string, using the SQL database.

Additional details:

- License: Free
- Download link: `http://appvtools.codeplex.com/releases/view/63642`
- Requirements:
    - Microsoft .NET Framework 3.5

# PowerShell snap-in for Microsoft App-V Server 4.6 SP1

Even though it is not an application itself, the PowerShell snap-in could be quite useful when we are looking for ways to automate processes handling App-V server operations.

Some of the operations we can use by handling these Cmdlets are: setting App-V management server options, handling applications and packages, adding/removing servers as well as server groups, and so on.

Additional details:

- License: Free
- Download link: `http://posh4appv.codeplex.com/`
- Requirements:
    - App-V Management Server 4.6 SP1
    - PowerShell V2

# App-V Generator

App-V Generator, created by Infopulse, is a tool for fast creation and editing of App-V packages for the Windows OS family.

App-V Generator, in contrast to App-V Sequencer, uses snapshot-based package creation. It compares two system snapshots, detects system changes, filters out application data from system data, and creates a resulting App-V package.

Additional details:

- License: Paid (trial version available)
- Download link: `http://www.infopulse.com.ua/eng/Solutions/App-V-Generator/`
- Requirements:
    - Windows 2000, Windows XP, Windows 2003 Server, Vista, Windows 2008 Server, or Windows 7
    - Microsoft .NET Framework 3.5 SP1

# PkgView for App-V

This tool, developed by TMUrgent (Tim Mangan), lets administrators view and analyze the PKG files from any user or in the global directory.

This tool is focused for advanced sequencer professionals, since by using it, we can evaluate whether the files sequenced are running in their right environment (as user data or application data).

Detailed information about PkgView can be found on Tim's blog at `http://www.tmurgent.com/TmBlog/?p=166`.

Additional details:

- License: Free
- Download link: `http://www.tmurgent.com/download/PkgView_1.5.0.zip`
- Requirements:
  - Any 32-bit Windows OS

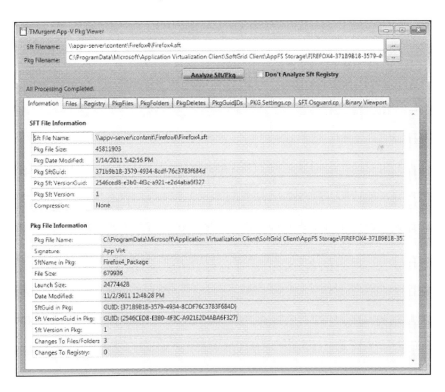

# PimpMy for Softgrid and App-V

The PimpMy suite, developed by TMUrgent (Tim Mangan), contains a set of two applications: PimpMy for SoftGrid Real-Time Monitoring package and PimpMy for SoftGrid Help Desks package.

The Real-Time Monitoring package offers information on-the-fly about current utilization of App-V packages. The tool also integrates with System Center Operations Manager.

The Help Desks package provides a user interface that is oriented for Help Desk operators to easily identify problems in App-V packages deployed to clients.

Additional details:

- License: Paid (trial version available)
- Download link: `http://tmurgent.com/PimpMy/PimpMy4SG.aspx`
- Requirements:
    - Windows Server 2003 or later
    - Microsoft .NET Framework 3.5

# Failure to Launch

The Failure to Launch app is actually a web app that we can use from any browser that supports Silverlight. This web app was developed by TMUrgent (Tim Mangan) and contains a detailed explanation and use cases about App-V errors.

Failure to Launch provides some great guidance about common App-V client errors. It covers general information about error codes, flow charts about issues with launching apps, information about errors during execution, and so on.

Additional details:

- License: Free
- Download link: `http://www.tmurgent.com/AppVirt/FTL/Ftl.aspx`
- Requirements:
    - Browser compatible with Silverlight

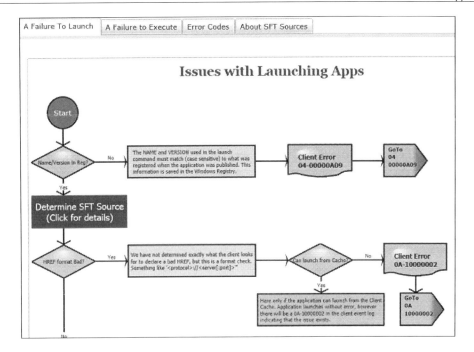

| A Failure To Launch | A Failure to Execute | Error Codes | About SFT Sources |

## Issues with Launching Apps

# sftImport

sftImport, created by DeNamiK (a software company), is a tool to automate the process of importing applications into the App-V management server, using their OSD file.

The application supports using **CSV** (**Comma Separated Value**) files to import a large number of applications.

Additional details:

- License: Free (registration required)
- Download link: `http://www.denamik.com/en/downloads/cat_view/8-denamik-free-downloads`
- Requirements:
  - Undocumented

# Advanced Installer

Advanced Installer is not an App-V-oriented suite; it is in fact used in several scenarios as an alternative to application virtualization. It offers the way to package applications into an MSI to facilitate the deployment.

However, it includes the possibility to create your own App-V packages manually by editing the file system, registry, and other components in the virtual environment. To review this process, take a look at `http://www.advancedinstaller.com/user-guide/tutorial-appv.html`.

Additional details:

- License: Paid (trial version available)
- Download link: `http://www.advancedinstaller.com/download.html`
- Requirements:
  - Windows XP SP3 or superior
  - Windows Installer 2.0 or superior

# DSC Management Utility

The DSC Management Utility, developed by add3 consultants, adds more functionality to the Microsoft DSC Composition tool.

DSC provides the way to link package dependencies in App-V. With this tool, we can edit those links and dependencies, but we can also retrieve the exact applications included in each package to gain more understanding in the dependencies we are setting.

Additional details:

- License: Free
- Download link: `http://www.add3.co.uk/content/app-v-dsc-management-utility`
  - The application should be requested by e-mail sent to `dsctool@add3.co.uk`
- Requirements:
  - Undocumented

# App-V Import tool

The App-V Import tool, available in CodePlex, is used to browse for App-V packages and import them into the App-V client as a standalone configuration. This app, of course, does not require for any App-V server to be present.

Additional details:

- License: Free
- Download link: `http://appvimport.codeplex.com/`
- Requirements:
  - Undocumented

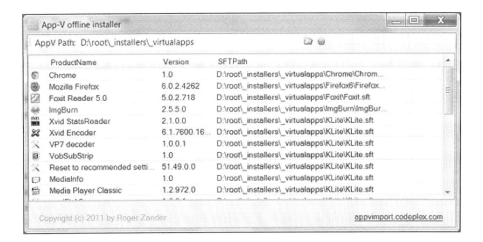

# Summary

Within this appendix, we had quite a complete reference about the set of tools and add-ons we can find in App-V, including Microsoft and third-party downloads available. We analyzed common features, characteristics, requirements, and download links available for each of the tools and add-ons.

Regarding Microsoft tools, a great thing to note is that all of them are free and available in Download Center. There are some important tools available, such as the Application Virtualization Dashboard, which is the recommended tool available to obtain reports and statistics.

There are also advanced tools, such as SFT Parser tool, from which we can retrieve detailed information about SFT files. It is recommended for advanced professionals and inexperienced administrators to avoid using these tools, since any change executed could result in damaging an App-V package.

Among the third-party tools available, we find a large number and variety. We also find that several of those execute similar tasks but using different interfaces; this, of course, depends on each administrator and their preferences.

Not all of the third party tools are actually freeware; there are several that are paid. But of course, we can find several alternatives that we can implement in order to save a lot of time and effort in various App-V processes.

# Index

## Thank you for buying
## Microsoft Application Virtualization Advanced Guide

# About Packt Publishing

Packt, pronounced 'packed', published its first book "Mastering phpMyAdmin for Effective MySQL Management" in April 2004 and subsequently continued to specialize in publishing highly focused books on specific technologies and solutions.

Our books and publications share the experiences of your fellow IT professionals in adapting and customizing today's systems, applications, and frameworks. Our solution based books give you the knowledge and power to customize the software and technologies you're using to get the job done. Packt books are more specific and less general than the IT books you have seen in the past. Our unique business model allows us to bring you more focused information, giving you more of what you need to know, and less of what you don't.

Packt is a modern, yet unique publishing company, which focuses on producing quality, cutting-edge books for communities of developers, administrators, and newbies alike. For more information, please visit our website: www.packtpub.com.

# About Packt Enterprise

In 2010, Packt launched two new brands, Packt Enterprise and Packt Open Source, in order to continue its focus on specialization. This book is part of the Packt Enterprise brand, home to books published on enterprise software – software created by major vendors, including (but not limited to) IBM, Microsoft and Oracle, often for use in other corporations. Its titles will offer information relevant to a range of users of this software, including administrators, developers, architects, and end users.

# Writing for Packt

We welcome all inquiries from people who are interested in authoring. Book proposals should be sent to author@packtpub.com. If your book idea is still at an early stage and you would like to discuss it first before writing a formal book proposal, contact us; one of our commissioning editors will get in touch with you.

We're not just looking for published authors; if you have strong technical skills but no writing experience, our experienced editors can help you develop a writing career, or simply get some additional reward for your expertise.

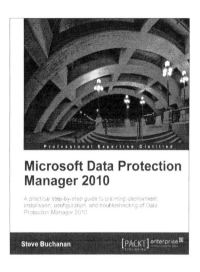

**Microsoft Data Protection Manager 2010**

ISBN: 978-1-84968-202-2    Paperback: 360 pages

A practical step-by-step guide to planning deployment, installation, configuration, and troubleshooting of Data Protection Manger 2010

1. A step-by-step guide to backing up your business data using Microsoft Data Protection Manager 2010

2. Discover how to back up and restore Microsoft applications that are critical in many of today's businesses

3. Understand the various components and features of Data Protection Manager 2010

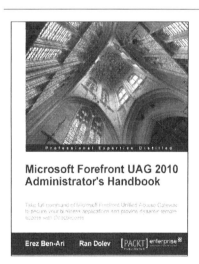

**Microsoft Forefront UAG 2010 Administrator's Handbook**

ISBN: 978-1-84968-162-9    Paperback: 484 pages

Take full command of Microsoft Forefront Unified Access Gateway to secure your business applications and provide dynamic remote access with DirectAccess

1. Maximize your business results by fully understanding how to plan your UAG integration

2. Consistently be ahead of the game by taking control of your server with backup and advanced monitoring

3. An essential tutorial for new users and a great resource for veterans

Please check **www.PacktPub.com** for information on our titles

## Windows Phone 7 XNA Cookbook

ISBN: 978-1-84969-120-8       Paperback: 450 pages

Over 70 recipes for making your own Windows Phone 7 game

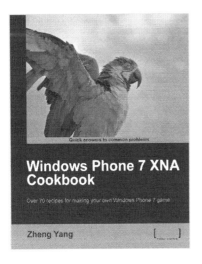

**Windows Phone 7 XNA Cookbook**

Over 70 recipes for making your own Windows Phone 7 game

Zheng Yang

1. Complete focus on the best Windows Phone 7 game development techniques using XNA 4.0

2. Easy to follow cookbook allowing you to dive in wherever you want.

3. Convert ideas into action using practical recipes

## Getting Started with Microsoft Application Virtualization 4.6

ISBN: 978-1-84968-126-1       Paperback: 308  pages

Virtualize your application infrastructure efficiently using Microsoft App-V

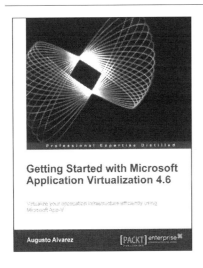

**Getting Started with Microsoft Application Virtualization 4.6**

Virtualize your application infrastructure efficiently using Microsoft App-V

Augusto Alvarez

1. Publish, deploy, and manage your virtual applications with App-V

2. Understand how Microsoft App-V can fit into your company

3. Guidelines for planning and designing an App-V environment

Please check **www.PacktPub.com** for information on our titles

16635487R00252

Made in the USA
Lexington, KY
03 August 2012